With Interest

How to profit from
interest rate fluctuations

————————

With Interest

How to profit from interest rate fluctuations

Joseph E. Murphy, Jr.

DOW JONES-IRWIN
Homewood, Illinois 60430

ISBN 0-87094-927-6
Library of Congress Catalog Card No. 86–71475

Printed in the United States of America

2 3 4 5 6 7 8 9 0 K 4 3 2 1 0 9 8 7

To Diana, Michael, and John

Preface

This book answers three basic types of questions. First of all, and perhaps paramount to most people, it tells how to profit more from fluctuations in interest rates. Second, it gives specific methods to estimate how much rate changes are likely to affect you. Third, it tells how to avoid common strategies that are not likely to be profitable in the long run. Taken together, this knowledge can make a big difference in dollars earned or saved—for you or your firm—as interest rates change.

With Interest gives a state-of-the-art presentation of interest rate risk management through its pioneering analysis of the volatility of changes in yields. Among other things, it shows how to estimate interest rate risk for different bond maturities and time periods and provides tables of interest rate risk. Based on this data, it provides tables on bond price and total return risk. The viewpoint and new methods shown in this book are more accurate and useful for forecasting interest rate risk than those commonly used.

This book had its origins in my work when I was a researcher and investment manager. I concluded that professionals in the field of finance should have tools to make better forecasts of fluctuations in interest rates. Millions of dollars were at stake.

For help in investigating this matter, I turned to Maury Osborne, who had done similar work on stock prices. Together we unraveled some of the fundamental characteristics of fluctuations in interest rates. How we arrived at and tested our findings was published in the *Journal of Portfolio Management*, Winter 1985.

The article didn't tell how to apply the results, and obviously that needed to be done and was the logical next step. This book now shows how to use the practical results of that research for investment, for taking out a loan, or for lending money. The difference that can make can be worth a considerable amount of money now or in the future.

Joseph E. Murphy, Jr.

ACKNOWLEDGMENTS

I was privileged to work with Maury Osborne for nearly a decade studying fluctuations in interest rates. This book is really the practical application of the empirical and theoretical foundation laid by that earlier work. Without Maury, neither that work nor this book would have been done. Neither he, nor anyone else, should be blamed for any shortcomings here.

I learned how to write this kind of book from Marlin Bree, who provided much editorial assistance. I am also indebted to Jim Harris, Peter Heegaard, Carol Huss, Jerry Jurgenson, Pierce McNally, Bill Ogden, John Rogers, Dick Schall, Dennis Senneseth, and my wife, Diana, for reading the manuscript, making corrections, or for help and encouragement.

J. E. M.

Contents

PART ONE

Discovering the Laws that Govern Fluctuations in Interest Rates

1

Profit and Loss from Fluctuations in Interest Rates

Contrary to what most people think, it is possible to make a fortune from fluctuations in interest rates, even from buying and selling the highest grade securities in the world, U.S. government securities.

For example, "smart money" bought 30-year U.S. government bonds in the summer of 1984 and unloaded the bonds a year later for a whopping 30 percent return, three times the usual on the stock market and more than three times what's usual on bonds. The smart buyers had simply forecast a sharp decline in interest rates over the next year and rolled in a 30 percent return.

Not bad at all, but peanuts compared to what a big financial institution could do if it could just call the shots. For example, I learned that if one of the largest banks in the world could just forecast interest rates, it could increase its earnings from $100 million to $1 billion.

"Not only that," said a financial specialist, "but if the bank could simply forecast the direction of interest rates, it could raise its earnings from $100 million to $700 million."

Obviously, the average investor isn't going to worry about upping his return in quite this dramatic fashion. On the other hand, to get started on a financial course that will pay you handsome sums doesn't take all the financial brains in New

York or, for that matter, unremitting bottom-line luck. Money invested wisely multiplies in obedience to the laws of interest.

You can look to all sorts of charts in the money books and magazines for inspiration on how you can make up your own success story. For example, if you put $13,000 down at 15 percent on a noncoupon bond when you are 20, you will have $1 million by the time you are 50. Rates were 15 percent a year ago. Even at 10 percent rates, you will end up with $1 million on a $53,000 investment. You don't have to be 20 to get that million; you can start at 35 and still have it by the time you retire.

The key, of course, is to know when the rate on bonds is attractive, to know when not to speculate on higher rates, and to make the commitment.

This book will give you no "get rich quick" schemes. It does not tell you how to turn a quick buck in interest rates. It doesn't contain any secret clues on how to surpass the Rockefellers, or H. L. Hunt before he lost a good part of his fortune speculating in silver futures. It doesn't tell you how to forecast the next direction of interest rates.

But it does give you new data that can be very helpful in dealing with interest rates—whether you are a small investor, a big institutional investor, a bank, or anyone who is affected by interest rates. What you are about to read is not contained in any other source.

In part, this book is about odds. When you decide to make the investment, there are certain odds for you and against you. Specifically, there are certain odds that you will avoid giving up a certain amount, avoid losing, and certain odds that rates will drop after you buy that bond. What you want to know is what the cost is if you're wrong and what the gain is if you're right.

Those risks and rewards can't be known, but they can be estimated for different kinds of bonds (maturities), for different future periods which we call forecast periods, for different sets of coupons, and for different kinds of odds.

If you change the maturity, alter the forecast period, move the coupon up or down, shift the odds, or move the probabilities, then the risks and rewards will change. Put all of these things into the kettle and you know what kind of stew you're likely to get: what you gain by investing, by lending, or by borrowing now. You can also see, bubbling away, what you might also lose, or what you might gain or lose by waiting.

Put all that together and you have hard information to help you make a more intelligent, more profitable, and wiser decision in handling your own money or in managing other people's money.

Other books may give you hypothetical answers to hypothetical questions based on a certain set of assumptions. They will tell you what you might gain if rates rise a certain amount, or if rates fall a certain amount. But they don't tell you how much rates are likely to rise or likely to fall for a certain probability, for a certain set of odds, or a certain period of time. Nor do they tell you what your actual risk and reward are, because no one has ever calculated that before, or figured it out correctly. We present calculations in tabular form. Because our tables are based on parameters that have held for 250 years, they are reliable within reasonable limits.

Whether you invest on your own account, manage money for others, borrow, lend, arbitrage, trade securities, or pursue other interests that are influenced by interest rates, this book will help you. It will help you most if you invest or lend, for yourself or for others. It will help you in ways that nothing else will, by giving you a much better idea of what will happen if you make one decision now, and not another; or, of what will happen to the rates after you decide. It will give you a better picture of probable future fluctuations in interest rates, of fluctuations for various maturities over various time intervals, a portrait of what is to come. You can improve your judgement of the risks and returns when you decide: to invest, to lend, or to wait.

That can be profitable.

2

Discovering the Laws of Interest Rates

Jerry, a bank executive stopped at my door, an intense look on his face.

"Murphy," he said with an undertone of personal anxiety. "The bank needs a better handle on future rates. It's for our asset allocation committee."

He shoved a sheath of papers in front of me and I immediately knew what he was worried about. Fluctuations in interest rates had a huge impact on the bank's profits, and the committee had the same problems we faced: advising clients on managing their money and investing their funds in bonds.

The problem was that we really didn't know much about the fluctuations in interest rates, even though that knowledge was fundamental to improvement.

"Jerry," I said as he left, "Let me think about your problem. I'll see what I can come up with."

After some reflection, I realized that over the years I had scanned a lot of academic research on interest rates for answers; but very little of it was useful, or it was too particular to apply in the future. We needed something that was general, not restricted to a single historical period, but applicable in the future. That hard criterion was not easy to meet or simple to find.

I began with the conviction that we could not predict the direction of interest rates and would merely waste our time trying.

Then, it occurred to me that if you can't predict the direction of interest rates, you might be able to predict how far rates might go up or down over a given period (for example, a month or a year). There might be a set relationship between the time interval and how far rates moved, whatever their direction. If there were such a relationship, it would help to gauge the risk: to know whether going short on buying money or long on selling money was dangerous—and how dangerous. I knew that some of the savings & loans (S&Ls) had gotten in trouble on just that sort of thing.

Excitedly, I realized the first thing to do was to call Maury Osborne. Osborne is a physicist who had applied the principles of physics to this kind of problem. In fact, he and I had collaborated in another area: bankrupt corporations and predicting bankruptcy. Our solution turned out to be different than the solutions of others; but I felt that ours was conceptually better, mathematically sounder, and tested out best. If you looked at it from the right angle, the interest rate problem was the same as the bankruptcy problem and the same as the common stock problem that Osborne had done pioneering work in years before. It would be a financial detective story to unravel all the clues.

No one had ever used Osborne's solution the way I felt it should be used now; no one had envisioned the wonderful possibilities in using it to better gauge common stock risk. Everyone had gone off in other directions, directions with much less potential.

"Maury, it's Joe, Joe Murphy," I almost shouted into the receiver.

"What is it?" the voice came back, sharp and clear, slightly high pitched.

I explained the problem, as Maury put to me one penetrating question after another. I knew Osborne wanted to look at the data in the same way he looked at stock market data, the same way we looked at earnings data in studying bankruptcy.

"How much does it fluctuate," he probed. "How much does the fluctuation increase as you look further out? . . . We need data," he muttered finally. "We need the data, we can't do anything without the data."

He was hooked and I was delighted. Osborne had worked on problems ranging from ocean currents to the flight of insects. A retired physicist for the Office of Naval Research, U.S. Department of Defense, he had one of the most probing and original minds in the country. And he was absolutely honest in his evaluation of data and in drawing conclusions from it. Nothing hoodwinked Osborne. And he would yell if he thought you misinterpreted the facts.

"Jerry," I said when I got him on the phone. "Can you get your hands on some long series of bond yields? Very long series, with as frequent datings as possible. And no changes in the series—they have to be as uniform as possible throughout."

"I'll see what I can do," he said, somewhat perplexed. "I'll look around upstairs."

In the meantime I scrounged through the investment department library. It had most of the current material on bonds: brokerage house reports, government publications, consultants reports, a whole host of books and articles, including Standard & Poor (S&P) reference guides and Moody's manuals. It was all good stuff, if you could find what you were looking for.

Then I turned to my home library, to the scores of financial journals that I'd kept like a pack rat for years, and to the books I'd accumulated over a lifetime of working in investments.

There were three sources that I knew were good, among the best: Sidney Homer, David Durand, and Frederick Macaulay. Each had collected long historical interest rate series, Homer going back to the Greeks and the Romans, Macaulay from the Civil War up to the early 1920s, and David Durand from the turn of the century to the 1960s.

They had what we needed for historical purposes: long series of data, monthly in some cases, annual in others. The longest series was the British consol yield data, perpetual bond yields running back to 1720; the next longest was Macaulay's, nearly a century; and the shortest was Durand's, 65 years. Each series had strengths and weakness: the consols gave us perspective, the ability to see if fundamental changes occurred over 250 years of war and peace, boom and bust; the Macaulay data gave us two series, a short commercial paper series and a long high-grade bond series, each with monthly data. The Durand data provided annual yields on a half dozen different maturities, ranging from 1 year to 30.

"Maturity will definitely be a factor," Osborne had warned me, "but what kind of factor we have to find out."

Osborne was not alone in knowing the importance of maturity on volatility. Everyone who was even generally familiar with interest rates knew about it, but there was a big difference between knowing there was an effect and knowing exactly what it was. We had to find out exactly what the effect was. That no one knew—precisely.

"I've got just what you need," Jerry announced one day as he plunked a big loose bound volume on my desk.

As I opened the covers, I saw the Salomon yield indexes, page after page, maturity after maturity, U.S. governments, corporates, municipals, all with monthly data going back to 1950. It was perfect, for it gave us a wonderful data base on which to examine the post–World War II era.

"Be careful," Jerry cautioned me in an earnest tone. "That's the only copy. They only give it out to big customers. It's not for distribution."

Duly impressed, I promised not to pass it out on the street. Jerry's anxieties seemed to be appeased.

Soon, all of the data was punched into the computer, yield after yield, one series after another, until I had a data base that could be used to find what we needed to know, that could dig the secret out of the deep. The trick was in asking the right questions.

We had three questions, deceptively simple questions, but probing enough to get what we wanted: (1) What was the volatility of changes in yields? In other words, how much did yields fluctuate? (2) Did the volatility change with time? (3) Did the volatility change with maturity? These three questions would not only be enough for Jerry's problem, but they also would be enough to help manage a bond portfolio.

It's almost like a murder mystery, I thought to myself. When you think you've got the criminal identified, you have to collect confirming evidence. The clues all have to point in the same direction to the same person.

We needed the same consistency of evidence—evidence pointing to the same characteristic, time and time again, in all periods. In that way, we would know that what we had was likely to happen in the future as it had in the past.

"We're on the right track," I finally confided to Osborne. "We're going in the right direction."

The trick lay in giving the data a common dimension, measuring it in a way that put everything on the same scale, so to speak. In this case the trick was quite simple: Don't take the original yields. Instead, take the logs, for if you do you can measure the speed of change, and you get the rate of change in yields. When you do that, the rate of change in periods of low interest looks much like the rate of change in periods of high interest. The volatility looks very similar. And our measure of volatility, the standard deviation, cranked out roughly similar numbers in different periods for the same kind of maturity. This was terrific.

I was delighted since the British consols in the 1700s looked liked the British consols in the 1800s and like the British consols in the 1900s, and they looked like Macaulay's long-term after the Civil War or Macaulay's long-term before World War I. And the volatility of that was similar to the volatility of S&P's long-term high-grade after 1900, after 1930, and like the Salomon U.S. government long-terms after 1950 or like the Durand long-term before 1965 and after 1900.

Maybe I was getting strange, but it was very exciting to know that we had something on interest rates that held true in a rough way over very long periods of time for different countries, for different kinds of securities, and for very different economic eras. It was astounding and at the same time comforting. Best of all, it indicated that we were looking in the right direction. With that bit of information, we headed for the next.

Test the short bonds, I said to myself. Test the short bonds to see how they behave.

So I turned to the shorts: the short U.S. governments, the Macaulay commercial paper, the Durand one-year bonds, and on and on, for different periods, different economic climates.

"The volatility is high," I said to Jerry. "And roughly the same for all the series." Jerry looked interested, but a little perplexed. "It means we have something that is constant," I said, trying to hide my excitement, "and therefore something we can use when we put it all together."

It had already taken a long time. But more time was needed to fit the pieces together and to derive the simple equation that, could make it all useful.

We had two solid pieces of crucial information that suggested we were moving in the right direction and that we would have something useful when the work was done: (1) We had discovered that the volatility of interest rates, measured in our way, held over long periods; (2) We had found that the long maturities had consistently much lower volatility than the short maturities. There was a fundamental and persistent difference between the longs and the shorts.

Both pieces of information were encouraging. But we needed measures for more maturities and we needed measures for time intervals of other lengths than the yearly or monthly measures. We needed measures of volatility for every maturity in our data base and we needed measures for time intervals running from 1 month to 5 to 10 years.

We didn't know what the effect of maturity would be on volatility of yields, except the general notion that volatility would drop as maturity increased. We knew this from the study of the long and short maturities. But we did have an idea about the effect of time, about what happened when you lengthened the forecast period, when you changed the length of the period of time over which you measured volatility. We had an idea from work on common stock prices, from studies of earnings, and from the underlying nature of random processes which we suspected mirrored changes in interest rates.

"Let's see what happens when we go from monthly changes to annual changes, or when we increase the differencing interval," Osborne suggested.

"Volatility should double if you go from quarterly to annual changes," I added.

"Yes," he said. "That's what I'd expect."

To find out, we had to compute measures of volatility for a lot of different time intervals, from one month to six years. Then we had to plot the measures. The plots would show exactly how volatility rose as the length of the time interval increased. I computed the volatility and Osborne plotted the figures. We ran the computations and plotted the figures for every series where we had enough data. It was a lot of data to plot.

After sending bundles of tables to Osborne in Maryland, I waited for the tables to come back. They came back, accompanied by long letters detailing what looked as I had expected, what was different than expected, and what the reason might be. Osborne's analysis, written in fine ink, ran to a couple of two-inch volumes over the course of several years.

After we plotted the data on charts, we wanted to know three things: (1) Were the lines straight? (2) Was the slope of the lines one half? (3) Did the lines for the same maturities coincide? If the lines were straight, we had a regular relationship. If the slope was one half, we had the relationship expected from probability theory: volatility increased with the square root of time. And if lines from the same maturity coincided, even though the series came from different time periods, the results were general and we could be confident that they would hold in the future.

We knew already that for short bonds and long bonds the lines would start at the same point, but we did not know if their slopes would be the same; this had to be the case if they were to coincide.

"Look at the slope of the line," Osborne would say. "See that it's not quite one half. But it's in the same general region. Look at it."

I would scan through his charts, redraw them so I could see what was going on, and then compare one against the other. It was hard to imagine how one could become so fascinated by a piece of paper with dots and lines drawn on them, looking at the lines, trying to see if they remained straight or curved off at the ends, trying to see how well the dots fit, what the precise slope was. As the evidence came in, one piece confirmed the other, the pieces of the jigsaw puzzle fit together, and the pattern became clear.

Changes in interest rates fluctuated much like a random series, the degree of fluctuation rose more slowly than time, the volatility rose roughly with the square root of time ($t^{\cdot 5}$), in a way that could be described and predicted with a simple equation. Certainly not all the evidence was perfect, not all the slopes were one half, not all the lines for the same maturities were exactly coincident. But they were very close—very, very close. Close enough to show us that we were on to something. Something that could be helpful and useful.

The last piece in the puzzle was the effect of maturity. We had less data, we took longer to figure out the effect of maturity, but we finally came up with a formula that fitted the data quite well, with a high correlation. We found, in general terms, that volatility varied inversely with the cube root of maturity:[1]

$$\left(\frac{1}{m}\right)^3$$

The pattern was there. We had discovered the underlying laws of volatility of changes in interest rates.

"Jerry," I shouted over the phone. "We've got it. We've solved the problem."

"What are you saying?" he asked, his voice betraying his excitement.

"We can predict the volatility of interest rates."

"What does that mean?" said Jerry, now growing cautious. "And how can we use it?"

---

[1]The formula is given at the end of Chapter 3, discussed in more detail in Appendix A, and is derived in References 8 and 12 (Appendix E).

3

Murphy's Three Laws—and How They Got That Way

"Jerry, you're always asking me how to put it to work," I began as we sat down in my office to go over what we'd come up with thus far.

"Certainly," replied Jerry, brightly. "What do you expect?"

"I'm not that fast. I can't do it that quickly. I've got to do the theoretical first. Then the practical. Only then," I added.

"What're you going to give me?" pursued Jerry. "Murphy's laws?"

I laughed. "You bet! Let's start with Murphy's new laws. Only let's call them Murphy and Osborne's laws. They're not just mine. And, the first one isn't ours, anyway. It's as old as the hills to those that know it. Here they are." '

With that, I summarized what Osborne and I had found out by studying the volatility of interest rates—rules that we drew from all the charts we'd constructed. These were axioms of general fact that would, I hoped, get to Jerry's practical concerns.

The laws are quite short and simple, I cautioned Jerry at the outset.

First law: You can't predict the direction of interest rates any better than the flip of a coin.

That means, I told Jerry, you can't make money by trying to guess the direction of interest rates. "You aren't smart enough," I said. "And there isn't anyone else smart enough or knowledgeable enough to be right more than half the time. That's because interest rates are too unpredictable, too volatile, and just too chaotic to be predicted." I shook my head. "So if you want to make money, and improve your investments that are affected by interest rates, you have to find something else to help you."

I paused for a moment to let my next point sink in. "And that something else can be found in the next two laws which deal with the underlying characteristics of interest rate volatility."

Second law: The volatility of changes in interest rates rises with the square root of time.

Jerry shook his head, then began to listen carefully.

"Sounds complicated, but it's not; and it can be translated into tables so you don't need to have it memorized," I continued. "The importance of the law, its significance, is that volatility does change in a predetermined fashion with time. From today, from tomorrow, or from next year, the range of values that future interest rates will take in the future increases with time."

Jerry was becoming alert now.

"Not only does the range increase, but it increases in a regular manner, with probabilities that can be determined with reasonable accuracy. The range rises, but it rises in a peculiar fashion, one that can be calculated only by using the logs of interest rates, not the original rates. The logs can then be converted back to normal rates for use and interpretation. All you really need to use the second law is a set of tables."

I came now to my third law, which covers maturities.

Third law: The volatility of changes in interest rates varies inversely with (the cube root of) maturity.

"The third law does for maturity what the second law does for time," I said. "It states how the increase in volatility, measured from today, or some future date, is affected by the maturity of the issue. And it shows in quantitative terms how powerful the effect of maturity is. Maturity is a key factor that must be taken into account."

I sat back now, a little tired.

"The three laws are the result of our study in a nut shell," I said. "They are three simple statements about the behavior of interest rates, three laws that summarize all we have found—three laws."

Jerry looked impressed, but a little puzzled. "How did you find the effect of maturity?" he asked after a few moments.

"It seemed simple once we had the answer," I said. "But it was not easy getting to the answer. It's like finding your way through a strange city where you don't speak the language. Before you've done it, the place seems like a maze, impossible to navigate. But once you've done it, it seems simple. It was like that working on maturities."

I then went on to explain what we had done. It all seemed so easy now, having done it. The trick turned out to be looking at maturity and time at the same time. Fortunately we had data for that, two sets of data in fact, the Durand corporate data from 1900 to 1965 and the Salomon government data from 1950 to 1979. For each set we had a lot of yields, annual in the former case, monthly in the latter.

With the yields at hand, all we had to do was compute measures of volatility changes in interest rates for different intervals, running from 1 to 60 months in one case and from one to seven years in the second. This gave us a matrix of volatility measures, or standard deviations, for a series of time intervals and a series of maturities.

That left a very solvable problem, fitting the measures of volatility to time and maturity simultaneously, which gave an equation. The second and third laws simply state the equation in words, words that approximate the real thing, though the real thing is best captured by the equation.

When you run an equation like that, you want to be sure the equation fits the data; you don't want a sloppy fit, for example, a size 42 for a size 25 person. But, our fit was good, nearly as high a correlation as you could get. This was satisfying and gave us confidence in the results of the equation.

The good fit gave the new equations the ability to help Jerry in his work on asset allocation, to help us in investments and in our evaluation of the best bond policy for the individual. There was a lot of usefulness here.

At Jerry's insistence, I stated the general formula.

"Wait till you see the tables," I concluded. "The tables will show you the potential values future interest rates can take. You'll see how you can use them. But first you must fully understand the first law and why we can't predict the direction of interest rates," I said.

The equation has the form:

$$\log_e (\text{Standard deviation}) = \log_e c$$
$$+ a[\log_e (\text{Difference interval})]$$
$$- b[\log_e (\text{Maturity})]$$

When we transform the logarithmic equation we obtain the equation:

$$\text{Standard deviation} =$$
$$c (\text{Difference interval})^a/(\text{Maturity})^b$$

The standard deviation is the standard deviation in changes in the natural logarithm of yields. When $a = .5$, the standard deviation rises with the square root of time; when $b = .3$, the standard deviation varies inversely with the cube root of maturity. The coefficient of correlation is 0.98 for the Salomon data and .99 for the Durand data.[1]

---

[1]See Appendix A and References 8 and 12 (Appendix E).

4

Don't Bet on the Direction of Interest Rates

Certainly, no one will argue with you that the easiest and the fastest way to make a killing on a bond portfolio is to correctly choose the direction interest rates will go. Any number of history lessons reveal the enormous riches you could reap if you play your cards right.

But is it that easy? Perhaps not, considering the many other players in the interest rate game, all of whom have a stake in forecasting the direction of interest rates.

The two biggest players in the game—the U.S. government and the banks—don't bet on the direction of interest rates. Though they are in a better position than anyone to know what's going on, they don't gamble on the direction of rates.

The biggest player is the U.S. government. The Treasury continually issues new bonds to finance its seemingly insatiable appetite. To do that, it has to print money in the form of new bond issues, using its prime credit.

Timing plays a critical role. If the government deferred a new issue of bonds until rates dropped, for example, from 10.25 percent to 10.00 percent, it could save millions, even billions, of dollars.

Or, if not that, why doesn't the government just buy back outstanding issues when rates are high and its bonds are cheap, or put out new issues when rates are low and bonds are dear? It would certainly be a good tactic to juggle inventory by buying and selling at the best times. The New York Federal Reserve Bank, which does most of the government's trading, doesn't have to worry about the underlying quality of its inventory.

Uncle Sam could certainly help out the poor taxpayer and resolve its budget dilemmas by playing the interest rate game. There is only one uncertainty, a single variable that you have to forecast: the direction of interest rates. The federal government can't make money in the above ways because it can't forecast the direction of interest rates.

If the federal government is too chicken to play the interest rate game, there are thousands of banks that could. With trillions of dollars in assets, the chief business of bankers is making money on interest rates. They do it all year long, buying money at one rate in the form of savings accounts, deposit accounts, and certificates of deposit, and then lending the money out at another rate, hopefully higher. The banks can hire the brightest and best MBAs from Harvard Business School, the shrewdest bond traders from Wall Street or the Fed, and the cleverest academicians from the University of Chicago, to tell them how best to play the interest rate game. They could say to those specialists: "Just tell us how to predict the direction of interest rates, and we will reward you lavishly."

In truth, the big banks do have big staffs to whom they pay big bucks to tell them about these things. A large regional bank hired a young expert directly from a high government office. They charged him with the responsibility of forecasting the direction of interest rates, and he had the guts to make such forecasts: not hedged forecasts, but predictions straight from the shoulder. Quite courageously, he pronounced the direction of rates. His wisdom on interest rates was sought throughout the Federal Reserve district, and beyond.

But did the bank bet its own money on those forecasts? It did not. The bankers were too smart for that. They simply didn't bet on interest rate forecasts, or, at least not often. It was too likely to get burned: the bankers knew that from experience, for it had happened more than once.

A friend of mine ran the bond department in the same bank. At that time the bond department managed the bank's bond portfolio. That was the bank's own money, not somebody else's. When the bank's money was not all out in loans, the bond department had some currency to play with. The department couldn't just let that cash sit idle, for idle cash to a bank is heresy, like leaving land unplanted or not charging rent on a condo if you happened to be lucky enough to find a renter.

My friend was not timid, nor was he afraid to make interest rate forecasts. He was certain enough in his own mind about the direction of rates to be able to convince not only himself but also his bosses. Now that is no easy thing, for bankers, from years of experience, know it is not safe to forecast interest rates if you're actually going to put your own money on the line. Knowing that, they generally stay short and buy short-term bonds. By doing this, they are willing to accept lower rates in return for avoiding the huge price drop that could arise if they bought long bonds.

Banks do allow their trust departments to buy long bonds and bear the risk. But that is done with *other peoples money.* The *bank's own money* is entirely another matter: No, the bank is leveraged enough without betting on the bond market. Besides, the bank usually doesn't have much of its own money anyway; it is kept as equity for its own huge liabilities. The general strategy is that it's best not to risk that little equity on such a crapshoot as predicting the direction of interest rates.

Nevertheless, my friend had the courage to put money down and the persuasive power to get others to accept his plunge into long bonds. Predicting that rates would fall, he bought very long bonds so the bank could make a real killing.

He was right about one thing: There was a killing. But it was the bank that got killed; its losses ran into the millions. The interest massacre was duly reported in the local newspapers and revealed to incredulous stockholders. The blood flowed, and my friend got fired. "He left the bank for personal reasons," or something like that, were the official parting words.

Not many years thereafter, the holding company that owned that bank got caught hedging in the futures market and lost $40 million. That loss was splashed in headlines across the national press. The person directly responsible for the loss was "fired"; not resigned, but "fired." This was blunt language for a bank caught in an unbankerlike act. And within the year the chief executive officer of the holding company had found a replacement for himself. There was no connection of that departure with playing the futures market, according to the official explanation; but there obviously was a connection. Once again, bank officials learned that managing a bond portfolio by forecasting the direction of interest rates was not wise, if it meant placing much of the bank's equity behind it. Gambling on the futures market is even worse.

If betting on interest rate forecasts is taboo, then why hire consultants to make forecasts? Why put down cash for highly paid economists to forecast the direction of rates, or to make pronouncements about the direction of Fed policy?

Bankers know there is an outside chance that the economists they hire, or the outside consultants they engage, might just have some inside track; or, that they might discover some course of events that would affect interest rates. This is useful information, not just for managing the bank portfolio, but for running the bank, and for borrowing and lending money.

Even though economists are expensive, the cost of not having the economist might be even greater. Besides, the additional cost is not that much compared with the potential loss of not knowing something that you might otherwise be in a position to know.

Bankers have another reason for hiring economists. Customers and the general public expect bankers to know which way interest rates are going. They think if anyone should know, the bankers should know. But the bankers don't know, and the way they handle that situation is to hire an economist. The economist can make the forecast. If the economist is correct, the bank can take the credit. And if the economist is wrong, the bank needn't take the blame. After all, it was the economist's forecast, not the bankers'.

Besides that, having an economist is good for one's image. It makes the bank seem more like a full-service bank, a bank that has everything the customer needs. If other banks have economists, it is particularly important to have one, if the bank can afford it.

Economists who predict interest rates do not work only for banks. Some work for brokerage houses, others for investment managers, still others for the government. The art of forecasting is rampant among those who manage money, either their own or other people's money.

But the use of interest rate forecasting is confined primarily to the care and handling of *other people's money.* People who manage their own money, or the money on which they depend directly for their own livelihood (like the bank's equity) are very careful not to use interest rate forecasts.

For years I thought changes in interest rates were random. I knew it in my mind from studying other financial data. But I also knew that no one would say that changes in rates are random, completely unpredictable. That is close to heresy. But I also knew that banks don't bet on their forecasts: they always hedge. They don't bet the bank on their interest rate forecast: or, if they do, they don't bet a lot.

It seems to me that there is simply no way to forecast the direction of rates with more than a 50 percent accuracy. And that's not good enough for a bank, for a money manager, or for anyone to win in the long run.

The direction of interest rates can't be predicted any more than the flip of a coin. You might come out ahead on a single bet, for the odds are 50 percent, but if you do it a lot or for a long time, the odds of doing well fall quite dramatically.

The two major players in the interest rate game are the federal government and the banks. If anyone should know how to bet on the direction of interest rates, they should. But they don't bet on the direction, and if they don't you shouldn't.

The lesson is clear cut: Don't base your bond investments on forecasting the direction of interest rates. Don't listen to anyone who says you should, and, above all, don't put *your money* with anyone who says he can.

5

The Laws Graphed

"Take a look at these figures, Jerry," I said, "because they show how volatility changes with time and maturity."

Once he saw the material, Jerry recognized immediately what I meant. These were calculations of public and bank data. The curves clearly showed that volatility rose with time but dropped with maturity. It was not a simple arithmetical correlation, yet nonetheless the figures grew steadily and perceptibly.

"That's it," he said, growing excited. "That shows what happens—how much future rates fluctuate."

In this chapter, you will see one figure for each of a number of maturities. Though we can't show them all here, we do cover nearly all maturities in tables later on.

The figures are arranged in order of maturity: first you will see the short maturities, then the long maturities.

Look at the *first* maturity, Figure 5–1, for *one year*. This is drawn for a beginning yield of 10 percent and calculates how far rates might rise and how much rates might fall from an initial yield of 10 percent.

Note all of the conditions we've charted. We've stated the initial yield (10 percent), the maturity of the bond (one year), and a particular probability. The probability is two out of three that rates will not rise higher than the upper line shown

FIGURE 5–1

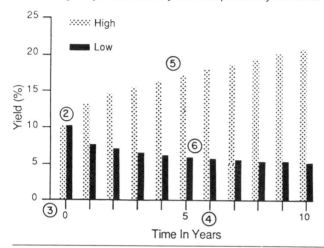

on the figure—or fall lower than the lower line shown on the figure.

We selected a probability of two thirds for all the figures and all the tables in this book because that is the normal range used. We could have selected another probability which would have caused the lines to lie elsewhere on the figure. If we had used a wider probability, like three fourths, the high and low would lie further apart; and if we had used a smaller probability, they would lie closer together.

Each figure shows the range of future yields for a single maturity for a 10-year period when the present yield is 10 percent. Figure 5–1 shows the following:

1. The maturity of the bond: 1 year.
2. The present yield on the bond: 10 percent.
3. The present time: year 0.
4. The number of years in the future: 5 years.
5. The *high* probable yield 5 years from now: 17 percent.
6. The *low* probable yield 5 years from now: 6 percent.

The figures are a summary picture of actual changes in yields in the past. If you plotted changes in yield over a particular period, (for example, a day or a month), you would find many small changes, up and down, and only a few large changes. If you then figured the changes from smallest to largest, you would obtain a curve that looks like a normal curve. In a normal curve there are many small changes and few large changes.

Figures 5–2 and 5–3 and the tables that follow confine themselves to two lines showing the range within which two thirds of the probable changes will fall. They only summarize what has happened in the past and what is likely to happen in the future. They do not tell the full story.

As you look through the figures, you will see that with each longer maturity, the lines are closer together. This reflects the lower volatility of yields of longer maturities, a decline in volatility described by the third law.

Figure 5–2 is based on the Salomon U.S. government yield data, 1950 to 1979. For this data, volatility rose somewhat more slowly than we expected, in fact, slower than for other series in our data base, and even more slowly compared with the Durand corporate data covering the first half of the century, 1900–1965 (see Figure 5–3).

Because of the slower rate of rise, the first figures understate the degree to which yields can change, the height to which they can rise, and the depth to which they can fall.

FIGURE 5–2

Range of Future Yields*

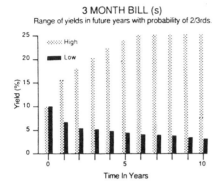

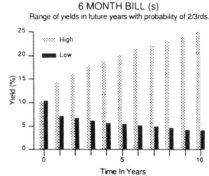

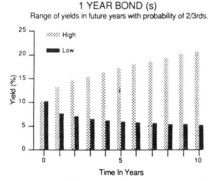

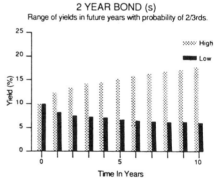

*For initial yield of 10 percent for maturities of ¼, ½, 1, 2, 5, 10, 15, 20, and 25 years for 1 to 10 years in the future with probability of two thirds of being within range.

Based on Salomon U.S. yield index data, 1950–1979.

FIGURE 5–2 *(concluded)*

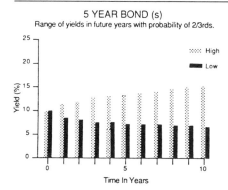

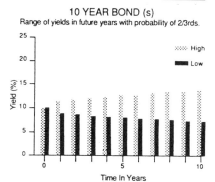

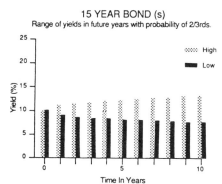

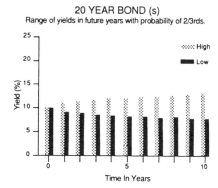

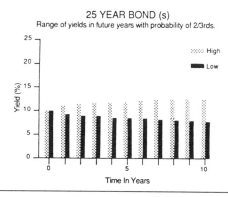

FIGURE 5–3 _____
Range of Future Yields*

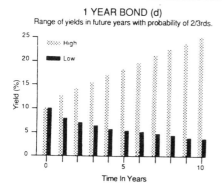

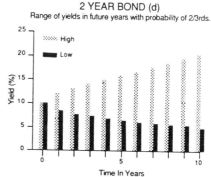

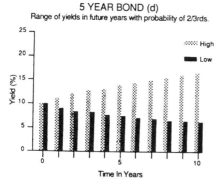

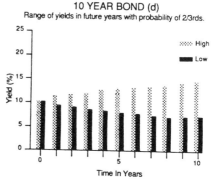

*For initial yield of 10 percent for maturities of 1, 2, 5, 10, 15, 20, and 25 years for 1 to 10 years in the future with probability of two thirds of being within range. Based on Durand corporate yield index data, 1900–1965.

FIGURE 5–3 (concluded)

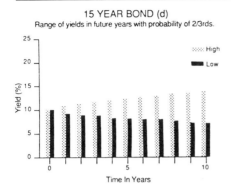

15 YEAR BOND (d)
Range of yields in future years with probability of 2/3rds.

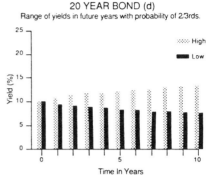

20 YEAR BOND (d)
Range of yields in future years with probability of 2/3rds.

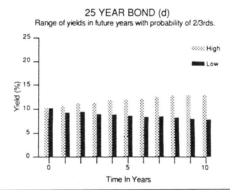

25 YEAR BOND (d)
Range of yields in future years with probability of 2/3rds.

6

The Laws in Table Form

Each table shows the range of future yields for seven maturities and six future years. Table 6–1 shows the range when the present yield is 10 percent; examples 1–4 are illustrated by Tables 6–2 through 6–5.

WHAT TABLE 6–1 SHOWS

1. The maturity of the bond: ¼-year.
2. The present yield on the bond: 10 percent.
3. How many years in the future: 1 year.
4. The high probable yield: 15.5 percent.
5. The low probable yield: 6.4 percent.

The range of yields shown in the tables have a two-thirds probability. Thus, for the one-fourth-year maturity, the probability is two-thirds that yields a year from now will lie between 6.4 percent and 15.5 percent. There is a 1-in-6 chance that yields will drop below 6.4 percent and a 1-in-6 chance that yields will rise above 15.5 percent.

EXAMPLES USING TABLE 6–1

Table 6–1 shows just how much more volatile short maturities are. The three-month Treasury (one-fourth-year) is perceptibly more volatile than the one-year Treasury and a lot

TABLE 6–1

BOND MATURITY	Initial Yield	RANGE OF FUTURE YIELDS Years					
		1	2	3	4	5	6
1/4	10.0	15.5	18.0	20.1	21.9	23.7	25.4
	10.0	6.4	5.6	5.0	4.6	4.2	3.9
1	10.0	13.1	14.4	15.3	16.2	17.0	17.7
	10.0	7.6	7.0	6.5	6.2	5.9	5.6
5	10.0	11.7	12.3	12.8	13.2	13.5	13.9
	10.0	8.6	8.1	7.8	7.6	7.4	7.2
10	10.0	11.3	11.8	12.1	12.4	12.7	12.9
	10.0	8.9	8.5	8.3	8.1	7.9	7.7
15	10.0	11.1	11.5	11.8	12.1	12.3	12.5
	10.0	9.0	8.7	8.5	8.3	8.1	8.0
20	10.0	11.0	11.3	11.6	11.8	12.0	12.2
	10.0	9.1	8.8	8.6	8.4	8.3	8.2
25	10.0	10.9	11.2	11.5	11.7	11.9	12.0
	10.0	9.2	8.9	8.7	8.5	8.4	8.3

Range of yields with probability of two thirds.
Based on Salomon U.S. yield data, 1950–79.

TABLE 6–2

BOND MATURITY	Initial Yield	RANGE OF FUTURE YIELDS Years					
		1	2	3	4	5	6
1/4	10.0	15.5	18.0	20.1	21.9	23.7	25.4
	10.0	6.4	5.6	5.0	4.6	4.2	3.9
1	10.0	13.1	14.4	15.3	16.2	17.0	17.7
	10.0	7.6	7.0	6.5	6.2	5.9	5.6
5	10.0	11.7	12.3	12.8	13.2	13.5	13.9
	10.0	8.6	8.1	7.8	7.6	7.4	7.2
10	10.0	11.3	11.8	12.1	12.4	12.7	12.9
	10.0	8.9	8.5	8.3	8.1	7.9	7.7
15	10.0	11.1	11.5	11.8	12.1	12.3	12.5
	10.0	9.0	8.7	8.5	8.3	8.1	8.0
20	10.0	11.0	11.3	11.6	11.8	12.0	12.2
	10.0	9.1	8.8	8.6	8.4	8.3	8.2
25	10.0	10.9	11.2	11.5	11.7	11.9	12.0
	10.0	9.2	8.9	8.7	8.5	8.4	8.3

Range of yields with probability of two thirds.
Based on Salomon U.S. yield data, 1950–79.

more volatile than the five-year maturity. The table also shows how volatility rises with maturity, particularly for short issues. For example, looking at the figures, you'll see that the one-fourth-year maturity has a range of 6.4 percent to 15.5 percent after one year, the one-year maturity a range of 7.6 percent to 13.1 percent, and the five-year maturity a range of only 8.6 percent to 11.7 percent. If you look at the 25-year maturity, you will see that the range is very slight after a year, 9.2 percent to 10.9 percent. Clearly, the short maturities have much more volatile yields.

HOW TO USE THE TABLES TO CALCULATE FUTURE YIELDS

Now, let's use the tables to solve some real-life problems. Here you'll see how the calculations will work with a short-term investment.

The first example (Table 6–2) deals with the problem of using a short maturity if you want the income.

Example 1. You may need your money anytime in the next year for a specific purpose, such as buying a house or making an investment. But you may not buy the house or make the investment immediately, and you might wait as long as five years. In the meantime, you want to earn a return and you need that income, actually nearly as much as current rates (now 10 percent) provide. You want to know how much loss in income you might take if rates drop.

Use the first line of the table for the three-month maturity (one-fourth-year). Rates could drop from the present 10 percent to 6.4 percent in a year, a 36 percent drop in income. In three years rates could drop to 5 percent, meaning a 50 percent loss of income. As you can see, that's an enormous drop in income.

The tables show you just how large that drop in income might be if you invest in the very short (one-fourth-year) security. After looking at the table, you may decide that you do not need the money so soon and can buy a slightly longer maturity (for example, a one-year maturity) so your income would be more stable.

TABLE 6–3

BOND MATURITY	Initial Yield	RANGE OF FUTURE YIELDS Years					
		1	2	3	4	5	6
1/4	10.0	15.5	18.0	20.1	21.9	23.7	25.4
	10.0	6.4	5.6	5.0	4.6	4.2	3.9
1	10.0	13.1	14.4	15.3	16.2	17.0	17.7
	10.0	7.6	7.0	6.5	6.2	5.9	5.6
5	10.0	11.7	12.3	12.8	13.2	13.5	13.9
	10.0	8.6	8.1	7.8	7.6	7.4	7.2
10	10.0	11.3	11.8	12.1	12.4	12.7	12.9
	10.0	8.9	8.5	8.3	8.1	7.9	7.7
15	10.0	11.1	11.5	11.8	12.1	12.3	12.5
	10.0	9.0	8.7	8.5	8.3	8.1	8.0
20	10.0	11.0	11.3	11.6	11.8	12.0	12.2
	10.0	9.1	8.8	8.6	8.4	8.3	8.2
25	10.0	10.9	11.2	11.5	11.7	11.9	12.0
	10.0	9.2	8.9	8.7	8.5	8.4	8.3

Range of yields with probability of two thirds.
Based on Salomon U.S. yield data, 1950–79.

The problem of short rates affects not only the investor, but also the borrower. The borrower doesn't want rates to rise because that will cost him money.

Recently banks have been offering borrowers floating rates: rates that fluctuate on a daily, monthly, or quarterly basis. Often the floating rate is tied to the prime rate, or to some other rate.

The next example deals with the problem of the borrower faced with a floating rate. We use the one-fourth-year maturity as a proxy for the prime rate (Table 6–3).

Example 2. The corporation was arranging a $50 million leveraged buyout at a time when rates were 10 percent. When the bank offered only a floating rate, the president of the company asked the chief financial officer to project cash flows and determine the maximum rate the company could afford, based on a conservative projection. The financial chief made his calculations and determined that the maximum interest the company could afford in any year was $10 million. That meant the company could stand a future yield of 20 percent. If interest rates rose above 20 percent, it could not meet its interest and principal obligations.

The president then asked: How likely are rates to go above 20 percent?

Using the first line of the table for the one-fourth-year maturity as a proxy for the prime rate, the financial chief said short rates could reach 20 percent in three years. The odds of going above 20 percent (the upper figure shown in the chart) are 1-in-6. Since the loan was for 10 years, there was a fair chance of hitting the 20 percent rate.

Based on the analysis of the table, the president considered the floating rate too risky. He decided to find another lender that would offer a fixed rate of interest.

The decision to wait for a rise in rates is more complex than either of the above examples. If you want to wait for rates to rise, you have to invest the funds in the meantime and you have three separate questions facing you. Will rates rise as you expect? Will rates fall? Or, what is the danger that rates will drop while your funds are temporarily invested short-term? The three questions are interrelated.

Example 3. Yields are 10 percent. You want to buy a 10-year bond, but you think it's too early because you believe yields on those bonds will return to 13 percent, where they were a year ago. While waiting for 10-year bond yields to rise, you plan to put your money in three-month bills which also now yield 10 percent.

You're betting that rates will rise, but you know you might be wrong. You want to know the risks. Before you make your move, you want to know three things:

1. How likely is it that yields on 10-year bonds will rise to 13 percent?
2. If yields drop instead, how far might they drop?
3. How far could short rates drop while you are waiting?

Table 6–4 answers your questions:

1. It's not very likely that rates on 10-year bonds will rise to 13 percent very soon.

TABLE 6–4

BOND MATURITY	Initial Yield	RANGE OF FUTURE YIELDS Years					
		1	2	3	4	5	6
1/4	10.0	15.5	18.0	20.1 ③	21.9	23.7	25.4
	10.0	6.4	5.6	5.0	4.6	4.2	3.9
1	10.0	13.1	14.4	15.3	16.2	17.0	17.7
	10.0	7.6	7.0	6.5	6.2	5.9	5.6
5	10.0	11.7	12.3	12.8	13.2	13.5	13.9
	10.0	8.6	8.1	7.8	7.6	7.4	7.2
10	10.0	11.3	11.8	12.1	12.4	12.7	12.9 ①
	10.0	8.9	8.5	8.3	8.1	7.9	7.7 ②
15	10.0	11.1	11.5	11.8	12.1	12.3	12.5
	10.0	9.0	8.7	8.5	8.3	8.1	8.0
20	10.0	11.0	11.3	11.6	11.8	12.0	12.2
	10.0	9.1	8.8	8.6	8.4	8.3	8.2
25	10.0	10.9	11.2	11.5	11.7	11.9	12.0
	10.0	9.2	8.9	8.7	8.5	8.4	8.3

Range of yields with probability of two thirds.
Based on Salomon U.S. yield data, 1950–79.

2. If you wait a year, rates are likely to stay above 9 percent. And if you wait six years, rates will probably remain above 8 percent. So you risk a loss of one or two full percentage points. That's a 10 percent to 20 percent loss in income. But it may be something you can sustain.
3. While you stay in short bonds, there is a considerable risk of income loss. Rates could drop to 6.4 percent in a year and to 5 percent in three years. The maximum likely risk is a 40 percent to 50 percent loss in income.

Your best bet? Your best bet is to buy the long bonds, either now, or within a year—whether your hunch is right or wrong. To stay short permanently is the worst possible thing to do because there is high risk of a substantial drop in income.

Lending, perhaps more than any other field, provides a good use for the tables. In lending, a banker wants to know what return he will obtain on a loan. If he loans at the floating rate (for example, prime plus a quarter point) the return to the bank will depend on fluctuations in the prime. Let's see how it might work.

TABLE 6–5 _____

BOND MATURITY	Initial Yield	RANGE OF FUTURE YIELDS Years					
		1	2	3	4	5	6
1/4	10.0	15.5	18.0	20.1	21.9	23.7	25.4
	10.0	6.4	5.6	5.0	4.6	4.2	3.9
1	10.0	13.1	14.4	15.3	16.2	17.0	17.7
	10.0	7.6	7.0	6.5	6.2	5.9	5.6
5	10.0	11.7	12.3	12.8	13.2	13.5	13.9
	10.0	8.6	8.1	7.8	7.6	7.4	7.2
10	10.0	11.3	11.8	12.1	12.4	12.7	12.9
	10.0	8.9	8.5	8.3	8.1	7.9	7.7
15	10.0	11.1	11.5	11.8	12.1	12.3	12.5
	10.0	9.0	8.7	8.5	8.3	8.1	8.0
20	10.0	11.0	11.3	11.6	11.8	12.0	12.2
	10.0	9.1	8.8	8.6	8.4	8.3	8.2
25	10.0	10.9	11.2	11.5	11.7	11.9	12.0
	10.0	9.2	8.9	8.7	8.5	8.4	8.3

Range of yields with probability of two thirds.
Based on Salomon U.S. yield data, 1950–79.

Example 4. The lending officer reviewed the loan and found the company to be solid: he knows the principal officers. After analyzing the company's record and the industry, he recommended the extension of a $1 million loan to the bank loan committee. The committee accepted his recommendation. Now the lending officer is concerned about the rate. He had agreed with the customer to prime plus 25 basis points. He asked himself; What will that rate be in a year?

We can take the one-fourth-year maturity as a proxy for the prime. The loan officer has the option of deciding how often the rate will be set: once a year or every six months. Looking at Table 6–5, he can see that the rate could drop to 6.4 percent in a year. It could go higher, of course, but the banker is concerned about the lowest return he might get. He decides the risk of 6.4 percent is acceptable and agrees to the floating rate.

Table 6–6 provides a range of future yields for a much broader spectrum of initial yields.

TABLE 6-6

BOND MATURITY	Initial Yield	RANGE OF FUTURE YIELDS Years					
		1	2	3	4	5	6
1/4	1.0	1.6	1.8	2.0	2.2	2.4	2.5
	1.0	.6	.6	.5	.5	.4	.4
1	1.0	1.3	1.4	1.5	1.6	1.7	1.8
	1.0	.8	.7	.7	.6	.6	.6
5	1.0	1.2	1.2	1.3	1.3	1.4	1.4
	1.0	.9	.8	.8	.8	.7	.7
10	1.0	1.1	1.2	1.2	1.2	1.3	1.3
	1.0	.9	.9	.8	.8	.8	.8
15	1.0	1.1	1.2	1.2	1.2	1.2	1.2
	1.0	.9	.9	.8	.8	.8	.8
20	1.0	1.1	1.1	1.2	1.2	1.2	1.2
	1.0	.9	.9	.9	.8	.8	.8
25	1.0	1.1	1.1	1.1	1.2	1.2	1.2
	1.0	.9	.9	.9	.9	.8	.8

BOND MATURITY	Initial Yield	RANGE OF FUTURE YIELDS Years					
		1	2	3	4	5	6
1/4	2.0	3.1	3.6	4.0	4.4	4.7	5.1
	2.0	1.3	1.1	1.0	.9	.8	.8
1	2.0	2.6	2.9	3.1	3.2	3.4	3.5
	2.0	1.5	1.4	1.3	1.2	1.2	1.1
5	2.0	2.3	2.5	2.6	2.6	2.7	2.8
	2.0	1.7	1.6	1.6	1.5	1.5	1.4
10	2.0	2.3	2.4	2.4	2.5	2.5	2.6
	2.0	1.8	1.7	1.7	1.6	1.6	1.5
15	2.0	2.2	2.3	2.4	2.4	2.5	2.5
	2.0	1.8	1.7	1.7	1.7	1.6	1.6
20	2.0	2.2	2.3	2.3	2.4	2.4	2.4
	2.0	1.8	1.8	1.7	1.7	1.7	1.6
25	2.0	2.2	2.2	2.3	2.3	2.4	2.4
	2.0	1.8	1.8	1.7	1.7	1.7	1.7

For initial yields of 3 percent to 16 percent for maturities of ¼, 1, 5, 10, 15, 20 and 25 years for 1 to 6 years in the future with probability of two thirds of being within range. Based on Salomon U.S. yield index data, 1950–1979.

TABLE 6-6 (continued)

BOND MATURITY	Initial Yield	1	2	3	4	5	6
		RANGE OF FUTURE YIELDS Years					
1/4	3.0	4.7	5.4	6.0	6.6	7.1	7.6
	3.0	1.9	1.7	1.5	1.4	1.3	1.2
1	3.0	3.9	4.3	4.6	4.9	5.1	5.3
	3.0	2.3	2.1	2.0	1.9	1.8	1.7
5	3.0	3.5	3.7	3.8	4.0	4.1	4.2
	3.0	2.6	2.4	2.4	2.3	2.2	2.2
10	3.0	3.4	3.5	3.6	3.7	3.8	3.9
	3.0	2.7	2.6	2.5	2.4	2.4	2.3
15	3.0	3.3	3.5	3.5	3.6	3.7	3.7
	3.0	2.7	2.6	2.5	2.5	2.4	2.4
20	3.0	3.3	3.4	3.5	3.6	3.6	3.7
	3.0	2.7	2.6	2.6	2.5	2.5	2.5
25	3.0	3.3	3.4	3.4	3.5	3.6	3.6
	3.0	2.7	2.7	2.6	2.6	2.5	2.5

BOND MATURITY	Initial Yield	1	2	3	4	5	6
		RANGE OF FUTURE YIELDS Years					
1/4	4.0	6.2	7.2	8.0	8.8	9.5	10.1
	4.0	2.6	2.2	2.0	1.8	1.7	1.6
1	4.0	5.2	5.7	6.1	6.5	6.8	7.1
	4.0	3.1	2.8	2.6	2.5	2.4	2.3
5	4.0	4.7	4.9	5.1	5.3	5.4	5.5
	4.0	3.4	3.3	3.1	3.0	3.0	2.9
10	4.0	4.5	4.7	4.8	5.0	5.1	5.2
	4.0	3.5	3.4	3.3	3.2	3.2	3.1
15	4.0	4.4	4.6	4.7	4.8	4.9	5.0
	4.0	3.6	3.5	3.4	3.3	3.3	3.2
20	4.0	4.4	4.5	4.6	4.7	4.8	4.9
	4.0	3.6	3.5	3.4	3.4	3.3	3.3
25	4.0	4.4	4.5	4.6	4.7	4.8	4.8
	4.0	3.7	3.6	3.5	3.4	3.4	3.3

TABLE 6–6 (*continued*)

BOND MATURITY	Initial Yield	RANGE OF FUTURE YIELDS Years					
		1	2	3	4	5	6
1/4	5.0	7.8	9.0	10.0	11.0	11.8	12.7
	5.0	3.2	2.8	2.5	2.3	2.1	2.0
1	5.0	6.5	7.2	7.7	8.1	8.5	8.9
	5.0	3.8	3.5	3.3	3.1	2.9	2.8
5	5.0	5.8	6.1	6.4	6.6	6.8	6.9
	5.0	4.3	4.1	3.9	3.8	3.7	3.6
10	5.0	5.6	5.9	6.1	6.2	6.3	6.5
	5.0	4.4	4.3	4.1	4.0	3.9	3.9
15	5.0	5.6	5.8	5.9	6.0	6.1	6.2
	5.0	4.5	4.3	4.2	4.1	4.1	4.0
20	5.0	5.5	5.7	5.8	5.9	6.0	6.1
	5.0	4.5	4.4	4.3	4.2	4.2	4.1
25	5.0	5.5	5.6	5.7	5.8	5.9	6.0
	5.0	4.6	4.4	4.4	4.3	4.2	4.2

BOND MATURITY	Initial Yield	RANGE OF FUTURE YIELDS Years					
		1	2	3	4	5	6
1/4	6.0	9.3	10.8	12.0	13.2	14.2	15.2
	6.0	3.9	3.3	3.0	2.7	2.5	2.4
1	6.0	7.9	8.6	9.2	9.7	10.2	10.6
	6.0	4.6	4.2	3.9	3.7	3.5	3.4
5	6.0	7.0	7.4	7.7	7.9	8.1	8.3
	6.0	5.1	4.9	4.7	4.6	4.4	4.3
10	6.0	6.8	7.1	7.3	7.4	7.6	7.8
	6.0	5.3	5.1	5.0	4.8	4.7	4.6
15	6.0	6.7	6.9	7.1	7.2	7.4	7.5
	6.0	5.4	5.2	5.1	5.0	4.9	4.8
20	6.0	6.6	6.8	7.0	7.1	7.2	7.3
	6.0	5.5	5.3	5.2	5.1	5.0	4.9
25	6.0	6.5	6.7	6.9	7.0	7.1	7.2
	6.0	5.5	5.3	5.2	5.1	5.1	5.0

TABLE 6–6 (*continued*) _____

BOND MATURITY	Initial Yield	RANGE OF FUTURE YIELDS Years					
		1	2	3	4	5	6
1/4	7.0	10.9	12.6	14.0	15.3	16.6	17.8
	7.0	4.5	3.9	3.5	3.2	3.0	2.8
1	7.0	9.2	10.0	10.7	11.4	11.9	12.4
	7.0	5.3	4.9	4.6	4.3	4.1	3.9
5	7.0	8.2	8.6	8.9	9.2	9.5	9.7
	7.0	6.0	5.7	5.5	5.3	5.2	5.1
10	7.0	7.9	8.2	8.5	8.7	8.9	9.0
	7.0	6.2	6.0	5.8	5.6	5.5	5.4
15	7.0	7.8	8.1	8.3	8.4	8.6	8.7
	7.0	6.3	6.1	5.9	5.8	5.7	5.6
20	7.0	7.7	7.9	8.1	8.3	8.4	8.6
	7.0	6.4	6.2	6.0	5.9	5.8	5.7
25	7.0	7.6	7.9	8.0	8.2	8.3	8.4
	7.0	6.4	6.2	6.1	6.0	5.9	5.8

BOND MATURITY	Initial Yield	RANGE OF FUTURE YIELDS Years					
		1	2	3	4	5	6
1/4	8.0	12.4	14.4	16.0	17.5	18.9	20.3
	8.0	5.2	4.4	4.0	3.6	3.4	3.2
1	8.0	10.5	11.5	12.3	13.0	13.6	14.2
	8.0	6.1	5.6	5.2	4.9	4.7	4.5
5	8.0	9.3	9.8	10.2	10.5	10.8	11.1
	8.0	6.9	6.5	6.3	6.1	5.9	5.8
10	8.0	9.0	9.4	9.7	9.9	10.1	10.3
	8.0	7.1	6.8	6.6	6.4	6.3	6.2
15	8.0	8.9	9.2	9.4	9.6	9.8	10.0
	8.0	7.2	7.0	6.8	6.6	6.5	6.4
20	8.0	8.8	9.1	9.3	9.5	9.6	9.8
	8.0	7.3	7.0	6.9	6.8	6.6	6.5
25	8.0	8.7	9.0	9.2	9.4	9.5	9.6
	8.0	7.3	7.1	7.0	6.8	6.7	6.6

TABLE 6–6 (*continued*)

BOND MATURITY	Initial Yield	1	2	RANGE OF FUTURE YIELDS Years 3	4	5	6
1/4	9.0	14.0	16.2	18.0	19.7	21.3	22.8
	9.0	5.8	5.0	4.5	4.1	3.8	3.5
1	9.0	11.8	12.9	13.8	14.6	15.3	16.0
	9.0	6.9	6.3	5.9	5.6	5.3	5.1
5	9.0	10.5	11.1	11.5	11.9	12.2	12.5
	9.0	7.7	7.3	7.1	6.8	6.7	6.5
10	9.0	10.2	10.6	10.9	11.2	11.4	11.6
	9.0	8.0	7.7	7.4	7.3	7.1	7.0
15	9.0	10.0	10.4	10.6	10.9	11.1	11.2
	9.0	8.1	7.8	7.6	7.5	7.3	7.2
20	9.0	9.9	10.2	10.5	10.7	10.8	11.0
	9.0	8.2	7.9	7.7	7.6	7.5	7.4
25	9.0	9.8	10.1	10.3	10.5	10.7	10.8
	9.0	8.2	8.0	7.8	7.7	7.6	7.5

BOND MATURITY	Initial Yield	1	2	RANGE OF FUTURE YIELDS Years 3	4	5	6
1/4	10.0	15.5	18.0	20.1	21.9	23.7	25.4
	10.0	6.4	5.6	5.0	4.6	4.2	3.9
1	10.0	13.1	14.4	15.3	16.2	17.0	17.7
	10.0	7.6	7.0	6.5	6.2	5.9	5.6
5	10.0	11.7	12.3	12.8	13.2	13.5	13.9
	10.0	8.6	8.1	7.8	7.6	7.4	7.2
10	10.0	11.3	11.8	12.1	12.4	12.7	12.9
	10.0	8.9	8.5	8.3	8.1	7.9	7.7
15	10.0	11.1	11.5	11.8	12.1	12.3	12.5
	10.0	9.0	8.7	8.5	8.3	8.1	8.0
20	10.0	11.0	11.3	11.6	11.8	12.0	12.2
	10.0	9.1	8.8	8.6	8.4	8.3	8.2
25	10.0	10.9	11.2	11.5	11.7	11.9	12.0
	10.0	9.2	8.9	8.7	8.5	8.4	8.3

TABLE 6–6 (continued) _____

BOND MATURITY	Initial Yield	RANGE OF FUTURE YIELDS Years					
		1	2	3	4	5	6
1/4	11.0	17.1	19.8	22.1	24.1	26.1	27.9
	11.0	7.1	6.1	5.5	5.0	4.6	4.3
1	11.0	14.4	15.8	16.9	17.8	18.7	19.5
	11.0	8.4	7.7	7.2	6.8	6.5	6.2
5	11.0	12.8	13.5	14.0	14.5	14.9	15.2
	11.0	9.4	9.0	8.6	8.4	8.1	7.9
10	11.0	12.4	12.9	13.3	13.7	13.9	14.2
	11.0	9.8	9.4	9.1	8.9	8.7	8.5
15	11.0	12.2	12.7	13.0	13.3	13.5	13.7
	11.0	9.9	9.6	9.3	9.1	9.0	8.8
20	11.0	12.1	12.5	12.8	13.0	13.2	13.4
	11.0	10.0	9.7	9.5	9.3	9.1	9.0
25	11.0	12.0	12.4	12.6	12.9	13.1	13.2
	11.0	10.1	9.8	9.6	9.4	9.3	9.1

BOND MATURITY	Initial Yield	RANGE OF FUTURE YIELDS Years					
		1	2	3	4	5	6
1/4	12.0	18.6	21.6	24.1	26.3	28.4	30.4
	12.0	7.7	6.7	6.0	5.5	5.1	4.7
1	12.0	15.7	17.2	18.4	19.5	20.4	21.3
	12.0	9.2	8.4	7.8	7.4	7.1	6.8
5	12.0	14.0	14.7	15.3	15.8	16.2	16.6
	12.0	10.3	9.8	9.4	9.1	8.9	8.7
10	12.0	13.5	14.1	14.5	14.9	15.2	15.5
	12.0	10.6	10.2	9.9	9.7	9.5	9.3
15	12.0	13.3	13.8	14.2	14.5	14.7	15.0
	12.0	10.8	10.4	10.2	10.0	9.8	9.6
20	12.0	13.2	13.6	13.9	14.2	14.5	14.7
	12.0	10.9	10.6	10.3	10.1	10.0	9.8
25	12.0	13.1	13.5	13.8	14.0	14.3	14.4
	12.0	11.0	10.7	10.4	10.3	10.1	10.0

TABLE 6–6 (*continued*) _____

BOND MATURITY	Initial Yield	RANGE OF FUTURE YIELDS Years					
		1	2	3	4	5	6
1/4	13.0	20.2	23.4	26.1	28.5	30.8	33.0
	13.0	8.4	7.2	6.5	5.9	5.5	5.1
1	13.0	17.0	18.7	20.0	21.1	22.1	23.1
	13.0	9.9	9.1	8.5	8.0	7.6	7.3
5	13.0	15.2	16.0	16.6	17.1	17.6	18.0
	13.0	11.1	10.6	10.2	9.9	9.6	9.4
10	13.0	14.7	15.3	15.7	16.1	16.5	16.8
	13.0	11.5	11.1	10.7	10.5	10.3	10.1
15	13.0	14.4	15.0	15.3	15.7	16.0	16.2
	13.0	11.7	11.3	11.0	10.8	10.6	10.4
20	13.0	14.3	14.8	15.1	15.4	15.7	15.9
	13.0	11.8	11.5	11.2	11.0	10.8	10.6
25	13.0	14.2	14.6	14.9	15.2	15.4	15.7
	13.0	11.9	11.6	11.3	11.1	10.9	10.8

BOND MATURITY	Initial Yield	RANGE OF FUTURE YIELDS Years					
		1	2	3	4	5	6
1/4	14.0	21.7	25.2	28.1	30.7	33.2	35.5
	14.0	9.0	7.8	7.0	6.4	5.9	5.5
1	14.0	18.3	20.1	21.5	22.7	23.8	24.8
	14.0	10.7	9.8	9.1	8.6	8.2	7.9
5	14.0	16.3	17.2	17.9	18.4	18.9	19.4
	14.0	12.0	11.4	11.0	10.6	10.3	10.1
10	14.0	15.8	16.5	17.0	17.4	17.7	18.1
	14.0	12.4	11.9	11.6	11.3	11.0	10.8
15	14.0	15.5	16.1	16.5	16.9	17.2	17.5
	14.0	12.6	12.2	11.9	11.6	11.4	11.2
20	14.0	15.4	15.9	16.3	16.6	16.9	17.1
	14.0	12.7	12.3	12.0	11.8	11.6	11.5
25	14.0	15.3	15.7	16.1	16.4	16.6	16.9
	14.0	12.8	12.5	12.2	12.0	11.8	11.6

TABLE 6–6 (*continued*) _____

BOND MATURITY	Initial Yield	RANGE OF FUTURE YIELDS Years					
		1	2	3	4	5	6
1/4	15.0	23.3	27.0	30.1	32.9	35.5	38.1
	15.0	9.7	8.3	7.5	6.8	6.3	5.9
1	15.0	19.6	21.5	23.0	24.3	25.5	26.6
	15.0	11.5	10.5	9.8	9.3	8.8	8.5
5	15.0	17.5	18.4	19.1	19.8	20.3	20.8
	15.0	12.9	12.2	11.8	11.4	11.1	10.8
10	15.0	16.9	17.6	18.2	18.6	19.0	19.4
	15.0	13.3	12.8	12.4	12.1	11.8	11.6
15	15.0	16.7	17.3	17.7	18.1	18.4	18.7
	15.0	13.5	13.0	12.7	12.4	12.2	12.0
20	15.0	16.5	17.0	17.4	17.8	18.1	18.3
	15.0	13.6	13.2	12.9	12.7	12.5	12.3
25	15.0	16.4	16.9	17.2	17.5	17.8	18.1
	15.0	13.7	13.3	13.1	12.8	12.6	12.5

BOND MATURITY	Initial Yield	RANGE OF FUTURE YIELDS Years					
		1	2	3	4	5	6
1/4	16.0	24.8	28.8	32.1	35.1	37.9	40.6
	16.0	10.3	8.9	8.0	7.3	6.8	6.3
1	16.0	21.0	23.0	24.6	25.9	27.2	28.4
	16.0	12.2	11.1	10.4	9.9	9.4	9.0
5	16.0	18.7	19.7	20.4	21.1	21.6	22.2
	16.0	13.7	13.0	12.5	12.2	11.8	11.5
10	16.0	18.1	18.8	19.4	19.9	20.3	20.7
	16.0	14.2	13.6	13.2	12.9	12.6	12.4
15	16.0	17.8	18.4	18.9	19.3	19.7	20.0
	16.0	14.4	13.9	13.6	13.3	13.0	12.8
20	16.0	17.6	18.2	18.6	19.0	19.3	19.6
	16.0	14.6	14.1	13.8	13.5	13.3	13.1
25	16.0	17.5	18.0	18.4	18.7	19.0	19.3
	16.0	14.7	14.2	13.9	13.7	13.5	13.3

TABLE 6–6 (*continued*)

BOND MATURITY	Initial Yield	1	2	RANGE OF FUTURE YIELDS Years 3	4	5	6
1/4	17.0	26.4	30.6	34.1	37.3	40.3	43.1
	17.0	11.0	9.5	8.5	7.8	7.2	6.7
1	17.0	22.3	24.4	26.1	27.6	28.9	30.2
	17.0	13.0	11.8	11.1	10.5	10.0	9.6
5	17.0	19.8	20.9	21.7	22.4	23.0	23.6
	17.0	14.6	13.8	13.3	12.9	12.6	12.3
10	17.0	19.2	20.0	20.6	21.1	21.5	22.0
	17.0	15.1	14.5	14.0	13.7	13.4	13.2
15	17.0	18.9	19.6	20.1	20.5	20.9	21.2
	17.0	15.3	14.8	14.4	14.1	13.8	13.6
20	17.0	18.7	19.3	19.8	20.1	20.5	20.8
	17.0	15.5	15.0	14.6	14.4	14.1	13.9
25	17.0	18.6	19.1	19.5	19.9	20.2	20.5
	17.0	15.6	15.1	14.8	14.5	14.3	14.1

BOND MATURITY	Initial Yield	1	2	RANGE OF FUTURE YIELDS Years 3	4	5	6
1/4	18.0	27.9	32.4	36.1	39.5	42.6	45.7
	18.0	11.6	10.0	9.0	8.2	7.6	7.1
1	18.0	23.6	25.8	27.6	29.2	30.6	31.9
	18.0	13.7	12.5	11.7	11.1	10.6	10.1
5	18.0	21.0	22.1	23.0	23.7	24.4	24.9
	18.0	15.4	14.7	14.1	13.7	13.3	13.0
10	18.0	20.3	21.2	21.8	22.3	22.8	23.3
	18.0	16.0	15.3	14.9	14.5	14.2	13.9
15	18.0	20.0	20.7	21.3	21.7	22.1	22.5
	18.0	16.2	15.6	15.2	14.9	14.7	14.4
20	18.0	19.8	20.4	20.9	21.3	21.7	22.0
	18.0	16.4	15.9	15.5	15.2	14.9	14.7
25	18.0	19.6	20.2	20.7	21.1	21.4	21.7
	18.0	16.5	16.0	15.7	15.4	15.2	14.9

TABLE 6–6 (concluded) _____

BOND MATURITY	Initial Yield	1	2	RANGE OF FUTURE YIELDS Years 3	4	5	6
1/4	19.0	29.5	34.2	38.1	41.7	45.0	48.2
	19.0	12.3	10.6	9.5	8.7	8.0	7.5
1	19.0	24.9	27.3	29.2	30.8	32.3	33.7
	19.0	14.5	13.2	12.4	11.7	11.2	10.7
5	19.0	22.2	23.3	24.2	25.0	25.7	26.3
	19.0	16.3	15.5	14.9	14.4	14.0	13.7
10	19.0	21.4	22.3	23.0	23.6	24.1	24.5
	19.0	16.8	16.2	15.7	15.3	15.0	14.7
15	19.0	21.1	21.9	22.4	22.9	23.3	23.7
	19.0	17.1	16.5	16.1	15.8	15.5	15.2
20	19.0	20.9	21.6	22.1	22.5	22.9	23.2
	19.0	17.3	16.7	16.4	16.0	15.8	15.5
25	19.0	20.7	21.4	21.8	22.2	22.6	22.9
	19.0	17.4	16.9	16.5	16.2	16.0	15.8

BOND MATURITY	Initial Yield	1	2	RANGE OF FUTURE YIELDS Years 3	4	5	6
1/4	20.0	31.0	36.0	40.1	43.9	47.4	50.7
	20.0	12.9	11.1	10.0	9.1	8.4	7.9
1	20.0	26.2	28.7	30.7	32.4	34.0	35.5
	20.0	15.3	13.9	13.0	12.3	11.8	11.3
5	20.0	23.3	24.6	25.5	26.3	27.1	27.7
	20.0	17.2	16.3	15.7	15.2	14.8	14.4
10	20.0	22.6	23.5	24.2	24.8	25.4	25.8
	20.0	17.7	17.0	16.5	16.1	15.8	15.5
15	20.0	22.2	23.0	23.6	24.1	24.6	25.0
	20.0	18.0	17.4	16.9	16.6	16.3	16.0
20	20.0	22.0	22.7	23.2	23.7	24.1	24.4
	20.0	18.2	17.6	17.2	16.9	16.6	16.4
25	20.0	21.8	22.5	23.0	23.4	23.8	24.1
	20.0	18.3	17.8	17.4	17.1	16.8	16.6

7

How to Calculate the Volatility of Bond Prices

"If you buy a long bond," said the bond broker, "the price will fluctuate more than if you buy a short bond."

I nodded, in agreement.

Then he continued. "If you buy a 10 percent 20-year bond and yields rise to 12 percent, the bond will fall in price from . . ." And he gave the figures. "But if you buy a five-year bond with the same yield figure, the price will not drop as far." He proceeded to calculate the price fall for a five-year bond. Predictably, the fall was much less.

Of course, I knew that a change in interest rates caused much greater changes in prices on long bonds than on short bonds. Everyone in the business knows this as accepted fact.

The reason that long bond prices changed more than short bond prices, for a given shift in interest rates, was that the change in yield had to be made up by the change in price.

If yields rose from 10 percent to 12 percent on a one-year 10 percent bond, you needed an extra $2 per $100 at the end of the year to give you the 12 percent yield. That meant the bond price had to drop from $100 to $98, roughly speaking. But if the bond was a five-year bond, then you needed to add the equivalent of $2 for each of five years, or an additional $10. Getting the additional $10 means the price would have to drop to $90. The actual figure is higher than $90 because a

$10 coupon on $90 is more than 10 percent and you have to calculate the gain in principal at a compound rate. But the principal we are driving at is the same.

In going from 10 percent to 12 percent on a $10 coupon, the actual prices work out to $98.17 on a five-year bond and $92.64 on a 10-year bond—a much bigger change for the longer bond.

I knew all of this. You can find it in any book on bonds. But the matter is not as simple as that because yields on long-term bonds don't fluctuate as much as yields on short-term bonds. And you also have to take into account the difference in yield fluctuation.

The writers of bond books also know that and put it in their books, but they don't give you the actual figures. In one part of the book, they calculate the price effects of a given change in interest rates for two bonds of different maturities. In another part of the book, they tell you that interest rates fluctuate more for short bonds than for long bonds. But they don't take into account the different degree of fluctuation when they do the calculation for the price effect.

The reason is that they don't have the data for the second law. You need that to make the correct calculation, and they don't have it.

You have to take into account the actual degree that interest rates fluctuate for each maturity in order to talk accurately about the volatility of bond prices. The volatility of yields on a 20-year bond is much less than the volatility of yields on a five-year bond, or a one-year bond. You have to apply the greater volatility of price change for a given yield change to the much lower probable yield change on the long bond. On the short bond, you have the much lower price change with the much greater probable change in yields.

It isn't only the differences in yield volatility for different maturity bonds that you have to take into account. You must also consider continually declining maturity. When we looked at changing yields for reinvestment purposes, the decline in maturity of the bond was not a problem. That's because we were waiting to invest long, or reinvest short. But when we look at the actual question of long bond prices, then the declining maturity of the actual bond has an effect: The effect is dramatic.

Let's start at the beginning. From the date of purchase of a bond, two things happen that affect the price. The first thing that happens is that the maturity of the bond declines. The maturity declines steadily so that at the end of the first year, a 15-year bond becomes 14-year bond; at the end of the second year, the 14-year bond becomes a 13-year bond, and thereafter maturity keeps declining until at the end of 15 years the bond has zero maturity. At zero maturity, you can turn the bond in for its par value: when you do that, the price of the bond is again 100, its purchase price, if you bought an original issue at par.

The second thing that happens is that with the passage of time, the volatility of yields rises under the influence of the two laws of volatility, time and maturity. For a bond with declining maturity, both volatility laws affect the future yields on which the bond will be priced. Since both laws are at work, if you want to know the range of yields affecting the price of a 15-year bond, after one year you look at the volatility of yields of a 14-year bond, after two years you use the volatility of a 13-year bond. After 14 years you use the volatility of a one-year bond, because at the end of 14 years your bond is a one-year bond with only one year of life remaining.

In order to estimate the future range of prices of a 15-year bond, we need a yield table showing the future range of yields for a declining maturity instrument, a 14, 13, 12 . . . 2, one-year bond after 1, 2, 3 . . . 13, 14 years.

Table 7–1 shows such figures for a five-year bond.

HOW TO CALCULATE THE PRICE RANGE OF A BOND

To calculate the future price range of a five-year 10 percent bond purchased at par, you use the data shown in Table 7–1, which indicates the following:

1. The original maturity of the bond: 5 years.
2. The coupon of the bond purchased at par: 10 percent.
3. The number of years from purchase date: 2 years.
4. The remaining maturity of the original bond: 3 years.
5. The high yield on a 3-year bond 2 years from purchase data: 12.8 percent.

TABLE 7–1 _____

①

CALCULATION OF PRICE RANGE OF 5 YEAR 10% BOND

		Years from Purchase				
0	1	2 ③	3	4	5	
		Years to Maturity				
5	4 ④	3	2	1	0	
		Yield on Bond				
② 10.0	11.8	12.8 ⑤	14.0	16.2	.0	High
10.0	8.5	7.8	7.2	6.2	.0	Low
		Price of Bond				
100.0	94.5	93.4 ⑥	93.4	94.7	100.0	Low
100.0	105.0	105.6	105.1	103.6	100.0	High

Range of Yields with Probability of two-thirds.
Based on Salomon U.S. yield data, 1950–1979.

6. The price of that 10 percent bond yielding 12.8 percent: $93.4.

Note that item number 5 is derived from the high yield after two years on what has become a *three-year* 10 percent bond. We use a three-year bond because the bond at this time has only three years to maturity, even though it was originally a five-year bond.

All prices are calculated using annual rather than semi-annual compounding; they differ from prices obtained using semiannual compounding.

The graph of such a table is shown in Figure 7–1 for a 10 percent 15-year bond. The lines diverge faster because the maturity of the bond depicted on the figure is continually declining and, under the third law, the volatility of shorter bonds is much higher. Therefore, declining maturity makes bond price risk much greater than it otherwise might be.

Once you have the future yields for a 15-year bond, you can price the bond using the standard yield to maturity formula. The pricing formula takes into account the coupon, in this case 10 percent per year or par, the future yield, and the years remaining to maturity.

Using the yield figures from Table 7–1, we can estimate the range of prices of the 15-year, 10 percent coupon bond. The range of prices is shown in Figure 7–1. As you can see,

FIGURE 7–1

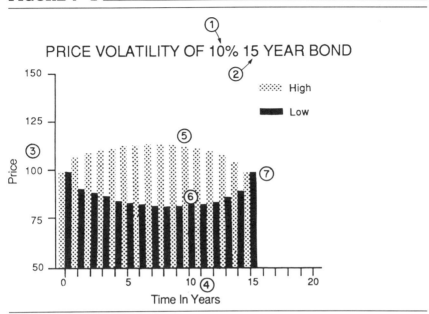

the price range is elliptical, increasing from purchase date, and then returning to par at maturity. The lines do not return to par until very soon before maturity, which may seem strange. The reason for the delay is that after 13 or 14 years, the range of rates on a one- or two-year bond is very high. That high volatility of the short rates delays the return of the bond price to par.

Maturity affects the volatility of a bond's price in two ways; first, maturity affects the price by its influence on the volatility of rates as the bond declines in maturity; second, the original maturity of the bond affects the volatility of the bond's price. It is the original maturity of the bond that most people talk about when they talk about the effect of maturity on the bond's price. When they talk about the original maturity, they talk about the most important effect of maturity; but the other effect is important, as we have just seen.

The effect of maturity can be seen in Figure 7–2. The figures show the range within which the price of the bond should lie, two-thirds of the time. The figures are constructed to reflect the range of future yields, high and low, after the passage of time and as the bond declines in maturity. Figures are drawn for different maturities so you can see the effect of maturity. All of the figures are based on a 10 percent coupon bond purchased at par, so that you can see the effect of different maturities.

EXAMPLES USING FIGURE 7–1

Each figure shows the range of future prices for a single maturity and various future years when the present yield is 10 percent.

WHAT FIGURE 7–1 SHOWS

1. The coupon of the bond: 10 percent.
2. The maturity of the bond: 15 years.
3. The price at date of purchase: $100.
4. The number of years from now: 10 years.
5. The *high* probable price 10 years from now: $114.
6. The *low* probable price 5 years from now: $83.
7. The price at maturity: $100.

Maturity has one effect on prices; the general yield level has another. For bonds selling near par, low yields result in low price volatility; high yields give high price volatility because high yields are more volatile than low yields. You can see the effect of differences in yields in the next set (Figure 7–3) which run from very low to very high yields. As you can see, the bond with the 1 percent yield shows very little volatility whereas the high yield bond is very volatile in price.

It is also true that for two bonds of similar yield, the low coupon, deep-discount bond will have a more volatile price.

FIGURE 7–2
Range of Future Prices*

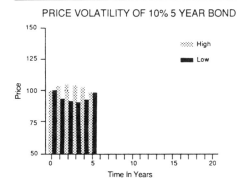

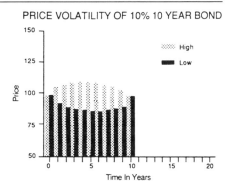

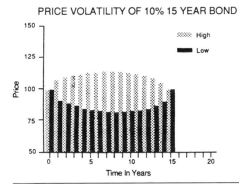

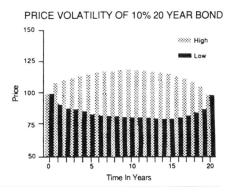

*For initial yield of 10 percent for maturities of 5, 10, 15, and 20 years with probability of two-thirds of being within range.
Based on Salomon U.S. yield index data, 1950–1979.

FIGURE 7–3
Range of Future Prices*

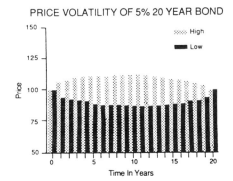

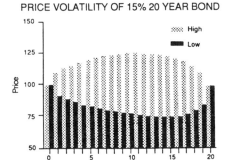

*For 1 percent, 5 percent, 10 percent, and 15 percent 20-year bond with probability of two-thirds of being within range.
Based on Salomon U.S. yield index data, 1950–1979.

PART TWO

Putting the Laws to Work on Your Behalf

8

Setting Objectives

The Russians defeated the Germans in World War II by turning a weakness into a strength, by retreating. They gave up land and time to the Germans, who in seizing the land exhausted themselves in the cold Russian winter. As a result, the Germans died not from bullets, but from exposure. The Russians had calculated what they could give up and devised a successful battle strategy based on that loss.

Success in the bond investment battle is analogous. By being able and willing to lose on one front, you can gain on another. The key is knowing what to give up and what not to give up, in distinguishing what is essential from what is not essential. If you think you need everything and try to get everything, you may lose all. In bond investment, the most critical thing is to know what you can do, what you cannot do, and to distinguish what is important from what is not important. Only then can you determine which strategy will work for you.

Of all the questions that you could ask to determine what is important, the following three questions are critical: (1) Will you need the principal soon? (2) Do you need the income and will you depend on it? (3) Are you only interested in total return?

The first question determines your alternatives, whether you can wait to get your money back, or not wait. If you can wait, then your time frame can be long, and you can buy long bonds. If you need to have the principal back the next month, or the next year, or in two years, then you are a short term investor and will have to buy short-term bonds, or their equivalent. Your choice of instruments is severely restricted. You don't have an option, analogous to the Russians' ability to retreat, to take your time.

From the answers to the second question, you can determine the kinds of bonds you can buy and the kind you should buy. Do you need the income that the bond will generate? Will you depend on that income, or do you want to depend on that income? An affirmative answer to this question implies that you will not need the principal soon. If you do need the principal in a short time, then you can't depend on the income.

Dependence on the income implies a long-term investment, and also an investment where interim fluctuations in principal are not of concern. It suggests a long-term, or an intermediate-term, income oriented investor. It means that income is more important to you than a stable market value of your principal, that you can give up stability of principal in order to have stable income. It is like the Russians who could afford to give up land to the Germans in order to allow that land to inflict exhaustion on the enemy. The result was not painless, just as interim fluctuations in the value of your bond are not painless. But the sacrifice is less valuable to you, the investor, than the gain: stable income. In order to achieve stable income, you must give up the stable principal; knowing which is more important during the life of the bond is critical to devising a bond maturity strategy. For this reason, being clear on what you want and do not want is critical. Investors should note that a strategy requiring income precludes certain types of long bonds, such as deep-discount bonds or zero coupon bonds.

The investor who says yes to the third question should have answered no to the other two questions. If you are interested in total return, your perspective is probably not short term; you do not need to keep principal stable, and you do not need income. Thus, your perspective is long term, or should be if you have thought out your needs carefully. A long-term, total return investor can give up interim fluctuations in market value and interim fluctuations in income. In fact, he can give up all income altogether and go straight for a zero coupon bond that gives him a certain return to maturity. Total return investors can secure a predetermined and certain return, provided they are willing to give up fluctuations in return prior to maturity. Like the income investor, they too must know what they want and what they don't want.

Frequently, total return investors, and the accountants and tax writers who make rules for the guidance of total return investors, fail to distinguish the important from the unimportant. Pension funds are total return investors with long-term horizons and no need for income and also little need for stability of principal. Yet they measure their bond portfolios on short-term total return performance, in complete disregard of what is important or not important to them over the long run.

Although we have not listed a fourth objective, capital appreciation, we have not forgotten it. Capital appreciation has no place among bond portfolio objectives, except under certain unusual circumstances. A bond is an instrument that pays a fixed coupon and returns the principal at maturity. Unless you buy discount bonds, or zero-coupon bonds, the only way to secure capital appreciation is to forecast interest rates with better than even odds of success. Though interest rate forecasting is practiced by many investment managers, it is not possible to correctly forecast the direction of interest rates over the long run with odds any better than telling when heads will come up on the next flip of a coin.

The only way to secure bond appreciation is to purchase default bonds, or very low rated bonds at discounts from par. That is a viable objective, and it can be very successful. But in general, capital appreciation is not a good objective for bond investment.

A final question, implied by the other four, is how long your investment horizon is. Is it 1 year, 5 years, or 20? For most people it is going to be 5 or 10 years, and for most institutions it will be longer. To determine the best maturity of the bonds to be selected, a decision on the length of the investment period is essential.

You must decide whether you need your principal soon. If you don't need the principal soon you must decide whether your main interest is long-term income or long-term total return. If you can wait to get your original investment back and rates are attractive, then you can invest long for the income it generates or the total return it promises. But first, you must decide what your primary objective is and what you can give up to get it.

9

Classic Bond Strategies You Can Use

Just as every field commander needs a strategy to execute his battle plan, the investor in bonds needs a strategy to gain his investment objective. Though the military strategy depends on the objectives of the general, the terrain and army opposing him, the successful bond strategy depends on the objectives of the investor, the characteristics of the bond instrument and interest rate fluctuations.

As the number of viable military strategies is fixed, since there are only so many within the constraints of war, the number of bond strategies is limited to the investor under the constraints and characteristics of bond obligations.

What you can do is limited. You cannot control the present level of interest rates; you cannot control the future level of rates; and you cannot control the shape of the yield curve. These powerful influences on your results are like terrain and the enemy order of battle: out of your hands and unchangeable.

But you can control how you use them. The primary weapon which you, as a bond investor, have to control the outcome of the investment battle is your ability to determine the maturities of the portfolio.

The initial choice of maturity strategies is restricted to four alternatives: short maturities, intermediate maturities, long maturities, or staggered maturities. Like picking employees by height, you can select only short men, only tall men, or a full range from short to tall. If you are selecting jockeys or basketball players, the height you select makes an enormous difference. If you are purchasing bonds, the maturities you choose at the outset has an enormous effect. This is because different length maturities behave differently under the laws of fluctuations in interest rates.

A short-maturity bond pays a fixed coupon for a short time and returns the whole amount of principal after a short interval. The short maturity strategy is a nearsighted strategy with a nearsighted result; its effects on you are quick and ephemeral.

For example, if you buy a 10 percent one-year bond for $1,000, you will receive two coupons ($50 in six months and $50 at the end of a year) plus your original $1,000 investment.

If you sell the one-year bond before the year is up, the price under the influence of changing interest rates may rise or fall. But it will not rise or fall as much as the price of a long-term bond, because at the end of a year, when the bond matures, you or the buyer will receive $1,000.

If you intend to liquidate your investment at the end of a year and use the cash for something else, you are a short-term investor. You don't want to gamble on the price you might get if you buy a long bond and have to sell a year after purchase. You want the original $1,000 you invested. You should buy the one-year bond. When your investment horizon is short, don't buy long: Buy short.

But when you are a long-term investor with a long-term horizon, a short maturity strategy gives you something quite different. It preserves principal, since the bond is always redeemed each year at the end of the year for $1,000. But the certainty of year-end principal is achieved at the cost of changing reinvestment rates when the $1,000 received at maturity must be reinvested in a new bond at a new rate. If the new rate is higher, you gain, but if the new rate is lower, you lose.

A short-bond strategy for a long-term investor brings stability of principal at the cost of unstable income; you get somewhat constant principal in exchange for volatile income. It's like the bank savings account kept for years on end: your principal never varies, but your income goes up and down, fluctuating under the laws of the volatility of bank interest rates, as volatile as a flopping fish on the end of a fishing line.

Since the intermediate-maturity strategy falls midway between the short and long strategies, and is simply a compromise between them, we will turn to the long-maturity strategy. The long strategy consists of buying long bonds. Some investors call any bond over 10 years long; others call 20 or 30 years long. Which definition applies depends on your needs and interests. Since the underlying principles are not affected by the precise definition, we will call long 20 years.

If you buy a 20-year bond at a 10 percent yield, you will receive $50 every six months, and at the end of 20 years, your bond will be redeemed for your original investment of $1,000. Thus, you will get $100 per year for 20 years no matter what happens to interest rates. That gives you $2,000 in interest, plus the return of your original $1,000 at the end of 20 years. If you do not need the original investment until maturity, and if you do not sell the bond in the intervening years, not only do you receive a constant flow of income, but you secure a fixed rate of return: 10 percent.

The long-maturity strategy is a farsighted strategy for a farsighted investor, an investor who will not need the principal for a long time but who wants constant income for a long time. It's for someone who wants constancy in income, who wants constancy in total return, but who has an unvarying long-term objective that can withstand the intervening vagaries in the value of principal. The long strategy is for certainty of income and uncertainty of interim market value of principal: stable income, but intervening high volatility of principal.

We shall turn to the precise volatility of principal of long bonds in a later chapter, but for now it is only important to discuss the general principals. An intermediate-maturity policy has the same characteristics as a long strategy, but for a shorter number of years. If the maturity of the bond is five years, income remains constant for five years and principal is paid off at the end of five years. The degree of volatility of principal during the intervening years does not approach the volatility of a 20-year bond, but it is still much greater than the volatility of a one-year bond. If the investor invests in intermediate bonds and reinvests in the same maturity bonds when the first bonds mature, and again when the subsequently purchased bonds mature, income will vary and income volatility will be higher than if a long-term bond were purchased.

The fourth strategy, a staggered or laddered strategy, combines the short, intermediate, and long policies, giving a portfolio of bonds that has staggered, or laddered, maturities. An initial staggered strategy might have bonds of 5, 10, 15, and 20 years; or, you might have a staggered strategy in which you bought bonds of 1, 2, 3, 4, 5, 6, and 7 years maturity.

The staggered policy combines the characteristics of the short, intermediate, and long bonds. Income on a staggered portfolio is more stable than for a short policy, but less stable than for a long policy. Principal in a staggered portfolio is less stable than on a short portfolio, but more stable than on a long portfolio. The staggered strategy reduces the income volatility over a short portfolio, but increases the income volatility over a long portfolio.

Since bonds on a staggered portfolio are continually maturing, if you need part of the principal before the maturity of the last bond, you should have bonds maturing whose proceeds you can use for other purposes than investment or investment in bonds.

In summary, bond maturity strategies may be reduced to four: short, intermediate, long, and staggered. If interest rates never changed, none of these strategies would differ in their effect on the investor. But because interest rates do fluctuate, and since interest rates are volatile, each strategy results in different income, principal, and total return characteristics for the investor. Which strategy you select—short, intermediate, long, or staggered—depends on your objectives.

Once you've selected a maturity strategy, then you must also decide what you do to the portfolio in subsequent years. For example, if you buy a 10-year bond, do you hold that bond to maturity? Or do you try to keep the maturity constant by selling the 10-year bond at the end of each year and buying a new 10-year bond?

The first strategy, holding to maturity, we call a *to maturity* strategy. The second strategy we call a *constant maturity* strategy because we hold the maturity of the portfolio constant. Each of these strategies, (To maturity and constant maturity) can be applied to any of the initial maturity strategies: short, intermediate, long, or even staggered. If you think about it, you will note that a *To maturity strategy* could be called a *declining maturity strategy,* since the bonds continually decline in maturity.

These bond management strategies are not all used, but we will want to examine them to see what their effect is on the initial maturity strategies: short, intermediate, long, and staggered. This will illustrate the impact of actual investment practice.

10

How Much Can You Lose by Going Short?

Eric Kurz, aged 44, inherited $500,000 from his father, who had died in early December. Once the estate was closed, Eric was ready to invest the remaining balance, which amounted to nearly $400,000 after payment of estate and inheritance taxes.

Having lost an early investment in the stock market, Eric was determined not to risk his funds again. No more stocks for me, he reassured himself. Bonds it will be.

Eric was determined not to permit the loss of his principal. Moreover, with growing government deficits, he was certain that interest rates would rise. "If not over the short term, then over the long term . . . five years or more," he had declared.

With that forecast in mind, and girded by the firm prediction of three of his adviser's leading economists, Eric planned his strategy with care. I am a long-term investor, he told himself. I do not intend to retire until I reach age 65. That is over 20 years from now. I have a lot of time.

Lehman, the adviser Kurz had selected after interviewing several possible investment firms for advice, seemed to agree. "If you buy short bonds now," Lehman advised Kurz, "you will protect your investment. At the same time, as interest rates rise, which we definitely expect, your income will go up."

A man of his own convictions, Kurz approved placing his entire investment in short U.S. government bonds in January.

"No risk of default on the governments," said the adviser. "You have the safest investment anyone could possibly devise." But was it?

The current rate on short U.S. government was then 7 percent. That brought the income on the $400,000 to $28,000 annually. During February, rates rose slightly to 8 percent, confirming the adviser's forecast. But in March, after some sharp fluctuations, rates dropped back to 7.5 percent, then 7 percent, and finally down to 6 percent. "A temporary correction," said the adviser.

Kurz's initial concerns were allayed by the reassurances. He calculated his annual income on the $400,000 invested at approximately $24,000: it was down $4,000 from the return at the old 7 percent level.

In April, rates crept up. But then the short U.S. government rate dropped again, to just over 5 percent, a full 200 basis points below the original 7 percent level.

Kurz was not informed of the drop by his investment manager, but he noticed it late in the month when he happened to pick up a copy of *The Wall Street Journal.* He had turned to the back pages to look at interest rates on U.S. government bonds, swallowed hard, and then called his adviser the first thing the next morning.

"Rates are down to 5 percent!" Kurz said as evenly as he could, trying to hide the concern in his voice. He had calculated the effect on his income.

"Yes," asserted the adviser. "The correction I mentioned to you earlier has been deeper than we expected. But, as you know, your principal has been protected."

Kurz was not soothed by the remark. He had done some reading on the bond market after the April fall in rates, and he knew that had he bought 10-year U.S. governments not only would his income have remained at $28,000 per year, but the principal value would not have fallen. On the contrary, principal would have risen.

Although he had not intended to point these facts out to his adviser, the word *correction* had irritated Kurz not a little.

"Mr. Lehman," he said, his voice tight with anger. "My income has been reduced by 30 percent on an annual basis. Not only that: Had I invested in long bonds, my principal would be up substantially. Your advice to place the $400,000 has cost me $8,000 per year in income and a significant amount of principal."

Lehman had no ready answer for Kurz's question. Yet he remained firm in his own conviction that interest rates would rise. "Our economist follows interest rates closely," he asserted in an authoritative tone. "I understand your concern about the temporary loss of income and the lost potential of market appreciation. But we have not changed our interest rate outlook, despite the decline in short-term rates from 7 percent to 5 percent in the last four months.

Lehman ended on a hopeful note: "We believe that higher future rates will much more than offset the temporary loss of income which you have suffered." The words were nearly reassuring, and Kurz decided to let the matter drop. He had to attend to his own business, matters which kept his attention for the next few months.

But when a statement arrived from Lehman's firm giving the latest status of the account, Kurz remembered his concerns. Although he had forgotten what the rates were a year ago January, he vaguely recalled that they had declined. Opening the envelope, he turned quickly to two pages: one showing income for the past year, the other recording the expected yield. He did not look for the principal value, for he knew what that would be—the $400,000 originally invested.

Income for the year was approximately $22,000—the return on the government bonds. He now recalled the original yield, 7 percent, and he quickly discovered that the past year's income was $5,000 below the original estimate of $28,000 based on the original 7 percent yield.

Nothing can be done about that, thought Kurz, wearily. The investment was made, and the income has already come in. There is no way to change it.

Choosing to let the past disappear, he turned to the estimate of future income. A year ago it had been $28,000 on a 7 percent yield. What was it now? With a bare trace of apprehension in his brow, Kurz turned to the expected yield and income. He found it on the back page of the report. It was hard to find in the confusing display of his account, but the facts were inescapable once he located them. He was not prepared for the shock of the figure. The yield figure he read was 4 percent.

"Four percent!" he repeated to himself, almost unbelieving. "How could short-term yields have fallen that much? How could they?" Kurz could hardly believe his own words.

Slowly he calculated in his own mind the implications of the 4 percent yield projected in income. He was half afraid to do so, but his mind ran to the number almost automatically.

Four percent of $400,000 was $16,000. He counted the digits. That's $12,000 below the original estimate made a year earlier. Slowly he reviewed the implications in his mind. By playing short bonds, yields had dropped from 7 percent to 4 percent, and within a year his expected income had dropped from $28,000 to $16,000.

To Kurz the figure was perturbing, almost shocking. He knew that short rates fluctuated wildly, but he simply would not have believed that they could drop so fast or that the drop could have had such a jarring effect on his income.

He started to consider another aspect of the impact. Had he invested a much lesser amount at 7 percent, he now would have the same income. He took out his pen and calculator and made the calculations.

Now he expected $16,000 in income from the investment. The principal needed to obtain $16,000 at 7 percent was $230,000. He considered the implication. Because yields had dropped so far from an income standpoint, the effect was the same as cutting the principal value from $400,000 to $230,000—a $170,000 decline. It was hard to comprehend the difference; it was so substantial, and so fast. He repeated the results out loud to himself.

"Mr. Lehman," he began, sitting upright and looking straight into the eyes of his financial adviser. "From your report, I see that my expected income on the original investment of $400,000 for the next year is $16,000."

"That is correct," Lehman replied, trying not to show his own concern over what he knew was in Kurz's mind.

"You realize," Kurz went on, "that the drop in rates from 7 percent to 4 percent meant the same loss in annual income as if principal had plunged from $400,000 to $230,000."

Not knowing quite what to answer, Lehman picked up the latest interest rate forecast by the firm's economist. As he began turning the pages, his mind went quickly back over certain facts.

Some months ago, Lehman had ceased taking his own firm's economist's forecast with the same interest he had a year ago. He had been disturbed by the conflicting spectacle of the actual and very deep fall in short-term rates and the opposite prediction of a rise in rates by his firm's economist.

The fall in short-term rates had not been steady, Lehman knew, but it had been severe, after one took out the intermediate fluctuations. Moreover, Lehman knew that economists for some other firms had correctly forecast the fall in rates, unlike the incorrect forecast of his own economist. It particularly disturbed him because he had seen clients leave his firm for the other firms.

Lehman had recently begun to read with more than passing interest the interest rate forecasts of other economists, forecasts he thought must be better than those of his own firm. Some of these were hard to secure. He had even adopted the strategy of lunching every week or so with a friend and competitor from another firm, ostensibly for old time's sake—but really to find out the interest rate forecast of his competitor's economists.

There were subtle ways of finding out what the other economist was thinking, and Lehman used those ways, not in a underhanded way, but instinctively from years of having discussed with others in the business the ins and outs of finance.

Lehman would begin with the economy: the outlook of the Federal Reserve Bank; the latest reported maneuvers of the secretary of the Treasury and whether they were in the right direction; and the poor performance of the economic consensus forecast on interest rates.

"A rise," the friend had said almost perfunctorily. "Our economist foresees a rise in short-term rates—gradual at first, then more pronounced as the year unfolds."

As Lehman looked at his economist's report for the first time in over a week, he nearly started. The forecast had changed. Although the economist had forseen a rise for the past year, he now predicted a continuation of the fall in short-term rates. Moreover, the economist bravely stated that he had been wrong— completely wrong over the past year.

Lehman was now faced with a dilemma: Should he report the reversal in his own economist's forecast, a forecast he had come to distrust; or should he use the forecast of his competitor's economist, a forecast much easier to use since it was consistent with the information he had recently been giving his clients?

Lehman also faced a moral question, one which would affect not only his relations with Mr. Kurz, but his relations with all his other clients. The other economist had been right; his own economist had been wrong. Lehman argued with himself that the most prudent thing to do—in his client's own interest, as he phrased it to himself—was to use the economist who had shown the best past advice.

"The best economist forecast that I know of," Lehman began, "is for a rise in rates—gradual at first, but increasing at the end of the year."

Kurz had not forgotten the poor advice received earlier from the firm's economist, and he wanted to nail down the guilt. "Is that your firm's economist's forecast?" Kurz asked, looking directly at Lehman.

Lehman felt a pain in his stomach. He feared that question, and he had hoped somehow he would not have to answer it. He fidgeted with his pencil in order to give himself time to decide how to handle the awkward question. He knew he was cornered. He wished he had some time to think about these critical issues.

"No," said Lehman. "It is not our own economist's forecast. As you know our economist has been consistently wrong for the past year. Last week he reversed himself, admitted his past error, and stated that he now sees a continuation in the fall of short rates."

Kurz had not expected such a frank answer. Underneath he admired the direct and truthful statement he had received from Lehman. But he had to get to the truth: "If you are not relying on your own economist, then exactly who are you relying on? Yourself?"

"Not myself," Lehman responded. "No, certainly not myself. I am not expert in making interest rate forecasts. I am relying on an economist who has been correct for the past year."

Lehman's frankness impressed Kurz favorably. Also Kurz hoped that rates would rise, for he considered part of the decision to invest in short bonds his own responsibility, though he would never admit that to Lehman, who was being paid to be the adviser. Therefore, he postponed any decision on switching advisers. Kurz considered changing advisers to be a major event. He had gone to plenty of trouble in selecting Lehman, and right now he lacked the time for another search. Finally, he didn't like to admit, even to himself, that the selection of Lehman had been a mistake.

"What do you advise, Lehman?" he finally asked, gathering up his papers to leave. "Do we stay in short bonds—and anticipate—(or hope for)—a rise in rates above the original 7 percent?"

"That sounds fine," replied Lehman.

Kurz's business began to take increasing amounts of his own time, so much so that over the next year he scarcely noticed his investment or the income from it.

When tax time came around a year later, he noted that income on his investment was $18,000, slightly above the $16,000 forecast a year earlier.

But in the third year his business began to take less time, not because it was being extremely successful, but rather because it was not doing well. In consequence, Kurz's earnings dropped and his need for return on the investment rose.

With more time to look into the income from his inheritance and more need for the income, he returned to the matter. During the past two years he had watched interest rates fluctuate, particularly short-term rates, but he had not studied the matter carefully.

At the end of the third year, Kurz scheduled a meeting with Lehman, to look at the results. He was particularly interested in how much income the investment would generate, for family requirements meant he had to have that income.

When the time for the meeting arrived, Kurz, in his matter-of-fact way, opened the meeting with the question that was foremost on his mind: "How much income did my investment of $400,000 generate last year?"

Lehman turned the pages of the portfolio review to the last page and answered quietly: "$10,000."

"And what income can I expect next year?"

Lehman scanned his client, guessing what was in Kurz's mind. "Just over $8,000," he replied.

"Less than one third of what we would have had, if we had originally invested in longer term 7 percent bonds," responded Kurz. Kurz reflected how in the brief course of three years short-term rates had dropped from 7 percent to 2 percent. He could hardly believe it. Nor, for that matter, could Lehman.

What happened to Kurz is a hypothetical illustration of how much you can lose by going short. If your main desire is income, and you want income over a long period, you should buy as long a maturity as you need if the income on that bond seems reasonable to you. Certainly you can gamble on higher future rates by going short. But if you do that, you risk future loss of income.

If you are uncertain of your objective, you can stagger the maturities, using the so-called ladder approach. In this approach, you might buy maturities of 5, 10, 15, and 20 years, for example, or, if your maximum bond is 10 years, you could have maturities of 2, 4, 6, 8, and 10 years. The ladder strategy represents a compromise on income, but it also ensures that you will have some bonds near cost in case you need the principal.

11

Strategies for the Income Investor

The two King brothers sold their business for nearly $1,000,000 and shared the profit. Now they were anxious to make a wise investment. The major desire of each was long-term income. Shortly after the sale, yields on long corporate bonds moved up from 9 percent to 11.1 percent. John, the older brother, decided to settle on the 20-year bonds and placed his funds at the November rate.

Tom, the younger brother, noting that commercial paper rates were even higher at 11.5 percent, decided to wait. He decided to employ a short strategy when he should have picked a long strategy. He put his funds to work in short-term commercial paper in November, expecting yields to rise to the higher levels that had prevailed in October. Long rates had been as high as 11.93 percent that month, following a steady upturn from 9.64 percent at the beginning of the year.

"I can keep the funds short," he reasoned, "if long rates don't rise." He believed his approach was more aggressive than his brother's approach, and would prove superior in the long run.

In December, short rates dropped sharply to 8 percent, and long rates declined slightly to 10.66 percent. During the succeeding months, short rates continued to drop, sharply and steadily, plunging to 3.64 percent in May. Long rates fell too: not as far, but just as steadily.

John, who had nailed down the long-term bond, thanked his good fortune while his younger brother worried over a chance to recoup his loss. The return to double-digit yields on long bonds did not occur. Long rates fell below 9 percent two years later, and did not return to 9 percent for a long time. Short rates fluctuated wildly, often dropping below 5 percent and only occasionally returning to the 11 percent level of that initial November.

The case we have just reported is hypothetical. But the purchase yields are actual: they prevailed in November 1857. Long rates did not again exceed 10 percent until the 1980s—120 years later.

John, who invested in the long bonds, enjoyed a steady income for 20 years. Tom, who stayed short, received a much lower and more volatile level of income during the same period.

Although Tom could have moved into the long bond market in subsequent years and secured a higher and more stable rate than he got on commercial paper, he did not.

John, the long-term income investor who bought long, secured stable income. Tom, the long-term income investor who stuck to short maturities, got volatile income. Long bonds ensure stable income, short bonds give unstable income. These two characteristics of bonds must be kept in mind.

Unfortunately, it is not possible to purchase a yield that is certain to be high in retrospect. Whatever yield you buy in at, future yields can always rise higher. But you can select a level of income that is certain to be stable. This is one of the few things in investments that you can do with perfect foresight.

We chose the dates of purchase for the above example with hindsight because we wanted to illustrate the point. We wanted to make the lesson dramatic in terms of the impact on future income of failing to purchase long bonds. To illustrate the impact of maturity on the stability of income, we could have picked any historical period we wished—any period at all.

The income investor who wants stable income, but defers purchase of long bonds, is helped by an important rule derived from the third law:

Long rates are not as volatile as short rates.

If you do go short, believing that rates will rise, and rates drop, you may be hurt. But you will not be hurt as badly as you might think. It depends on what you do next.

Under the second law, long rates fluctuate less than short rates. If rates drop, short rates will tend to drop much more than long rates. If you stay short and get a fall in rates instead of the rise you expected, you will find that long rates fell less than short rates. So you will have a chance to move back into long bonds. Long bond rates will be lower, but generally not as low as the short bond rates.

But, if you still keep your money invested short, the long rates can continue to fall. If you still stay short and never go long, then your income will continue to be unstable. By not going long, initially or later, you risk a big drop in short rates. For the long-term income investor, the safest policy is long, the next safest is to go long after a delay, and the riskiest of all is staying short.

By risk, we don't mean that the expected return is lower. The highest expected return is the maturity with the highest yield. We mean only that there is greater danger of a sharp drop in income. Future income is less constant, less stable.

So far we have given an example and talked in general terms. We have not said how far short rates can drop or how far long rates can drop. We have not discussed the magnitude of income loss to the income investor if he gambles on long rates rising. Knowing the magnitude is crucial to making an informed decision. Telling you the magnitude is the purpose of this book. Knowledge of the magnitude is all you really need to decide on your strategy, once you know what you want.

Let's start with the risk of change in short-term, one-year bond rates. We will use the Salomon U.S. Government bond data as the basis. Another data base will give us somewhat different figures, though not that much different. We want to get a feel for the numbers.

We will start from a current yield on one-year bonds of 10 percent. If the current yield were 5 percent, rates would rise or fall less in basis points, but the same proportionally. If rates were 16 percent, we would see greater increases and decreases in basis points. But the proportional change would be the same. You can see that in the tables in Appendix B.

You'll also see that, given the numbers for a 5 percent initial yield, you could easily calculate them for any other initial yield. The numbers for a starting yield of 5 percent are five times the numbers for a starting yield of 1 percent.

We will use a 1-in-6 probability for a rise, or a fall. That is one standard deviation. We could use another probability, but one standard deviation is easy to deal with. It means a 1-in-6 chance, or a 16 percent probability.

If short yields are 10 percent today, there is a 1-in-6 chance they could fall to 7.6 percent a year from now. That's nearly a 25 percent drop in income in one year. There is the same probability that rates could rise to 13.1 percent, a 31 percent increase.

You see that the percentage rise is higher than the percentage fall. That is always the case. The log changes are not different, but are the same. When you convert the log differences back to yields, you get a greater percentage rise than fall. This phenomenon—equal log changes, but with higher percentage increases than decreases—is not limited to interest rates. It also characterizes stock prices and, quite possibly, the consumer price index.

For example, the odds are the same of a rise to three halves of the old yield, or a fall to two thirds of the old yield. Both changes have the same probability. Both represent equal log differences. Both are related mathematically. As you can see, the latter change (two thirds) is the reciprocal of the former (three halves). But the three-halves change is a 50 percent rise, and the two-thirds change is a 33 percent fall.

The rise and the fall have the same probability, but the percentage gain in the rise is greater. Because the probabilities are the same, but the percentage rise is greater, the yield index tends to increase over long periods of time. It has a tendency to increase just as other indexes, such as stock indexes, have a tendency to increase. But the log of the index does not tend to increase. It is only the actual index that tends to increase. For stocks, the rate of increase is about 5 percent per year.[1]

---

[1] M. F. M. Osborne, and J. E. Murphy.

If we look further ahead, say to five years, rates can rise or drop more with the same probability. Five years from now rates could drop from 10 percent to 5.9 percent or rise to 17 percent. That's a 40 percent drop and a 70 percent rise. Again the log changes are the same, but give quite different percentage differences. If we move ahead to 10 years, yields could double to 20.3 percent, or halve to 4.9 percent. In each case, we are talking about a 1-in-6 chance of changes that great or more, up or down. There is a smaller probability that you will get more substantial changes. And there is a greater probability that you will get smaller changes. You can actually calculate the odds of a change of any magnitude, up or down, for any probability.

If we take another initial yield, we get a different, but comparable set of numbers. There is a 1-in-6 chance that an initial yield of 5 percent will double in 10 years (to 10.2 percent) or halve (to 2.5 percent). An initial yield of 16 percent could drop to 8 percent in 10 years, or double to 32 percent, with the same odds.

If we shift our attention to a five-year bond, the potential changes in yield are less, under the second law. The second law says that the volatility of yields declines with maturity. With a one-sixth probability, a 10 percent yield could go to 15 percent or drop to 6.7 percent, a rise to three halves of the former value, or a fall to two thirds. This compares with a doubling or a halving for the one-year bond.

A 20-year bond could rise from 10 percent to 12.8 percent in 10 years, or fall to 7.8 percent. That is a much less dramatic change than we saw in the one-year bond. In fact, the one-year bond has the potential for a greater change in one year than the 20-year bond has in 10 years.

You should keep the general idea of these differences in mind. The easiest way to do it is to remember that it is not an arithmetic scale. Going from 1 to 10 years in the future does not increase the potential rise or fall by a factor of 10, but by the square root of 10, or approximately by 3.

Going from a 1-year bond to a 10-year bond does not reduce the potential drop by a factor of 10, but by a factor more like the log of 10, or to one third the former value instead of one tenth the former value. The percentage increase and decrease is not the same, but the log increases and decreases are the same. Thus, if the fall is to one half the former value, the rise is to the reciprocal of one half, or to two times the former value.

The full force of the volatility of changes in interest rates is apparent in the tables. There you can see how fast rates could rise, or fall, for different maturity bonds and for different time intervals. The tables don't tell you which way interest rates will go. No one can do that. They only tell how far they might go up or down. If you are an income investor, it is important to know how far rates might fall if you don't invest now. The tables also show you how much risk you bear of lower future income if you don't buy long bonds today.

We've talked about the future risks of not buying long bonds: the risk of a future decline in interest rates. We have not talked about evaluating the current level of yields. We haven't told you how to tell whether the current level is satisfactory, or not. You have to make that decision. You have to decide whether a 5 percent yield, a 10 percent yield, or a 15 percent yield is satisfactory. We have said that you cannot make that decision on the basis of future rates because there is no way of knowing what future rates will be. The odds are 50 percent that rates will fall and only 50 percent that rates will rise. Guessing the future direction of interest rates is not the way to do it.

You can compare current yields to historical yields. If yields in the past were rarely above 10 percent, and they were, then a yield of 10 percent is attractive, on a historical basis. You can also compare yields of one maturity bond against another. Your highest expected return (excluding consideration of risk) will be the maturity with the highest yield. You can compare yields on bonds with yields on stocks. You can compare yields on bonds with what the average corporation earns on its equity or its assets. If bonds are yielding 15 percent and most corporations are earning 12 percent on assets, the bond yield is attractive.

Your final evaluation of whether a long bond is a good buy, of whether you should go short, or put the money into some other instrument, depends on how you feel about the current level of yields in relation to other options and what the risk of changes in yields is. But in general, a long-term bond for an investor that wants income is a good investment at historically high yields, say 10 percent or more.

12

How to Guard Your Principal

Crilly sold his company and was negotiating for another. He received $1.5 million in cash for the business that had taken him most of his working life to build. He couldn't make that much again, and he was thankful that he had been paid top price. He wouldn't have sold, except the value was there, the buyer was there, and the opportunity was too great to miss. Now his working life was not over, and he had the chance to invest in another company in a different line that would give him more time off to do the things he wanted to do, yet offer a real challenge and much better income.

But the deal was not yet ready, and he had to park the money and earn something on it in the meantime. Safety of principal was paramount. He knew that.

"Certainly you can put the money in certificates of deposit (CD's) or Treasury bills," his friend, a local broker, told him. "The yield curve slopes sharply down and you'll get 5 percent on your money—not much, to be sure, but something."

Crilly frowned, then asked. "What would you suggest?"

"Yields have been dropping and will plunge further. I'd buy seven-year governments, now yielding 8 percent. You will get 60 percent more on your money, and you'll make a killing when yields drop."

Crilly hesitated, but then did as his friend had suggested. Not one to second-guess his own decision, he forgot about the matter. Settling the deal took a year. At the end of the year, he needed the money again and stopped by at his broker's office to pick it up.

"I need my money," he said to the broker, "to buy the company I told you about. I need the full $1.5 million. Can I have it today?"

The broker stepped back thoughtfully. "You know what's happened to yields?" he asked.

"No, but what difference does that make?" returned Crilly, surprised at the question.

"Yields rose—substantially. You earned more interest on your million and a half. But the market value of the principal has dropped."

"Dropped," returned Crilly. "What do you mean by that?"

"When yields rise, prices of long-term bonds fall. Yours fell a lot."

Crilly looked puzzled, then frustrated. With an unmistakable touch of anger, he asked: "How much can I get?"

The answer was slow in coming. The broker, realizing his error in recommending the long bonds, was reluctant to admit the truth. After some minutes, he replied, looking away as he did. "Just over a million," he confessed. Then, to soften the blow, he added. "But if you wait six years . . ."

Crilly didn't hear those words. He couldn't bear to. The deal he had agreed to and wanted was off. Worse, he had lost nearly one third of his principal.

What poor Crilly and the broker did not take into account was the difference between the income and principal investor. The income investor, the person that wants long-term, stable income, must be willing to withstand a drop in the value of his bond portfolio. The principal investor cannot stand that drop because he will need the money soon, or because he will not be willing to experience the portfolio loss.

Some investors absolutely need stability of principal. Others need it psychologically. Still others may need stable principal for legal, accounting, tax, or other reasons.

The converse of stable principal is unstable income. If your principal is to be stable, your income will be volatile. For the income investor (described in Chapter 11) principal will be volatile. You cannot achieve stable income and stable principal at the same time, or with the same portfolio of bonds. It simply cannot be done.

We have seen in the previous chapter how unstable income will be if you purchase short-term bonds. Basically, the short-term investor gets the volatility of the one-year bond portfolio. But the longer he holds the short portfolio, the more future yields are likely to depart from original yields.

If instead of one-year bonds, you buy six-month, or three-month, or daily money market funds, your future income will be even more volatile. And the principal will be correspondingly more stable.

The back side of the blade of constant principal is inconstant income. Short rates are highly volatile and will always be so. And the degree of nominal volatility will reflect the level of yields. When yields are high, shifts in dollar income will be high. And vice versa.

If the principal investor stays in money market funds, very short-term bonds, CD's, or other short-term paper, he need not worry about market fluctuations in the value of his investment. The value will be there when he needs it. Uncertainty of principal poses no problem.

But what if the principal investor decides to try to stabilize income? What if he may need the principal, but decides to risk it by lengthening maturities? We have said that this is not a good policy, but let's see what kind of risk going long entails.

The general principles are similar to those for the volatility of yields. In fact, the volatility of bond prices can be derived from the volatility of yields. That is the case because once we know the future yield risk we can calculate the future price risk. The price is determined by the maturity of the bond, the coupon rate, and the yield. We know the coupon and maturity. Just as yields change with time, the price of a bond will change.

Take, for example, a five-year bond with a 10 percent coupon. It will fluctuate in price if yields change. In Appendix B we gave the levels to which yields could rise, or fall, with a probability of 1-in-6. We can use that same table to calculate future prices on the five-year bond if yields do reach those levels. We can use the same probability. We can use the initial yield for the coupon, a 10 percent bond. We could use a bond with another coupon, but the principle would be the same. The price would differ a little. Since the price of a bond drops if the yield rises, we can see what happens just by looking at the rise in yield.

We are concerned about loss of principal, not appreciation. After a year the yield on a five-year bond could rise to 11.66 percent. Our bond had an original maturity of five years. A year later it has a maturity of only four years. So we have to look at how much yields change for a four-year bond. We will assume that initial yields were the same on all maturities. We will also assume that all yields were 10 percent when we started the investment. You could change the assumptions to reflect the prevailing yield curve, but the principle will be the same.

In a year, yields on a four-year bond could rise to 11.81 percent. And if yields rose to 11.81 percent, the price on a 10 percent coupon bond would drop to $94.36. Now lets take the yield two years from the start.

Two years from the time of original investment our five-year bond has only three years remaining to maturity. So it is a three-year bond. We need the yield of a three-year bond two years after original investment. With the same odds, 1-in-6, yields of three year bonds could rise to 12.79 percent after two years. If yields rose that much, the price on a three year bond would be $93.22.

Now you see what we are doing. We have used the general equation to calculate future yields for 10 percent coupon bonds. We start with a five-year bond that after one year becomes a four-year bond. With the estimated change in yield of a four-year bond, we can price the bond. We continue in this fashion until we have the price each year, from year zero to year five. Each of these prices is calculated from the yields given by our formula, the original yield and coupon, and the number of years remaining on the bond.

We end up with the price volatility of the bond. Note that there are two forces acting on bond price: (1) The increasing volatility of yields; (2) The declining maturity of the bond. As the bond approaches maturity, the bond price returns to par or $100.

The net effect of all of this is that as yields rise, the bond price falls and then rises once again, returning to $100 at maturity. The price returns to par because maturity declines to zero.

If yields fall, then the bond price rises. The price keeps rising until the maturity becomes short enough to more than offset the lower yields. The price returns to par at maturity.

PART THREE

Investing for Total Return

13

Freedom of Choice in Total Return

Stewart glanced down the figures.

No question, he thought. I've got plenty of leeway. The oldest person in the company has not passed 60. The controller flipped the page and then scanned the exit forecast.

No one will retire for five years. The average worker is barely 40. Whether I earn income on the portfolio or not makes no difference. Only the total fund counts. Since not a farthing must be paid out, the fund will grow rapidly for 10 years. After that, the cash received will surpass cash paid out for another decade.

Stewart continued to think about the matter. The company pension fund enjoys great freedom of choice. It can reap the luxury of shooting for total return. No need for income restricts it; no preference for capital gain bridles it; no tax or accounting rules bind it. And to a degree, we can weather the ups and downs of market fluctuations.

Stewart's investment portfolio could run with a freedom possessed by only certain kinds of funds. He could use income if he chose, but he did not need income. He could register capital gain or loss, but he was not bound by them. His fund paid no taxes and shelled out no early cash. The fund could conserve its principal and plow back its income for a long time. He had complete freedom of choice, for 20 years.

The freedom to choose income or principal appreciation as the source of growth meant that Stewart had a total return fund. If income dropped, he need not care. If principal fell, he need not sweat. If tax laws changed, he need not fret. He was free to take income, or capital gain, in any form and any combination. He had a total return portfolio.

Stewart was like the driver headed south with plenty of time to make the trip. Nothing bound him to the interstate highway. He was free: free to take the state highways, free to ply the side roads, and free to take the interstate—free to take whichever route he chose. As a total return investor, Stewart was able to secure his return from whatever part of the bond market he chose, income or principal, or any combination, to achieve total return.

Many investors lack Stewart's freedom of choice. They are not total return investors. They may depend on income; they may pay taxes on income, or they remit tax on capital gain. Their eye is on income, usually, or on appreciation: one or the other. They lack indifference to the form of payment. They are not total return investors.

The accounting rules of their business may preclude capital loss, or bring a penalty to capital loss, or raise shareholder ire. Or, even if the income is not needed, income may still be necessary for appearance, for law, for state rules, or for something. Men who run funds restricted in one way or another are bound by something other than total return. They lack freedom of choice in earning whatever seems best to gain the highest total return.

If you earn a salary, you may not need income from your own investment. If you receive a pension, you may not demand semiannual cash from your bonds. If you are a single investor, not a business, you may not need income. If you have no near-term need for capital, you may be a total return individual investor. But if you are not bound in any way, you are in a minority. Most individuals, unlike pension funds, are not total return investors. The total return investor is a special breed. He can select more options, use more types of bonds, or defer receipt of cash.

Not bound as others are in most ways, the total return investor is nevertheless bound in one special way: he must know when he wants his money back. He must know how long he can invest. Thus, he must have a time goal. This may be 20 years, like Stewart's; or it may be 5 years, or 10. But he must pick a time when he needs his money back: all of his money, or part. If he can't make a decision on how long he does not need his principal back, he loses his freedom of choice and limits the maturities he can hold.

Once you know you need neither income nor principal, once you know you want only total return, and once you pick your time period, then your investment options open up. You can select low-coupon bonds, discount bonds, or even zero-coupon bonds, bonds which pay no income. Or you can pick high-coupon bonds, or even bonds which have no maturity. You can use perpetuities. Since you do not need income or principal, you have a choice in the maturities you may use and the maturity structure you will employ.

What Measure of Results to Use?

The ocean chop sprayed the windshield of the boat as its bottom banged the waves, hitting rows of water like a machine gun. The helmsman peered at the compass, kept the throttle wide open, and then shouted back to the navigator: "What's our average speed since Miami?"

"Total time?" yelled the navigator.

"No. Average speed. It's the average speed I want," The answer came.

Soon the helmsman asked again: "Faster," the helmsman cursed, "We've got to go faster!" he repeated, as he jammed harder on the throttle.

He knew he had to average 103.5 miles per hour to beat the world record on the Miami–New York run. Whether he would or not hinged on his average speed from start to wherever he was on the long, demanding course.

In examining total return, the investor has the same problem that faced the helmsman of the race boat. Like the helmsman, you need to know more than the elapsed time, you need a measure like the average speed since the start.

Once you have the choice of looking only at total return, then you must have a means of gauging whether any particular strategy you select worked, or will work, or what its risks are. You must ask: how do I gauge my results? What measure do I use to tell if I have done well or ill with my cash.

In measuring your actual or potential results, there are several measures. You can measure the return each year; or you can measure the return from the start of your investment to a future period. For the purpose of evaluating alternative strategies, we have found that the best measure is the average annual compound return from the beginning to future dates. You can compare this figure with the promised yield to maturity. You can see how time affects this measure. And you can see how far above, or below, the return is in comparison to the promised yield to maturity.

Average return is what we need to gauge the result of our investment, from start to any future date. The average, measured as compound annual return, is what we need to know how well we have done—or might do. We need that total amount over the period of years, divided by the number of years, so we will have a standard notch to measure the growth. And that is what we shall use in this book to measure total return: the annual compound growth from the day we put down the money to the future date.

This measure is not the measure of a future year; it is not the result of one year; it is the average return from inception to a future year. Like the miles per hour of the speed boat from Miami to Charleston, or Miami to Newport, it measures the average speed from start to future. It is a mean change to various future points. It is not speed since the last town or in the last hour. The mean to various future times gives a barometer, a standard we can use to compare the promised return with the range of potential returns under fluctuating interest rates.

On a total return bond portfolio, we know the promised return to maturity. But it is not the promised return that we need to discover, but the probability of getting a return other than the promised return *if the bond is not held to maturity.* We shall measure the return we might get under the influence of changing interest rates. We shall use, in determining this, one standard deviation. We shall ask how far the return might fall with a 1-in-6 probability, or above what point it might rise, with a 1-in-6 probability. Equivalently, we can ask what is the likelihood that we will get a return two points higher than our expected 10 percent, or two percentage points lower. We shall ask for the risk profile within which our return should lie two thirds of the time.

Total return includes both income and change in principal. It is not just the one, or the other. We have looked at income separately and at change in market value separately. Constant income was achieved by buying a long bond. Volatile income was gained by staying in a short maturity. Constant principal was achieved by buying a short bond. Volatile principal was bought by getting a long bond.

When we measure total return to various future dates prior to maturity, we incorporate both income risk and principal risk. Since income and principal risk are the opposite for the same maturity bond, the total return combines the two influences and is moderated by them. Total return has neither full income risk nor full principal risk.

When we looked at income, and when we looked at market values, we showed what happened when interest rates rose above a certain point, or fell below a certain point. That point was the level of rates reached, or exceeded, with a probability of 1-in-6. We looked at what happened on the up side, and on the down side. The probability of not rising that high, or falling that low, was two thirds. The odds were 2-in-3 that the upper or lower levels would not be gained.

We can do the same thing in looking at total return. We can again use a probability of 1-in-6 that rates will rise that much or more, or that rates will fall that much or more. When rates rise, the return on reinvested interest rises, but the value of bonds held falls, except as modified by the shortening maturity of the bond portfolio. When we look at a bond after a rise in rates, total return is increased by higher rates on reinvested assets; total return is reduced by the fall in market values of bonds held so that the one effect moderates the other. If rates fall, the return on reinvested cash is cut, but the market values of bonds held rises.

Another thing happens that is caused by the way we measure. We measure on an annual basis from inception: We take an average. When we compute total return under this risk probability, three things happen at once:

First, rates depart from the initial rate, steadily, but more slowly than time.

Second, the market value of the bond rises if rates fall, and falls if rates rise. As maturity approaches, the market value of the bond returns toward 100, reaching 100 at maturity. Bond price risk creates an elliptical profile under the dual influence of changing interest rates and shortening maturity.

If rates rise and interest income is reinvested, the reinvested income earns a higher return than the original investment earned. This high return pushes up total return. But the rising rates also depress the market value of the bond, reducing total return. At first, and for some time, the depressing effect of lower market values is the most powerful influence and dominates the early rates of return, particularly if the portfolio is dominated by long bonds. Later on the high reinvestment rates on reinvested income begin to dominate.

Third, by measuring on an annual compound basis, we moderate all of the above influences.

What happens to the portfolio depends on the initial maturity structure of the portfolio. If the portfolio was short term, variations in the market value of the portfolio are small, and total return risk increases continuously. Risk increases continuously because the short maturities are continually maturing, and you must keep rolling over the portfolio. When the short bonds mature, you have to reinvest the proceeds. The volatility of changing interest rates continuously increases the risk on reinvestment rates. You are likely to get either higher or lower rates. Total return volatility ultimately becomes very high on a short portfolio.

Not only that, but short rates are much more volatile than long rates, as we have seen. So in addition to being subject to volatile returns on the rolled-over bonds, you are subject to the most volatile part of the maturity spectrum, to the highly volatile short bonds. Our method of measuring total returns, on an annual basis from inception, moderates volatility of total return. We will show less volatile total return figures than we would see if we simply looked at the future rates on short term bonds. But that is appropriate.

The total return risk of long bond portfolios is quite different from that of short bond portfolios. On the short bond portfolios, total return risk increases continuously. But on long bond portfolios, total return risk decreases and then increases. If initial rates are 10 percent and rates rise, the initial rates of return will be much less than 10 percent due to the drop in bond prices. If rates fall, the initial returns will be much higher than 10 percent due to the rise in the bond price. A long bond portfolio has very high *initial* total return risk because of the volatility of the bond prices.

But with the passage of time, risk declines on a long-term portfolio and keeps declining, reaches zero, and then begins to rise again, just as it does on the short portfolio. Risk rises again because the reinvestment rate on income, if income is reinvested, or on principal after the bonds mature, becomes the dominant influence. Thus, on a long bond portfolio, total return risk starts out high, declines to zero, and then rises again.

Contrary to what might seem to be the case, poor initial results are likely to produce good long return results, while good initial results are likely to produce poor long return results. Contradictory as it may seem, on a long-term total return portfolio, you want rates to rise because over the long run that increases the probability of increasing return. Early disappointment is likely to produce favorable long-term results because of higher return on reinvested income and principal.

These seemingly contradictory influences on bonds make it important that you know what your objective is, that you determine what your time horizon is, and that you understand exactly what is happening. You have to understand that it is better to have rates rise even though that will produce results that are initially bad. You must be able to withstand those adverse initial returns and you must be psychologically prepared for them. If you are a pension fund investor, or an endowment fund investor, you can't judge what is happening by looking at the return from last year. If you do only that, you will be tempted to sell all the bonds, fire the investment manager, and get a new manager. That is likely to be precisely the wrong thing to do.

The total return account must know what the objective is and what the time horizon is. The way to measure risk is from inception to various future dates on an annual compound basis. If your horizon is short, then you want a short bond portfolio. But if you have a short bond portfolio, and maintain it for a long time, it becomes a high risk portfolio. Over the long run, a long bond portfolio is the least risky portfolio. But the low risk comes only with time. Initial risk on a long bond portfolio is high, but it decreases continuously with time. Odd as it may seem, poor results on a long bond portfolio make it more likely that long run results will be good; and vice versa.

We have discussed total return risk before any adjustment for inflation, though inflation will affect all bond portfolios in the same manner.

14

Total Return for the Short-Term Investor

The investment committee of the pension fund was concerned about a near-term loss. If the fund declined in value, they must make up the difference. It was not that they didn't have the cash, but they had other priorities. It was expected to be a tough year for capital outlays. New plant and equipment requirements were expected to drain the cash position. Not only that, but short-term borrowing rates were high and the president didn't want interest payments on short funds to cut into earnings. "Investors will be unhappy," he said. "And the stock price will drop."

All of these concerns were passed on to the investment manager, who took them into account. "Your time horizon is long term," he said, wanting to be sure he understood the major requirement.

"Yes," said the chief financial officer of the company. "But for this year we don't want losses."

To be sure the money manager understood, the company official repeated the point. "Our horizon is long term, our need is total return, not income or appreciation separately. But this year we don't want to take a heavy capital loss from long-term bonds."

The portfolio was placed in short instruments where rates were high. Long-term rates were also high, but the short rates were even higher. So there seemed to be no harm done.

What the money manager knew, but had neglected to impress on the company pension investment committee, was that a short-term maturity structure was the riskiest structure for a long-term, total return investment objective.

History has a tendency of repeating itself. The following year the desire for no loss continued. The portfolio remained short at the request of the investment committee. For some years thereafter, the maturities remained short, despite the sharp decline in short rates. As short rates fell, long rates followed, not as quickly, but just as surely. The dictum of the money manager, who followed the wishes of the committee, came to pass. The pension fund lost the high rates of the earlier years and the return dropped. The common shareholders, who might have overlooked heavy contributions to the fund in those early years, saw much higher contributions in later years. The higher later contributions eventually hurt earnings, dividends, and finally stock prices.

By running the pension fund contrary to its long-term objectives, by positioning the pension to meet company short-term objectives, the investment committee hurt both the long-term objectives of the fund and the long-term objectives of the company, its stockholders, and employees.

A short-term portfolio brings high risk over the long term. Short-term bond rates are highly volatile. Short-term rates are more volatile than long-term rates, under the third law. The odds of a decline in rates are high and increase with time. Since the portfolio assets must continually be reinvested in new short-term bonds, there is the risk that the reinvestment will be in lower yielding short-term maturities. This risk continues to rise with time, seen from the perspective of the first year of investment. Consequently, a short term portfolio is the highest risk portfolio for a total return account with a long-term investment horizon. The risk profile resembles an arrowhead, with the point today and high risk tomorrow.

So what is the answer to the investor whose objective is long-term total return? The answer is to invest in long-term bonds. If the objective is long term, stay away from short-term bonds. Stay away from bonds which have high long-term risk. If long-term yields are satisfactory, design the portfolio for the long term by buying the longer term issues. In that way, match the length of the bond maturity with the length of the objective: long-term maturities for a long-term portfolio, short-term maturities only for a short-term portfolio.

Most savings and loan companies have failed to consider the investment implications of their savings accounts. Since savings accounts represent short-term money, the proceeds should have been invested in short-term loans, not long-term loans. Instead the S&Ls placed the money in long-term mortgages. When volatile short-term rates rose, the money borrowed cost more than the money loaned, and many S&Ls went bankrupt. They had failed to realize that they had to be short-term investors.

15

When Storm Clouds Turn to Sunshine

When the Russians withdrew across the plains of their country in full retreat, it looked as though Napoleon had victory within his grasp. But a long, cold winter and the problems with an overextended supply eventually defeated Napoleon, turning apparent Russian defeat into victory. The Russian storm became eventual sunshine.

In many ways, a bond investor is in a similar situation because what appears to be disaster turns out to be a good thing. The best thing for a long-term total return policy is to have rates rise, particularly if income is reinvested.

The rise in rates will drive the price of the bonds down. Total return will be negative. The drop in bond prices will appear to be the worst thing that could happen.

But income that is reinvested will be put to work at higher rates. Soon the higher rates on reinvested income will gradually offset the depressing effect on market values. As the bond maturity shortens, the price will begin to return to par, even if rates continue to rise. After a time, total return will begin to increase.

On a single bond, total return portfolio, with income paid out, the actual total return will equal the promised total return at maturity. At maturity of the bond you get what you expected. Risk at maturity returns to zero.

For a portfolio with income reinvested, the minimum risk point will be achieved much sooner than maturity. This is because rising rates increase returns on reinvested income. On a long-term total return portfolio with income reinvested, minimum risk is reached at roughly half the maturity of the portfolio. Thereafter risk increases. The subsequent increase in risk is caused by the continuation of the probable fluctuation in interest rates.

Thus, for the long portfolio with a total return objective, risk is high at first, diminishes to zero, and increases thereafter if income is reinvested. If income is paid out, risk reaches zero at the maturity of the portfolio.

Like the retreat of the Russians before Napoleon, what appears to be initial defeat becomes the cause of victory. For a long-term bond portfolio where the objective is long-term total return with income reinvested, the best thing is a rise in rates that cuts down the value of the portfolio. What appears to bring defeat will be the cause of victory. The rise in rates will bring higher returns in the long run.

16

How Not to Pick a Bond Manager

It was obvious to people of Portugal that the world was flat. All you had to do was look, and if you looked you could see that the Earth was not round, but flat.

Columbus knew that appearances could be deceiving and that what seemed to be real to some might not be what it seemed. He knew, from his experience at sea, that the Earth curved slightly. Others before Columbus also observed that the Earth was round, and that the impression others had was not necessarily accurate. A lot depended on your viewpoint and where you had been.

Just as the world seemed flat to some, it would seem that the best way to pick a bond manager is to pick the manager with the best record. It would appear that the wise choice would be the manager who racked up the best bond return over the last year, or five years. Most investment committees that spend a lot of time selecting a bond manager do pick the manager with the best record. In doing so they often have the help of consultants who compile records of the performance of leading bond managers. They can tell you to the fraction of a percentile the past record of bond managers from all parts of the country. For a fee, they will help you get the manager with the best record.

This method of selection seems obvious. Not only does it seem obvious: It was borrowed from the method of selecting common stock managers. Before bond managers were selected by their records, the selection of stock managers by the best performance had grown from an art into almost a science. The method, which evolved into a mini-investment industry, was hardly questioned.

But what seems obvious in this method of selection is not. Once I listened to a prominent case study that had been presented at the Harvard Business School. It concerned a Fortune 500 company in my hometown that used this method to fire one set of common stock managers and to hire another. They fired the manager with a poor record and hired a manager with the best record. On the surface, that seemed the sophisticated and smart thing to do. The person responsible for doing it was one of the "best and the brightest," an articulate person with superb business school credentials. But the results were disastrous.

An old line investment person who had been burned enough times probably could have forewarned the company about the problem of using such a method. He could probably see, just as Columbus had seen from his experience at sea, that appearances were not what they seemed to be.

The problem in using the best record in selecting common stock managers is that you tend to get the big gamblers who have been lucky. They're smart enough to know what sophisticated fund owners and investment committees are looking for. They have enough guts to play that game, and not enough bad experiences to know the danger. They tend to be young and aggressive because they haven't had enough experience to learn the danger of such an approach. If that's what you want, if you want to gamble with the company pension fund, if you want to play roulette with the college endowment fund, fine. Go ahead, but recognize what you are doing for what it is.

In selecting bond managers by the numbers (for that is what you are doing if you go only by the best record) you have to know what the bond manager is doing and why. He may have the best record for very good reasons. If he does, you may have made a good choice.

What is the problem of selecting the bond manager with the best record? Whether there is a problem depends on how the record was achieved and why. It depends on whether the bond manager geared the portfolio to the preferences of the customer and the current level of rates, or whether he was gambling on his ability to guess interest rates in the future. If he was doing the former, you may have a reasonably good bond manager. If he was doing the latter, you may be in for trouble.

Let's look at the former situation first. An unusually high rate of return will go to a manager who invests long because he learns that your investment horizon is long term and then, subsequent to the investment, rates drop. The portfolio will experience very high short-term returns because when rates fall, long bond prices will shoot up. If the manager is smart, he will know that this effect is short term. He will know that the price of the bonds will come down when the portfolio approaches maturity. He will know that the high returns of the last year, or two years, or three years, are temporary and will not be achieved by the portfolio if it is held to maturity. He will also know that if you choose him on the basis of those short-term returns, you are probably making a mistake. And he may caution you about that; though he may not, knowing how quick many buyers of investment management are to change, particularly the ones who should be the most sophisticated but are not.

He will also know that if income on the high return portfolio is reinvested, the fall in rates that gave the good performance is precisely what he does not want. He does not want it for his client's sake because the lower rates that gave the higher returns will produce lower returns on the reinvested income. And those lower reinvestment rates will reduce future returns. All of this may be going through his mind when you tell him what a good job he has been doing. He knows that the appearance is deceiving. What appears to be good on a bond portfolio may in fact be bad. And what appears to be poor may in fact be good. Good near-term results may bode ill for long-term results, and vice versa.

But another thing can happen that is even worse. Suppose you looked at a set of results which were also good, equally good, and for the same cause. The manager bought long bonds, yields dropped, the bond prices rose very high, and short term rates of return were very high.

But in this case, the managers' objectives were entirely different. The manager did not buy long bonds because he learned that your investment horizon was long term. He did not buy long-term bonds because he felt current rates were attractive and wanted to lock them in. He bought long-term bonds because he felt interest rates would fall and he wanted to reap the benefit of a sharp rise in long bond prices. And he turned out to be correct. As a result of his correct guess on the direction of interest rates and his purchase of long bonds, the portfolio experienced very high rates of return. The rates of return were the same as those of the other portfolio manager, but the reasons they were achieved were entirely different. The facts were the same, but the methods of investment management were entirely different.

If you select the first manager, your portfolio will be well handled. But if you select the second manager, you may be in for trouble. The trouble arises from his next move. The second manager based his investment decision on something we say cannot be done consistently over the long run. The second manager based his decision on guessing the future direction of interest rates. We have said that by the first law he cannot do this. If he could, he is wasting his time working for the paltry sum he gets managing other peoples money compared to what he could get if he managed his own. And he doesn't need a lot of capital to make a fortune if he can forecast interest rates. He can deal in futures where little capital is needed.

The danger of the second manager lies in his next move. As one who bets on the direction of interest rates, he is likely to guess next that interest rates will rise. If he makes that bet, he will want to move out of the long bonds into short bonds. That is fine for preserving the capital gain he made on the first bet, but he will have to reinvest the proceeds at much lower rates. And, if he turns out to be wrong, then he will have to reinvest the proceeds at even lower rates. That means that he will lose the returns which the first manager locked in.

Of course you could pick the manager who showed the high returns for the wrong reasons. You could pick the manager who thought he could predict the direction of interest rates. And he could be correct in his forecasts of interest rates in running your portfolio. He could buy long-term bonds just as rates were falling and he could switch into short bonds just as rates were rising. And your portfolio could run up an extraordinary record. That could happen, but is unlikely. But it could happen.

Something else could happen that would be less desirable. The manager who had been lucky up to the point when you hired him could suddenly become unlucky. He could guess wrong on every move. He could move into long bonds just as rates were rising and shift back into shorts when rates were falling. He could lose your capital when bond prices fell and cut your potential interest by buying when rates were low. He could do all the wrong things. And the effect of all those wrong moves would be that your investment, or your company's pension, or your college endowment, would suffer.

That scenario is also unlikely. Just as a string of perfect hits by your risk-taking manager is unlikely, a string of misses is also unlikely. If his batting average in any particular move is 50 percent, we can calculate the probability of a string of completely right, or completely wrong, moves. The probability of three right moves in a row is 1-in-8. Those are the same odds of a set of three wrong moves in a row.

While you may select a manager who has been lucky, and who will continue to be lucky in investing your funds by betting on the direction of interest rates, you are certain to select a manager whose results will be volatile. You hope the volatility will end up in your favor. But the odds are that it will not. You will have picked a wild card. You will have picked the manager who is a gambler. If he follows his past practices, he will gamble with your money, or with the money entrusted to your care. By using a method which seems on the surface to be the most wise and prudent, by selecting the manager with the best past record, you may have in fact picked a bond gambler, a crapshooter who operates under the guise of an investment professional.

In order to determine that, you will have to inquire about how he invests and why he got the results he did. Otherwise your selection process becomes the prisoner of the numbers game.

There are other ways to score a home run in bond returns. There are other ways, and some of these other ways are legitimate. One way is to buy low rated bonds which have higher yields and to diversify the risk by buying lots of those bonds. There is nothing wrong with that, if the bond manager knows the risks, knows what he is doing, and if you know what you are getting into. Another way of getting superior returns is to buy bonds in default. Bonds in default, based on several studies, can give extraordinary returns. Some bond managers use this type of instrument, but to do it successfully you have to know the risks and cut them by diversifing the portfolio. And you have to realize that the good returns were probably helped not so much by the skill of the bond manager in picking the right issues and underlying companies, but by a rebound in the economy or a sector of the economy that bailed out the default companies. You should also be sure your bond manager is not simply buying some secondary issues, calling them low-rated bonds, and putting into your portfolio issues that have slightly higher yields for very good reasons.

Perhaps the most important criterion in picking a bond manager is that you know what a bond is and that your manager knows what a bond is. A bond is an instrument that pays a fixed coupon over a length of time and pays back the principal at the end of that time. It is a fixed income instrument. In effect you put your money out for hire. If the rent you get on your money is reasonable, then you lend it. If the rent is not reasonable, then you don't lend it. You don't buy the bond, and your bond manager doesn't buy the bond. That is what it is all about. The advantage of a bond is that you know at the start what the return is going to be, provided you have selected a borrower that will be able to pay the income, the rent, and repay the principal.

Once you forget those things, once you start gambling on your ability to guess interest rates, or your bond manager's ability to guess interest rates, you no longer have a bond. You have moved from an investment to the roulette table. If you want a roulette wheel for your pension fund or college endowment, that is fine. But you should be sure that you know what you have. You should be able to look through appearances and see whether the Earth is really flat, or something else. You should ask the right questions to determine whether your prospective bond manager got good numbers by dumb luck, or whether he knew what a bond was and how to use bonds to achieve his clients' real objectives.

17

A Bond Fund Is Not a Bond—and Don't Think That It Is

Most bond funds aren't like bonds at all. Certainly bond funds invest in bonds, so the underlying assets of a bond fund consists of bonds. But the funds themselves (and that is what you buy, you don't buy the bonds) behave more like stocks than bonds. They exhibit variable principal and even more variable income: not as variable as stock prices or income, but still quite variable.

Remember the two basic characteristics of bonds: (1) They pay a coupon every six months, the same coupon; it doesn't change; (2) They're an IOU—a promise to pay your principal back at maturity.

But *bond funds* don't pay coupons, and they have no maturity. They're more like perpetuities. They go on and on forever, with an unending life. Even if they were to be terminated, you wouldn't get your principal back because a lot of bonds in the portfolio wouldn't be at maturity and therefore would not pay off principal.

When you buy a bond fund, you have a share of the fund. You might buy a unit for $762. You buy on the open market, on the New York Stock Exchange, on the over-the-counter market, or directly from the mutual fund company that distributes the fund. Most of the time you get the bond fund right from your broker. You don't get the fund on a new bond offering, like you buy lots of other bonds. It's not issued by an underwriter or sold by the federal government.

You don't give it up at call price to the company or get reimbursed at maturity like a normal bond. Quite the contrary: You sell it through your broker just like a common stock. What you get is not $1,000 per bond, but whatever the market price is. There is no return of principal.

What you get when you sell depends on a whole lot of factors entirely out of your control and also out of the control of the fund manager, whether he knows it or not.

The main thing a bond fund manager can't control is what people like you do: buying and selling units of the fund. You may decide to come in at a certain point and others may do the same.

Suppose you went into the fund when it had $100 million of assets. Let's say you bought when yields were 8 percent and a year later yields rose to 12 percent. Good, you might think, my income will go up. But when yields go up, bond prices drop and that makes the fund go down in value. When the fund goes down in value, more people start to sell than buy. So the fund is hit by selling and by the drop in bond prices at the same time.

Bonds aren't as liquid as stocks, particularly long-term bonds. The fund manager will try to avoid selling the deep discount bonds by selling his short maturities, by liquidating his near cash items. If short rates are higher than long rates, his sale of the short bonds will lower income on the fund more than proportionally. So you will see your income drop, even though rates have gone up.

Tricky things happen to the fund. For example, if half the units are pulled out by investors who are disillusioned by the drop in the fund's value, if short money is pulled out, the composition of the fund will change. It will have more long bonds. Long bonds vary more in price than short bonds, so the fund will become more volatile in value. Your principal will fluctuate more in value. You've got a different animal now than you had when you first bought the fund, and you can't control that. Neither can the fund manager to any major degree.

Or, consider another example: Suppose, to raise cash for sellers who liquidate, the fund manager decides to sell off the long bonds instead of the short bonds; and suppose the market is sticky. Since the dealers have big spreads between bid and asked, the market is like a fire sale and the bonds are sold at a deeper discount than they ought to be. You, like the sellers, suffer the consequences.

A bond promises constant income, but a bond fund doesn't offer that. The 8 percent you are offered when you go in is not what you will get next year. Because other investors, over whom you have absolutely no control, go in and out of the fund, the fund manager is continually buying bonds and selling bonds at different prices and different rates. When you bought in, you bought at the average yield. The bond manager buys and sells at yields other than at the yield you bought. If yields fall, say to 5 percent, and a great deal of money is added to the fund—lets say it doubles—then the manager will have to purchase a lot of 5 percent bonds. The average income on the fund will drop and you will no longer get 8 percent on your original purchase, but something less. The same decline in income will be caused by the maturing of bonds in the portfolio.

A bond fund is not like a bond at all. The fund has no promise to pay at the end, even though the individual bonds do. And it lacks a fixed income.

In return for these disadvantages (and they are disadvantages) you get one definite advantage: Diversification. A bond fund is diversified. The eggs are scattered around, and that is a lot of protection. You never know which company will be faced with a billion-dollar lawsuit, like Union Carbide in 1985. You can't know in advance which municipality is on the ropes. You will not realize until too late which security Standard & Poor's will drop its rating on, from AAA to C or to unrated.

A bond fund protects you from all that because the fund has lots of bonds in its portfolio. If one egg goes bad, the rest will be OK. Your whole fortune isn't tied up in one town or a single company.

A bond fund is also managed and can deal in large lots, and the latter is certainly an advantage. Having someone manage the fund may help or it may not, depending on the skill, and more probably the luck, of the manager.

But it does save you the trouble of calling brokers and having to decide whether the yield is good, or if the credit is acceptable, or if the time is right to buy the bond. And having to keep track of the whole thing, pay the bills, collect the interest, and so forth. You also don't have to wonder at night whether the XYZ municipal pension fund is going to plunge that attractive little town underwater, or whether Chrysler Corporation will indeed make it and you'll get your principal back in 1992. Some of the worry of doing it yourself can be relegated to more global matters by buying U.S. government bonds which, for that reason, are often a very attractive investment.

The above remarks apply to the normal bond fund, but they do not apply to a unit trust, or to a closed-end investment bond trust which, unlike the usual bond fund, does have a fixed maturity and stable income.

But apart from closed-end investment trusts, which are a minority, the bond fund is not a bond. It doesn't have constant income. And it doesn't pay off at maturity. Both the fruit and the tree are in constant motion.

So be sure you know what you are getting if you buy a bond fund and if that is what you really want.

PART FOUR

Some Myths You Should Recognize

18

Is There Enough Trend in Interest Rates to Make Money On?

For years, stock chartists and at least half the people who bet on stock prices believed there were trends in stock prices, at least enough to make money on. In fact, most investors believed in trends until a couple of decades ago, when a finance professor published two stock market graphs on the same page.

His first chart was an actual replica of the stock market. But the second chart had been generated by flipping coins and adding up the heads and tails. Whereas the first chart was an actual portrayal of the stock market, the second was no more than the cumulation of random numbers. By definition, the cumulation had no trend. At each point in the chart the odds of it going up or down remained the same. It was one half in each case.

Yet the random number chart looked just like the real stock market chart. Both the random number chart and the real chart seemed to have definite and similar trends.

A few years later, another professor generated a new stock market chart from random numbers. That chart also seemed to have trends where none should exist.

But the few random number stock market charts didn't stop stock chartists from seeing trends, and it didn't stop people from betting on the stock market trends they believed existed. A glance at the record of the Dow-Jones Industrial Average charted on paper seemed evidence enough for many investors. Yet the intervening fluctuations in stock prices are very great, and the odds of an increase in the stock market are no greater than one half.

If that is the case with stocks, what about interest rates? Is there a trend to interest rates? And if there is a trend, is it enough to make money on?

You can generate random numbers and create interest rate charts that look pretty much like the real thing. The pseudo interest rate charts seem to have trends, often long trends that look like those that characterize interest rates. The real question is: How significant are the trends? Are the trends significant enough to profitably bet on?

One problem is that the fluctuation in interest rates is very great, particularly for short-term rates. The high short-term volatility tends to cut down the possibility of making a profit from betting on the trend. But the odds of an increase or a decrease in interest rates are just about what they are for stock prices: each fifty percent. Though even odds seem to fly in the face of what appear to be trends, that's what they are. One reason the odds are so even is that the fluctuations are far more pronounced than any trend.

It's a little like walking north from New Orleans to Minneapolis. By the time you get to Minneapolis, you will have risen roughly 400 feet, depending a little on where you start in New Orleans and where you end up in Minneapolis. In coming north you cover about 1,000 miles. Since there are 5,280 feet to the mile, you will walk over 5,000,000 feet horizontally, assuming you walked in a perfectly straight line. If you ended up 500 feet high above sea level, you walked 10,000 feet horizontally for every foot you gained in elevation. Now you can call that net increase a trend, and it is definitely a trend. But in making the trip you went up and down an awful lot for every mean foot you gained. In Minneapolis, in fact, its quite possible to go up and down 500 feet in a few blocks or a few miles.

In the same way, interest rates fluctuate a lot in comparison to the trend. The trend in interest rates may not be quite that small in comparison to the daily, weekly, and monthly fluctuations. But it is close. There is a great deal of intervening fluctuation to every mean point of rise, or fall, in the trend. You may need a detailed interest rate chart, like a daily chart, to see all the fluctuation, but the fluctuation is there.

You should recall that the trends are not always up. There have been long periods of downward trends, sometimes lasting a half century or more. And what appear to be trends may not be significant.

One way to check on trends is to look at the mean change and ask if it is significant. Statisticians have ways of determining whether an average change, up or down, is significant. Usually they call a mean significant if the chance of getting the figure is low, under 1 in 20. Using that test, which is fairly tough, roughly one third of the means that we worked with were significant. That is to say the average increase, or decrease, in interest rates was significant one time in three.

But saying a past change was significant is different than saying the direction will continue. It's also different than saying you can make money by betting on the past trend. We don't think you can bet on a continuation of the past trend and make money. If you make such a bet, you are just as likely to lose money as to make it.

If you look at a chart of past interest rates, you will think you see trends. But such charts are deceptive in that similar charts could be generated by flipping a coin, or generating random numbers. The apparent trends are deceptive. They are not sufficiently strong to bet on. The reason you can't bet on apparent trends is that the interim fluctuations, the volatility of interest rates, is too much. The volatility submerges the mean change, if any, to such an extent that the odds of increase or decrease remain no better than the flip of a coin. It's just like the walk north from New Orleans to Minneapolis. Even if you were rising, on average, you could hardly tell with all the hills you had to go up and down. And in any segment of the walk, there's a good chance you may be going down.

19

Are There Any Cycles To Interest Rates?

Everything in life seems to have a cycle, but many apparent cycles are just that: apparent, but not real. Interest rates are no exception.

Back in the 1920s a large and well-funded organization was established to research business cycles. And, in accord with the apparent law of "seek and you shall find," the researchers at the National Bureau of Economic Research discovered not only business cycles, but stock market and interest rate cycles. These cycles were carefully recorded and correlated with various other business cycles. We are fortunate that this work was done, for one of the by-products was the Durand interest rate series that is crucial for this book.

The cycles that appear in interest rate charts are more apparent than real. Charts made from random numbers have the same apparent cycles. Yet there are no cycles, but only the appearance of cycles. There seem to be cycles when there are in fact no cycles, and we are so accustomed to looking for cycles and to seeing cycles in things, that we find cycles where there are none.

Certainly in some kinds of business data there are definite cycles. There are seasonal components to agricultural production; for some kinds of agricultural products there may be seasonal cycles. But when we move beyond seasonal cycles, or annual cycles, the presence of such regularities diminishes. Demand for some kinds of credit is seasonal, but the number of factors which influence interest rates is probably so large that any seasonal effect is overwhelmed by other things.

In order to be useful, in order to be something that you can make money on, you need a regularity of one kind or another, something that tells you where the turning points are. Without that, you cannot bet, you cannot turn a profit.

Unfortunately, interest rates appear to offer no such regularity. While there are various statistical tests which you could make to discover whether any regularity exists, our tests of the dispersion of changes in interest rates are a sufficient test. If the second law holds, if the volatility of interest rates increases with time, then there can be no cycles to interest rates. If a cycle existed, then the standard deviation of changes in interest rates would cease to continue rising with time. The volatility of interest rates would fall back to zero at the end of a cycle.

But the volatility of interest rates does not return to zero. The dispersion of changes in interest rates continues to rise, and increases with each increase in time; the second law holds. Therefore there is no regular cycle to interest rates. The cycles we see are not real cycles, only mirages, the appearance of cycles that could as easily be generated by some kind of random process. You cannot bet on the cycles in interest rates and expect to make money over the long run.

20

The Mathematical Laws of Interest Rates

"Your paper," said the elder professor to the young student, "concerns a subject that is trivial."

The young student was shaken. It was a paper on which he had spent long hours and much thought over several years. He felt he had plowed new ground; he believed he married two important subjects with mathematical rigor. And he thought he had explained them in a pioneering doctoral dissertation.

But the department of mathematics of the University of Paris thought otherwise. Gambling was not a proper subject for its students. Nor was the sordid business of interest rates. Pure mathematics was all that counted; or, at the very least a more honorable branch of applied mathematics. But not the application of mathematics to gambling; and not the use of the pure science on the stock and bond exchange.

Bachelier's thesis was considered trivial when he presented it in 1900. Though the young student passed, he never received a proper teaching post. His work was forgotten for nearly half a century.

Six years later, in 1906, Albert Einstein developed the same kind of mathematics that Bachelier had developed, this time applying the formulas, not to interest rates, but to the motion of microscopic particles. For his work on *Brownian*

Motion, as this branch of physics was called, Einstein received the Nobel prize. Einstein did not know that Bachelier had covered much the same course a few years earlier.

What Bachelier and Einstein both knew was that mathematics can describe the formal characteristics of a wide range of applications, from fluctuations in interest rates to the motion of particles.

Other subjects that can be treated by the same mathematics include the weather, the topography of the Earth, certain branches of astronomy, oceanography, highway traffic, thermodynamics, and artillery firing. In fact, there is scarcely a major branch of science that is not subject to the same mathematical treatment that Bachelier gave to interest rates.

Strange as it may seem, the same treatment Bachelier received from the University of Paris mathematics department is being repeated today. But it is not gambling and the exchange that are considered trivial, but his mathematics. Interest rates are the serious subject and Bachelier's mathematics is considered the trivial part in an ironic twist of history.

It is not just that mathematics is considered trivial, for that is not quite so. Rather it is that Bachelier's specific mathematical method is neglected. While superficially accepted, his method has, nevertheless, not been understood; it has been ignored for the most part, and by some experts even forgotten.

But, unless you understand Bachelier's point of view and his approach, you may never understand fluctuations in interest rates. The formal mathematical properties of interest, which Bachelier sought to describe mathematically, constitute the essential nature of their fluctuations. It is this Bachelier mathematical model which is the core of this book.

Bachelier figured out the laws of fluctuations in interest rates by making an analogy with games, and this is easy to understand. Let's suppose you and I are flipping coins. Each time a head comes up, I get one penny. Each time a tail comes up, I lose a penny to you. We keep track of my total winnings or losings. After the first flip of the coin, let's say I'm ahead by one. It was fairly simple to predict on that first flip that the odds of my being ahead by one were exactly one half. And the odds of my being behind by one are exactly one half. After the first flip, I cannot be ahead by more than one, or behind by more than one. After the first flip, the limit of fluctuation in my total gain, or loss, is + 1 or − 1.

But, after the first two flips, the limits of fluctuation change, as well as the probabilities. For example, I could get two heads in a row, or two tails in a row, or a head and a tail, or even a tail and a head. Those are the four ways, and the only four ways, the coins could come up. Note that getting a tail and a head is different from getting a head and a tail, though both result in a net gain of zero.

As you can see, when we go from the results of one flip to the results of two flips, several things happen. First, there are more possible different results. There are in fact four: + 2, 0, 0, and − 2. The four results come from the four possible sequences: *hh, ht, th, tt.* Second, the range of results, the possible magnitude of fluctuation increases. After two flips, the extreme possibilities are + 2 to − 2, whereas after one flip the range was + 1 to − 1. The potential range has doubled. Third, the probability of being ahead or behind has not changed after the second flip. The odds of winning or losing are still the same, one half, irrespective of past gain or loss.

Fourth, we can find the probability of any result by simply counting the number of ways of flipping that give that result and dividing that number by the total number of ways of flipping the coin. For example, the probability of being ahead by two is the number of ways of getting that result (one way) divided by the number of ways of flipping the coin (four). The probability of being ahead by two after two flips is one fourth.

Bachelier and the people that worked on probabilities after him knew that you could calculate probabilities by counting the number of ways of getting a certain result, or set of results, by the total number of ways of flipping the coin.

When you start to play around with what happens in flipping coins, you get surprising and illuminating results. If we carry out the comparison with interest rates, the sum of my winnings (or your winnings) is analogous to the current level of interest rates. Fluctuations in that total are analogous to fluctuations in the level of interest rates. If we know something about those fluctuations, we will be able to estimate how high interest rates might rise, or fall, after a given interval of time.

After one flip of the coin, the maximum fluctuation in my winnings is $+1$ to -1. After two flips it is $+2$ to -2. After three flips it will be $+3$ to -3.

But while the magnitude of potential gain or loss goes up by one with each additional flip, the number of ways of flipping the coin goes up by 2^n. On one flip there are two ways to flip (heads or tails), on two flips there are four ways (*hh, tt, th, ht*), on three flips there are eight ways, on four flips there are sixteen ways. And so on. The probability of getting the maximum result, all heads or all tails, goes down very dramatically since the probability is the single way divided by the number of ways of flipping the coin, or 2^nth power.

Since the range of potential fluctuation in the sum of the flips rises with the number of flips, but not as rapidly, you might guess that the degree of fluctuation would also rise with the number of flips, but again not quite as rapidly. If you guessed that, you would be correct.

Or, if you took the converse, the probability of very little fluctuation would decline with the number of flips. For example, if the total were not to exceed $+1$ or fall below -1, the sequence of tosses would have to be heads, tails, heads, tails . . . etc. There is only one way to get that result out of 2^n ways of flipping a coin n times. Thus as n rises, the probability of little fluctuation also declines. This is contrary to what you expect, for you might think that ending up at zero gain is the most probable outcome. Actually it has only a small probability; the probability of no net change decreases with the number of flips, or with time, if we flip the coin at a steady rate. At the same time, the odds of winning or losing remain the same, one half, even though the odds of losing or winning more than $+1$ or -1 increase. These two assertions are not contradictory. It is the probable range of gain or loss, the volatility of the amount of gain or loss that change. The sum of all probable gains remains at 50 percent as does the sum of all probable loss. The odds of gain or loss remain equal, and the odds of larger gains or losses increase.

Just as we measured the standard deviation of changes in interest rates, we can measure the standard deviation of cumulative gains or losses in coin flipping. The standard deviation of my net gain after n tosses of the coin is the square root of the number of tosses. If tosses continue steadily through time, the standard deviation will rise with the square root of time.

The same square root rule describes the increase in volatility of changes in interest rates; the volatility of changes in interest rates also increases with the square root of time.

The coin-flipping model is analogous to interest rates in other ways. Though there appear to be trends if you chart the cumulative sum, there are none. Though there appear to be cycles, there are none. The probability of increase is one half.

The degree of volatility increases with the square root of time. All of these things characterize fluctuations in interest rates and fluctuations in coin-tossing games. The distribution of probable gains is normal for coin-tossing games (when there are many tosses) and approaches normal for changes in interest rates.

The analogy between fluctuations in interest rates and fluctuations in coin-tossing games, pointed out by Bachelier, still holds. Though Bachelier used only short-term securities called *rentes* and though he used the prices of those *rentes,* rather than yields to maturity, his basic findings were correct.

21

Is the Bond Market Efficient? Probably Not

Myths die hard, particularly myths that are part of our intellectual history, or that form the underpinnings of our basic beliefs about our country, our business, or our state of being. And the myths that die hardest are those that cannot be proved or disproved. If we cannot disprove them, and they are part of our culture, we tend to accept them, assert them, and even believe in them.

One such myth is the efficiency of the bond market. By efficiency is usually meant that all information is properly discounted by the market; that is, the information is known, understood, and properly reflected in the current rate of interest, the slope of the yield curve, and so on. This means that the market reflects the best estimate of the future based on everything known and knowable from what has occurred in the past. The market as a whole knows more than any individual, and future movements of interest rates will reflect future developments.

Academics teach that the bond market is efficient. They say that if yields are higher for long bonds than for short bonds, that is because the market as a whole knows something that the individual cannot know. It is probably because inflation will be higher in the future, and the market knows that and is taking account of it. The individual investor may not know that, but the market does. The market is smarter than the individual, it is more efficient, and it takes into account all available information.

This line of reasoning may have started a long time ago. It probably started with Adam Smith, the father of the theory of free enterprise. Smith argued that an invisible hand guided the actions of the marketplace so that goods and services were allocated in the most efficient manner possible. The individual acts of all the market participants, buyers and sellers, manufacturers and consumers, produced the greatest good for all, seen in the aggregate. In so doing, the market was efficient: more efficient than a government could be, or a state regulator could be.

That idea made sense and not only became one of the bulwarks of the system of free enterprise, but became one of the reasons why we think our economic system is better than other systems, such as a socialist system, for allocating resources. Unfortunately, the idea was extended to the market for stocks and bonds.

Teachers in business schools tell students that the bond market is efficient, and students who go into investment management accept these ideas. Students who go to work for large companies also accept it. Academic researchers try to prove that the theory is correct by showing that when some new information comes out, interest rates move. That proves, they say, that the bond market must be efficient. Rates change when new information comes out. Not only do rates change, they say, but they change in the right direction.

That the bond market is efficient cannot be proved or disproved, unless you define precisely what you mean by efficiency, and do it in a way that can be tested. Unfortunately, you cannot test the fundamental idea of efficiency—"reflects all information."

There is no way of knowing whether the market is efficient. How do we know whether all current information is reflected? How could we know whether all present information was reflected in bond yields?

But you can test whether the slope of the yield curve is properly aligned in relation to future markets. An upward slope is badly aligned (from a lender's standpoint) whenever future rates fall. And that happens roughly half the time. The converse is true from the investor's standpoint.

In retrospect, the market is not particularly smart, not very wise. It always goes up too high, or down too low, and it is impossible to predict with more than 50 percent odds where it will go next. Its random movements need not be ascribed to efficiency, but simply to the competitive nature of the bond market itself, to the effect of many buyers and sellers working opposite sides of every trade. The market need not be efficient to be random.

There are several things that happen that might cast doubt on the efficiency theory. Perhaps the most obvious is that interest rates are always jumping around, always changing. If the bond market is so efficient, why is it changing its mind all the time? If long-term inflation will be higher, why do long and short rates shift in relation to one another? If the market is so efficient, why do the prices of some bonds drop from 100 in the market to very low levels in the span of a year or two? If bond buyers are so smart, why didn't they foresee that?

I think the answer is that the bond market is actually not very efficient at all, that it is not very smart, that it is relatively inept in allocating resources. But that's my opinion. And, as I've said, it cannot be proved or disproved.

Why do I bring up the business of bond market efficiency? I bring the subject up because it has a very important effect on how bonds are managed. If you believe the bond market is efficient, then you will not take advantage of yield differentials in the yield curve. If long bonds have much higher yields, you may avoid them simply because you believe they are properly priced. The only way you may take advantage of yield differences is when yields of a particular maturity are higher than yields of neighboring maturities. Then you will buy that maturity. Or, if the yield is lower you will sell. That is what some current bond managers do under the guise of active bond management. When you think the whole bond market, except for those minor imperfections, is efficient, you don't make the trades you could make based on yield differentials and your own needs, or those of your client if you are a bond manager. You are hampered in what you do by an unprovable theory.

The problem of believing the myth of market efficiency is that you don't take advantage of the available yields in meeting the investment objectives you want to meet. You're a prisoner of your own beliefs; you're a captive of the beliefs of other investors or the academics. There is something that the market knows that you don't know, they say. You cannot beat the market at its own game, you can't know more than it does.

This line of thought, which may be pure nonsense, restricts your ability to act, to choose, and to decide which investment to make. But that is what many investors and many investment managers do.

One currently prevalent sign of this is the way bond managers purchase the highest yield of the shortest maturity. For example, if yields rise from 5 percent on the short end of the yield curve to, for example, 10 percent 10 years out and then if yields go no higher than 10 percent for maturities longer than 10 years, they will buy the 10 year bond. But if your investment horizon is 15 years and you are satisfied with a return of 10 percent, you should probably buy the 15-year bond.

It's much like buying potatoes. If you need potatoes, buy potatoes if the price is reasonable. Don't get turnips, or carrots because they have a better price. Get the maturity you need if the return is what you want and feel is a good return on your money. Don't try to base your decision on what some theory or other says about the market.

The bond market is not quite like the market for goods and services envisioned by Adam Smith. The farmer sells potatoes to earn money. The customer buys potatoes to eat. It's a two-way exchange of people wanting different things.

But the market for bonds is often dominated by professionals who trade to make a point or two. They don't have money to lend or need money to build something, but are simply traders who try to make money by gambling. These people, who are not investment managers, investors, or borrowers, are like gamblers in Las Vegas. To call them rational men who create efficient markets is to attribute to them something that is not present. They are gamblers, pure and simple. But their actions have an enormous impact on bond prices.

The wise investor cannot be swayed by the current myths of the market, but must know what he or she wants, see what is available, and match the two if possible.

22

The Slope of the Yield Curve Doesn't Necessarily Mean Anything

"If we line the children up by age, the most mature will be the tallest," the teacher said. "And it is rarely not so," she continued, to stress the point.

In the same manner, there is a correlation between maturity of the bond and yields. At the present time short-term bonds have low yields, intermediate-term bonds have intermediate yields, and long-term bonds have high yields.

You can plot yields on a grid, showing yield by the vertical distance from the origin and maturity of the bond by the horizontal distance. If you then connect the dots you've plotted with a line, you will see that the line often slopes up to the right. The long maturity yields, which appear on the right, are higher than the short maturity yields, shown on the left. Not only that, the line which connects the yields is continuous and smooth.

Economists argue that long-term money has more risk from inflation and should therefore be priced at higher yields. There is an economic basis, they say, for the upward sloping yield curve.

But to the contrary, there have been many periods in history when the opposite was true and long maturities have suffered lower yields than short maturities over extended periods. There have been other exceptions, also, in history when the yield curve went flat: sometimes it sloped up to the right and then bent flat, and sometimes there were irregularities in the curve itself.

Investment men say that the yield curve tends to smooth itself. They say that buying opportunities occur when there are blips in the yield curve; and that you should buy if the yield is higher than the line or sell if the yield is lower than the line.

They suggest that you should buy because irregularities in the yield curve line tend to correct themselves; the blips represent special opportunities because they tend to disappear.

Other investment persons say that if the yield curve slopes up and then levels off, you should buy where the bend is, for that is the highest yield for the shortest maturity. And thousands of investors do just this.

But you can visualize how the yield curve will look if you think about the third law. The third law states that the degree of volatility of changes in interest rates is highest for short-term maturities and lowest for long-term maturities. This means, basically, that there will be more fluctuations in short-term interest rates than in long-term interest rates. The fluctuation will be lower for long maturities (It will be inversely proportional to the cube root of the maturity). This explains why the yield curve is as it is.

What this means is that short-term yields will move up and down more than long-term yields. Short-term yields also will tend to rise higher and fall lower than long-term yields. Considering also that yields tend to move in the same direction, this activity will tend to produce a slope in the yield curve. It will tend to make short yields lower than long yields in some periods and make short yields higher than long yields in other periods. It will do this because the short yields fluctuate more than the long yields.

There is another way to look at the yield curve. Think of short yields in terms of your height above the ground compared to your active son's height. His position is more volatile as he jumps up and down around you; at times he will be sprawled on the ground below you; at times he will be seated next to you; and at still other times, he will be towering above you. In the same way, the movement of short yields will create a more volatile curve that leans down sometimes, lies flat in other periods, and rises up in other periods.

Nothing stands still. When the yield curve changes, the difference between long and short rates changes. This difference can change in the same way that interest rates change. These changes in the difference between long and short rates can be viewed in the same way that we viewed changes in interest rates.

We can examine the volatility of changes in rates (between long and short); we can compute the volatility of changes in the difference; we can calculate the standard deviation of changes in the difference; and we can then look to see how that measure of volatility (the standard deviation) changes with time. If the standard deviation increases with time, then the changes in the differences will be similar to changes in interest rates, a random variable whose volatility rises with time.

Since the volatility rises with time, a number of traditional ideas must fall. The slope of the yield will not always have an upward slope, but will continually change. The direction of the slope, up or down, will be subject to continuous mutation. It will rise and fall like the waves on the ocean: randomly, unpredictably, and continuously.

If the slope of the yield curve changes at random, there may be no such thing as the *term structure* of interest rates, but a state that is merely the result of random changes in the difference between long and short yields; if this should be called a term structure, so be it. But changes in the difference rise continuously with time which gives them more the character of a random variable than a structure. Thus, we should expect no such thing as a normal yield curve, or a term structure to the yield curve.

From a practical standpoint, we should be a little skeptical when an investment adviser starts to find all kinds of information in the *yield curve.* If he says that the yield curve indicates this about future inflation, or that about future interest rates, or something else about investor expectations, we should listen with caution and be skeptical.

We know that changes in the yield curve occur simply because short rates are more volatile than long rates. It's as simple as that, and the changes are random. To find greater meaning may be not only illusory, but unprofitable.

PART FIVE

Conclusion

23

How to Buy Bonds

Buying bonds is a lot like buying a house. For example, when you've found a house that meets your needs and bank account, don't wait: Buy it. If you look long enough, there may be a better or a cheaper house. But you may look forever and still not find what you want. You have to make a decision and then live with your decision.

Simple enough in theory, you say? Well, it's the same with bonds. If the level of interest rates seems good, buy the bonds. Don't gamble on a rise in rates that may never come: Invest the funds. Get the maturity that suits your needs. Then hold till the bonds come due.

Once you've bought, stand fast and don't fret if rates rise. In buying bonds, you'll be wrong half the time. Remember that the important thing is to get a return that is satisfactory—a yield to maturity that is reasonable.

How do you know if the rate you buy at is satisfactory? You can consider the rate to be satisfactory if it is higher than rates on other investments. For example, if bonds are yielding 10 percent and stocks are yielding 5 percent, then the bonds will be the better buy. Again, if bonds are yielding 12 percent, and the average corporate return on assets is 10 percent, then bonds will still be an attractive buy. But if bonds are yielding 5 percent and stocks are yielding 10 percent, then stocks will be the better buy.

Comparing rates to find the best buy may seem simple-minded, but it's not a bad rule and you would be surprised at how many investors ignore it. If they had followed my rule, instead of prevailing fads, it would have kept them out of bonds in the 1950s when bonds yielded 1 percent and stocks yielded 7 percent. But it would have put them into bonds in the early 1980s when bonds yielded 10 percent and stocks yielded 5 percent. And many wish they'd done just that.

The rule emphasizes what is most important: that before you put down your money you decide on the basis of actual, current return on investment. The rule pays no attention to some theoretical or hypothetical future return. Instead, you base your decision on the hardest facts around: the current yield to maturity.

"What about inflation?" the critics may cry. True, there is no question that inflation can cripple investment returns. In some periods, inflation has cut deeply into profits or has deepened losses. But remember that inflation affects all investments alike. A dollar earned from bonds gives no less, after inflation, than a dollar earned from stocks. To be a little hard-nosed, you shouldn't care where your dollar of investment profits come from. Simply stated, the investment with the best return—inflation or no inflation—is what counts.

The rule we stated earlier, to select the best current return, is the best rule for you to follow. When bonds are returning much more than stocks, buy bonds. When stocks are yielding more, buy stocks. Or, if it is certain return that you want, for a given period, buy bonds. But don't worry about inflation, except as it affects all types of investment equally.

There may be unusual periods, such as in Germany in the 1920s, or in Latin America recently, when inflation grows so rampant that it wipes out all rules. In these unusual circumstances, you might not want to invest at all. Or, you might want to get commodities; but here again, that too is risky during periods of rampant inflation.

Risk

As everyone is aware, risk is an important concern in investing. However, a lot of the mystery, and most of the emotionalism, can be removed by systematically analyzing the potential risk. A lot of information can be gathered in the Interest Rate Risk tables (see Appendix B). These tables can tell you what your risk is. For example, they can forecast what you risk in income loss if you invest. Or, conversely, they can show you the risk of income gain. You can also see what you risk in principal loss if you invest now. It also tells you what you might get on reinvested income.

One of the most interesting readings I get from the tables is that market losses are not necessarily bad. That's because market losses mean higher yields. In turn, higher yields will give higher returns on reinvested income. Consequently, your yield to maturity will be higher than you expected when you bought the bonds. The tables also show that poor initial results give good long-term results, if you reinvest income, and if you don't have to cash in the bonds.

The tables put a number on risk. They tell you how far rates can drop, or rise—for a given set of odds, time interval, and maturity bond. That's really all you need to evaluate interest rate risk.

Remember that the figures are a guide. They are approximate, since they are based on a sampling of the past. But they can be relied upon as a good rough approximation of the future. And that may be as good as you'll get.

Some Things to Remember

1. A bond pays a fixed coupon and has a maturity when you get your money back. Therefore, if a bond is held to maturity, there is no risk. You will get the yield you were promised.
2. Interest rates fluctuate. The degree of fluctuation (from now) increases with time. It is greater for short maturities.
3. The odds of a rise in rates are 50 percent: no more, no less. There is less than a 50 percent probability that rates will rise (or fall) to some former level. The probability can be found in the tables.
4. Interest rates are not cyclical, even though they may seem to be.
5. There is no limit as to how high rates can rise or fall. A checking account may have a negative rate.

6. The only thing the yield curve tells you is which rates are highest. You're kidding yourself if you think it means anything more than that.
7. If you borrow money at a variable rate, your risk may be very high. Check the tables to see how high.

Some Things You Might Do

1. If you don't need income, consider a zero-coupon bond. Check the tax implications first, or consider a municipal zero-coupon issue.
2. When U.S. government rates are the same as corporate rates, or higher, buy the governments. Skip the corporates. Even the best can go under.
3. Be careful when your adviser talks about *active management.* If he means watching the credit of corporate or municipal bonds, that's fine. If he means diversifying those bonds, excellent. But if he starts talking about shifting back and forth between short and long, get another adviser.

What You Should Not Do

What to avoid is no less important than what to do. The bond investment game is surrounded by as many myths and as much mythology as any exotic cult. There are certain of these myths you should avoid. If you don't avoid them, you could get hit by a large loss. The following things should be avoided:

1. Don't bet on the direction of interest rates. The odds of being wrong are high: 50 percent.
2. If rates are attractive, don't wait. Invest now. Rates are attractive when they are high in relation to current returns on other investments, or historical yields on bonds.
3. If you are a long-term investor, don't buy short bonds. Buy long bonds. A long-term investor is one who can wait a long time to get back his principal.

4. If you are a short-term investor, don't buy long bonds. Buy short-maturity bonds. A short-term investor is one who may need his money back soon.
5. Don't measure the performance of a long-term fund on a short-term basis. Gear performance measurement to the length of the fund. The yield to maturity is the best measure of future return; not last month's return.
6. Don't shift back and forth from long to short and short to long, trying to guess the direction of interest rates. That's the biggest gamble of all.
7. Don't buy a bond fund as a bond, unless the fund has a specific maturity; or, unless it's a money market fund.

24

What to Do with Your Fortune

I've often suspected that most people were more interested in speculation than investment. Investment connotes something conservative, reliable, and reputable, something more constant than is revealed by the high volatility of stock prices and interest rates. Speculation suggests a lack of prudence, the desire to make a lot of money fast, even gambling. But speculation is what most investors engage in, whether the investor is acting on his own account, managing money for others, serving on the board of an endowment fund, or making a loan for a bank.

Perhaps it is the sheer fascination of not knowing what the outcome will be, of putting down the money, your own or someone else's, and waiting for the wheel to turn, the next edition of *The Wall Street Journal* to reveal your winnings and losings. That it is speculation, and not something more prudent, is suggested by the words that are used: "earn the highest return," or "rank in the top quartile," or "beat the S&P 500."

But if it is speculation, then there are odds, and the odds are to a degree knowable. If you play roulette, gamble at poker, or play dice in the street, you can know the odds so that you then have the option of betting intelligently. If you play in bonds, you should know the odds as best you can of what will happen next in interest rates, of how far they can rise, or fall, in a given time or for a particular maturity.

In looking at the odds, you should be mindful of the uncertainty, be skeptical of those who say they know which way rates will turn, and be wary of past records.

Skepticism is the most valuable trait you can possess: skepticism that the record of others will be repeated, skepticism of what they say, knowing that there may be another alternative than those which happen to be suggested.

I remember my own introduction into the investment business many years ago. At that time stocks were selling at 20 to 25 times earnings, which made stock yields a bare 2.5 percent. To sell at those precious values, stocks had to have risen in price, and rise they did, making fortunes for many and imparting wisdom to the money managers who seemed to be able to do no wrong. My hometown was rife with newly minted millionaires elevated to new riches on the rise of hot local stocks.

When I questioned the continuance of those lofty prices, some of my more experienced and knowledgeable friends assured me that if earnings continued to rise at past rates, as surely they would, stock prices would double again in another few years.

Earnings did rise, though not as spectacularly as before, but prices did not rise. Instead prices fell gradually, uninterruptedly, and for many stocks, quite sharply. It was a full decade before common stock prices returned to their former levels. As a result, the average investor earned a negative return on his investment for many years.

The lesson is clear: Beware of what you hear on investments in general, and on interest rates in particular. Be a little leery of anyone who says he will make or has made fortunes forecasting swings in interest rates. Above all, try to assess the odds of this or that happening; be sure that you have decided in advance what you want, what you truly need, and what you can forego. If you don't need the money now, and rates are attractive, buy long bonds, or empower your investment manager to do so. And do not worry about the intervening rates of return, the monthly or quarterly performance figures: for those do not matter if you are only concerned in the long-term return on your investment.

If you've made a fortune, inherited one, or made a killing at the racetrack, hire a manager to decide which bond is best, to keep tab on your investments and make reports on your income for tax time. But in so doing, tell your adviser exactly what you want, what you need, and what you don't need. Do not, under any circumstances, let your adviser lead you into putting your money into the latest investment fad—which money managers are wont to do and will do unless the client makes clear what he, or she, wants.

If you have fewer funds to invest, as most do, put your money in U.S. government securities. Have your bank or broker buy them, first being sure about the maturity length that suits your financial needs (and temperament). Only you can decide that, and a major factor is how soon you will need the money back. If you might need the money soon, get a savings account or put the money in a money market fund.

Some people want certainty. You get certainty, and guaranteed return, if you buy a government bond and spend all the coupons and hold the bond to maturity. You don't get certainty from bonds if you reinvest the coupons or if you sell the bonds prior to maturity. You can't get certainty from any other form of investment—stocks or commodities.

Until a few years ago, you couldn't get a certain return from any investment if you reinvested the income. You were utterly dependent on future reinvestment rates. And, if your time horizon was long term, as it is for pensions and endowments and for many individuals, those volatile future reinvestment rates made your investment highly speculative.

Now that is all changed. Now it is possible to get certain returns for long term investments. It was made possible by the invention of *zero coupon bonds.* The zero coupon bonds permit you to nail down your future return precisely. In fact, if you are in a high tax bracket, you can buy a zero coupon tax exempt bond and do something no investment manager, mutual fund, or anyone else was ever able to do. The remarkable features of the zero coupon bond, particularly the U.S. government zero, makes putting money in bonds what it never was before: a zero risk investment (inflation aside).

It is often said that history never repeats itself. But that is only partly true, for there are aspects of history that do recur, just as surely as the sun comes up each morning. The general patterns of yield volatility which we have pointed out are universal and you can profit by knowing more about them.

APPENDIX A
Technical Notes

The purpose of the original study, done by M. F. M. Osborne and the author of this book, was to examine the volatility of changes in bond yields in order to: (1) determine the characteristics of that volatility; (2) ascertain the effect of time and maturity on volatility; (3) fit an equation to the data; and (4) find out how consistent or inconsistent the general characteristics were over time.

Very early we found that we should use the logs of the yields, instead of the original yields, as our basic data. It was also clear that the (logs of) yields could probably be represented as the cumulative sums of a random series. Suspecting this, we then concentrated on a study of the standard deviation of changes in the logs of yields. We paid particular attention to how the standard deviation (our measure of volatility) increased as the difference interval was lengthened. By doing this, we not only learned much about the underlying nature of yield volatility, but also derived equations which could be put to use in understanding what is happening to volatility of yields and to making decisions. Our method of examining and describing yield volatility is, I think, uncommon, but extremely useful.

The raw data of our study was a series of monthly (or annual) yields for a bond of a particular maturity. In nearly all cases, the yields were yield indexes, such as the Salomon U.S. Government Monthly Yield Index, 1950–1979, for a 10-year bond. We can define such a set of yields(y) as y_t where $t = 1$ to n. We looked up the natural logarithms of each yield to obtain a new series $\log_e(y_t)$

We then computed differences in the logs of yields for the difference interval (k).

$$\Delta \log_e(y_t) = \log_e(y_t) - \log_e(y_{t-k}) \qquad (1)$$

where

$$t = 1, n - k.$$

Equation 1 gives $n - k$ changes in the natural logarithm of yields over a particular difference interval (k) for a particular bond maturity (*m*). We performed the operation of Equation 1 for varying difference intervals, $k = 1, 2 \ldots$ and for different maturity bonds (*m*).

This gave us many sets of series of differences in the logs of yields. We wished to know the attributes of each series. We wanted to see whether they resembled random numbers, and what impact the historical era, the type vehicle (corporate or government), the difference interval (*k*), and the maturity (*m*), had on each series and what seemed to characterize all of the series, irrespective of historical era or vehicle type.

The most important step was to compute the standard deviation of the series obtained in equation 1 which gave

$$s\Delta\log y_{(k,m)}$$

In doing this, we obtained a set of standard deviations, one for each combination of difference intervals and maturities. For the Durand U.S. Corporate Bond Yields 1900–1965, for example, we obtained standard deviations for 8 difference intervals (1, 2 . . . 8 years) and 7 maturities (1, 5, 10, 15, 20, 25, and 30 years)—56 different standard deviations altogether.

We examined the relationship between the standard deviation (*s*), the difference interval (*k*), and the bond maturity (*m*) by regressing *s* on *k* and *m* (using multiple regression).

The equation which we derived from our two most extensive sets of data (the Salomon and the Durand data) is the following:

$$\log_e[\text{Standard deviation}\Delta\log_e(\text{Yield})] = \log_e c \qquad (2)$$
$$+ a[\log_e(\text{Difference interval})]$$
$$- b[\log_e(\text{Maturity})]$$

For the Salomon data, $a = .42$, $b = .35$, $c = .27$, and $r^2 = .93$.
For the Durand data, $a = .61$, $b = .40$, $c = .23$, and $r^2 = .99$.

The parameters of the equations (*a*, *b*, and *c*) shown above are based on difference intervals measured in years. Both coefficients of multiple correlation are significant at the .01 level.

For a random series, we would expect $a = 0.5$ (the square root of time rule). The above values (0.42 and 0.61) are fair approximations of the expected value, as are the values we obtained from the other yield series we examined.

This equation may seem theoretical. From a practical standpoint it is helpful to know, for example: if you wait for a year, will rates rise from 10 percent to 12 percent on a 10-year bond? The time you wait, the year, is the difference interval (k). Ten years is the maturity of the bond (m). The standard deviation (s) can be used to calculate the probability of rates rising from 10 percent to 12 percent, assuming a normal distribution of changes in the natural logarithms of yields. The distributions are not normal, but are approximately so.

Several points bear mentioning. First, there is a general consistency over long historical periods to volatility of yields. Certainly, the volatility of yields is affected by the historical period. But the effect is within limits, usually within a factor of two. Paradoxically, the historical period has more influence on volatility than the type issue (government or corporate). The mean change in yields, the trend, is not usually significant, yet it does affect volatility. It is not taken into account in the tables in this book and, to that degree, the tables understate volatility.

In examining volatility we are limited by our data. The shortest period for which we had good measures of volatility was a week; the longest was six or seven years. Yet, some of the tables in this book extend up to 20 years. Beyond six or seven years the results are based on the extrapolation of shorter term data.

This book does not use duration as a criterion, nor does it use expectational theory, or modern portfolio theory. The usefulness of the duration measure is reduced by using the logs of yields, while the yield indexes are less amenable to using duration than are individual bonds. Also, this book does not discuss inflation, the risk-free rate, or other related subjects which are treatable by the methods described here, but beyond the scope of this book.

Accounts of our original studies which describe the foundation for the above material and other things covered in this book are given in the References (Appendix E).

APPENDIX B _____
Range of Future Yields

The tables in this Appendix show the range of future yields for 25 maturities and 18 future years for present yields of from 4 to 16 percent.

WHAT TABLE B-1 SHOWS

1. The present yield on the bond: 10 percent.
2. How many years in the future: 1 year.
3. The maturity of the bond: 3 years.
4. The high probable yield: 12.02 percent.
5. The low probable yield: 8.32 percent.

The range of yields shown in these tables have a two-thirds probability. Thus, for the three year maturity, the probability is two-thirds that yields a year from now will lie between 8.32 percent and 12.02 percent. There is a 1-in-6 chance that yields will drop below 8.32 percent and a 1-in-6 chance that yields will rise above 12.02 percent.

The range of yields is based on Salomon U.S. yield index data, 1950–1979.

TABLE B-1
Range of Future Yields

RANGE OF FUTURE YIELDS FROM INITIAL YIELD OF 10%

BOND MATURITY	1	2	3	4	5	6	7	8	9	10	11	12	13	14	15	16	17	18
									Years									
1	13.10	14.35	15.35	16.21	17.00	17.74	18.43	19.09	19.73	20.34	20.94	21.53	22.10	22.66	23.21	23.75	24.29	24.82
	7.63	6.97	6.52	6.17	5.88	5.64	5.43	5.24	5.07	4.92	4.78	4.65	4.53	4.41	4.31	4.21	4.12	4.03
2	12.36	13.28	13.99	14.61	15.17	15.68	16.16	16.61	17.04	17.46	17.86	18.25	18.63	19.00	19.36	19.71	20.06	20.41
	8.09	7.53	7.15	6.84	6.59	6.38	6.19	6.02	5.87	5.73	5.60	5.48	5.37	5.26	5.17	5.07	4.98	4.90
3	12.02	12.79	13.39	13.90	14.35	14.77	15.16	15.53	15.88	16.22	16.54	16.85	17.16	17.45	17.74	18.02	18.30	18.57
	8.32	7.82	7.47	7.20	6.97	6.77	6.60	6.44	6.30	6.17	6.05	5.93	5.83	5.73	5.64	5.55	5.47	5.39
4	11.81	12.49	13.02	13.47	13.86	14.23	14.57	14.89	15.19	15.48	15.76	16.03	16.29	16.55	16.79	17.03	17.27	17.50
	8.47	8.01	7.68	7.43	7.21	7.03	6.86	6.72	6.58	6.46	6.34	6.24	6.14	6.04	5.96	5.87	5.79	5.71
5	11.66	12.28	12.76	13.17	13.53	13.86	14.16	14.45	14.72	14.98	15.23	15.47	15.71	15.93	16.15	16.36	16.57	16.78
	8.58	8.14	7.84	7.59	7.39	7.22	7.06	6.92	6.79	6.67	6.57	6.46	6.37	6.28	6.19	6.11	6.03	5.96
6	11.55	12.13	12.57	12.95	13.28	13.58	13.86	14.13	14.37	14.61	14.84	15.06	15.27	15.48	15.68	15.87	16.06	16.25
	8.66	8.25	7.96	7.72	7.53	7.36	7.21	7.08	6.96	6.84	6.74	6.64	6.55	6.46	6.38	6.30	6.22	6.15
7	11.46	12.01	12.42	12.77	13.08	13.36	13.63	13.87	14.10	14.32	14.54	14.74	14.94	15.13	15.31	15.49	15.67	15.84
	8.72	8.33	8.05	7.83	7.64	7.48	7.34	7.21	7.09	6.98	6.88	6.78	6.69	6.61	6.53	6.45	6.38	6.31
8	11.39	11.91	12.30	12.63	12.92	13.19	13.43	13.67	13.88	14.09	14.29	14.48	14.67	14.84	15.02	15.19	15.35	15.51
	8.78	8.40	8.13	7.92	7.74	7.58	7.44	7.32	7.20	7.10	7.00	6.91	6.82	6.74	6.66	6.58	6.51	6.45
9	11.33	11.82	12.20	12.51	12.79	13.04	13.28	13.49	13.70	13.90	14.09	14.27	14.44	14.61	14.77	14.93	15.09	15.24
	8.82	8.46	8.20	7.99	7.82	7.67	7.53	7.41	7.30	7.20	7.10	7.01	6.92	6.84	6.77	6.70	6.63	6.56
10	11.28	11.75	12.11	12.41	12.68	12.92	13.14	13.35	13.55	13.73	13.91	14.08	14.25	14.41	14.57	14.72	14.86	15.01
	8.86	8.51	8.26	8.06	7.89	7.74	7.61	7.49	7.38	7.28	7.19	7.10	7.02	6.94	6.87	6.79	6.73	6.66

RANGE OF FUTURE YIELDS FROM INITIAL YIELD OF 4%

BOND MATURITY	Years																	
	1	2	3	4	5	6	7	8	9	10	11	12	13	14	15	16	17	18
1	5.24	5.74	6.14	6.49	6.80	7.09	7.37	7.64	7.89	8.14	8.38	8.61	8.84	9.06	9.28	9.50	9.72	9.93
	3.05	2.79	2.61	2.47	2.35	2.26	2.17	2.10	2.03	1.97	1.91	1.86	1.81	1.77	1.72	1.68	1.65	1.61
2	4.94	5.31	5.60	5.84	6.07	6.27	6.46	6.64	6.82	6.98	7.14	7.30	7.45	7.60	7.74	7.89	8.03	8.16
	3.24	3.01	2.86	2.74	2.64	2.55	2.48	2.41	2.35	2.29	2.24	2.19	2.15	2.11	2.07	2.03	1.99	1.96
3	4.81	5.12	5.35	5.56	5.74	5.91	6.06	6.21	6.35	6.49	6.62	6.74	6.86	6.98	7.10	7.21	7.32	7.43
	3.33	3.13	2.99	2.88	2.79	2.71	2.64	2.58	2.52	2.47	2.42	2.37	2.33	2.29	2.25	2.22	2.19	2.15
4	4.72	5.00	5.21	5.39	5.55	5.69	5.83	5.96	6.08	6.19	6.30	6.41	6.52	6.62	6.72	6.81	6.91	7.00
	3.39	3.20	3.07	2.97	2.89	2.81	2.75	2.69	2.63	2.58	2.54	2.50	2.46	2.42	2.38	2.35	2.32	2.29
5	4.66	4.91	5.10	5.27	5.41	5.54	5.67	5.78	5.89	5.99	6.09	6.19	6.28	6.37	6.46	6.55	6.63	6.71
	3.43	3.26	3.13	3.04	2.96	2.89	2.82	2.77	2.72	2.67	2.63	2.59	2.55	2.51	2.48	2.44	2.41	2.38
6	4.62	4.85	5.03	5.18	5.31	5.43	5.54	5.65	5.75	5.85	5.94	6.02	6.11	6.19	6.27	6.35	6.43	6.50
	3.46	3.30	3.18	3.09	3.01	2.95	2.89	2.83	2.78	2.74	2.70	2.66	2.62	2.58	2.55	2.52	2.49	2.46
7	4.59	4.80	4.97	5.11	5.23	5.35	5.45	5.55	5.64	5.73	5.81	5.90	5.97	6.05	6.13	6.20	6.27	6.34
	3.49	3.33	3.22	3.13	3.06	2.99	2.94	2.88	2.84	2.79	2.75	2.71	2.68	2.64	2.61	2.58	2.55	2.53
8	4.56	4.76	4.92	5.05	5.17	5.28	5.37	5.47	5.55	5.64	5.72	5.79	5.87	5.94	6.01	6.07	6.14	6.20
	3.51	3.36	3.25	3.17	3.10	3.03	2.98	2.93	2.88	2.84	2.80	2.76	2.73	2.69	2.66	2.63	2.61	2.58
9	4.53	4.73	4.88	5.00	5.12	5.22	5.31	5.40	5.48	5.56	5.63	5.71	5.78	5.84	5.91	5.97	6.04	6.10
	3.53	3.38	3.28	3.20	3.13	3.07	3.01	2.96	2.92	2.88	2.84	2.80	2.77	2.74	2.71	2.68	2.65	2.62
10	4.51	4.70	4.84	4.96	5.07	5.17	5.26	5.34	5.42	5.49	5.56	5.63	5.70	5.76	5.83	5.89	5.95	6.00
	3.55	3.40	3.30	3.22	3.16	3.10	3.04	3.00	2.95	2.91	2.88	2.84	2.81	2.78	2.75	2.72	2.69	2.67
11	4.49	4.68	4.81	4.93	5.03	5.12	5.21	5.29	5.36	5.44	5.50	5.57	5.63	5.70	5.76	5.81	5.87	5.92
	3.56	3.42	3.32	3.25	3.18	3.12	3.07	3.03	2.98	2.94	2.91	2.87	2.84	2.81	2.78	2.75	2.73	2.70
12	4.48	4.65	4.79	4.90	5.00	5.09	5.17	5.25	5.32	5.39	5.45	5.52	5.58	5.64	5.69	5.75	5.80	5.85
	3.57	3.44	3.34	3.27	3.20	3.15	3.10	3.05	3.01	2.97	2.93	2.90	2.87	2.84	2.81	2.78	2.76	2.73

Years

	1	2	3	4	5	6	7	8	9	10	11	12	13	14	15	16	17	18
13	4.47 / 3.58	4.63 / 3.45	4.76 / 3.36	4.87 / 3.28	4.97 / 3.22	5.05 / 3.17	5.13 / 3.12	5.21 / 3.07	5.28 / 3.03	5.34 / 2.99	5.41 / 2.96	5.47 / 2.93	5.53 / 2.90	5.58 / 2.87	5.64 / 2.84	5.69 / 2.81	5.74 / 2.79	5.79 / 2.76
14	4.45 / 3.59	4.62 / 3.47	4.74 / 3.37	4.85 / 3.30	4.94 / 3.24	5.02 / 3.19	5.10 / 3.14	5.17 / 3.09	5.24 / 3.05	5.30 / 3.02	5.36 / 2.98	5.42 / 2.95	5.48 / 2.92	5.53 / 2.89	5.59 / 2.86	5.64 / 2.84	5.69 / 2.81	5.74 / 2.79
15	4.44 / 3.60	4.60 / 3.48	4.72 / 3.39	4.82 / 3.32	4.91 / 3.26	4.99 / 3.20	5.07 / 3.16	5.14 / 3.11	5.21 / 3.07	5.27 / 3.04	5.33 / 3.00	5.38 / 2.97	5.44 / 2.94	5.49 / 2.91	5.54 / 2.89	5.59 / 2.86	5.64 / 2.84	5.69 / 2.81
16	4.43 / 3.61	4.59 / 3.49	4.70 / 3.40	4.80 / 3.33	4.89 / 3.27	4.97 / 3.22	5.04 / 3.17	5.11 / 3.13	5.17 / 3.09	5.24 / 3.06	5.29 / 3.02	5.35 / 2.99	5.40 / 2.96	5.45 / 2.93	5.50 / 2.91	5.55 / 2.88	5.60 / 2.86	5.64 / 2.83
17	4.42 / 3.62	4.57 / 3.50	4.69 / 3.41	4.79 / 3.34	4.87 / 3.29	4.95 / 3.23	5.02 / 3.19	5.08 / 3.15	5.15 / 3.11	5.21 / 3.07	5.26 / 3.04	5.32 / 3.01	5.37 / 2.98	5.42 / 2.95	5.47 / 2.93	5.51 / 2.90	5.56 / 2.88	5.60 / 2.85
18	4.41 / 3.63	4.56 / 3.51	4.67 / 3.42	4.77 / 3.36	4.85 / 3.30	4.93 / 3.25	5.00 / 3.20	5.06 / 3.16	5.12 / 3.12	5.18 / 3.09	5.23 / 3.06	5.29 / 3.03	5.34 / 3.00	5.39 / 2.97	5.43 / 2.95	5.48 / 2.92	5.52 / 2.90	5.57 / 2.87
19	4.40 / 3.63	4.55 / 3.52	4.66 / 3.43	4.75 / 3.37	4.83 / 3.31	4.91 / 3.26	4.98 / 3.22	5.04 / 3.18	5.10 / 3.14	5.15 / 3.10	5.21 / 3.07	5.26 / 3.04	5.31 / 3.01	5.36 / 2.99	5.40 / 2.96	5.45 / 2.94	5.49 / 2.91	5.53 / 2.89
20	4.40 / 3.64	4.54 / 3.52	4.65 / 3.44	4.74 / 3.38	4.82 / 3.32	4.89 / 3.27	4.96 / 3.23	5.02 / 3.19	5.08 / 3.15	5.13 / 3.12	5.18 / 3.09	5.23 / 3.06	5.28 / 3.03	5.33 / 3.00	5.37 / 2.98	5.42 / 2.95	5.46 / 2.93	5.50 / 2.91
21	4.39 / 3.64	4.53 / 3.53	4.64 / 3.45	4.72 / 3.39	4.80 / 3.33	4.87 / 3.28	4.94 / 3.24	5.00 / 3.20	5.05 / 3.17	5.11 / 3.13	5.16 / 3.10	5.21 / 3.07	5.26 / 3.04	5.30 / 3.02	5.35 / 2.99	5.39 / 2.97	5.43 / 2.95	5.47 / 2.92
22	4.38 / 3.65	4.52 / 3.54	4.62 / 3.46	4.71 / 3.40	4.79 / 3.34	4.86 / 3.29	4.92 / 3.25	4.98 / 3.21	5.04 / 3.18	5.09 / 3.14	5.14 / 3.11	5.19 / 3.08	5.23 / 3.06	5.28 / 3.03	5.32 / 3.01	5.36 / 2.98	5.40 / 2.96	5.44 / 2.94
23	4.38 / 3.66	4.51 / 3.55	4.61 / 3.47	4.70 / 3.40	4.78 / 3.35	4.84 / 3.30	4.91 / 3.26	4.96 / 3.22	5.02 / 3.19	5.07 / 3.16	5.12 / 3.13	5.17 / 3.10	5.21 / 3.07	5.26 / 3.04	5.30 / 3.02	5.34 / 3.00	5.38 / 2.97	5.42 / 2.95
24	4.37 / 3.66	4.50 / 3.55	4.60 / 3.47	4.69 / 3.41	4.76 / 3.36	4.83 / 3.31	4.89 / 3.27	4.95 / 3.23	5.00 / 3.20	5.05 / 3.17	5.10 / 3.14	5.15 / 3.11	5.19 / 3.08	5.23 / 3.06	5.28 / 3.03	5.32 / 3.01	5.36 / 2.99	5.39 / 2.97
25	4.37 / 3.66	4.50 / 3.56	4.60 / 3.48	4.68 / 3.42	4.75 / 3.37	4.82 / 3.32	4.88 / 3.28	4.93 / 3.24	4.99 / 3.21	5.04 / 3.18	5.08 / 3.15	5.13 / 3.12	5.17 / 3.09	5.21 / 3.07	5.26 / 3.04	5.29 / 3.02	5.33 / 3.00	5.37 / 2.98

RANGE OF FUTURE YIELDS FROM INITIAL YIELD OF 5%

BOND MATURITY	Years																	
	1	2	3	4	5	6	7	8	9	10	11	12	13	14	15	16	17	18
1	6.55 / 3.82	7.18 / 3.48	7.67 / 3.26	8.11 / 3.08	8.50 / 2.94	8.87 / 2.82	9.21 / 2.71	9.55 / 2.62	9.86 / 2.53	10.17 / 2.46	10.47 / 2.39	10.76 / 2.32	11.05 / 2.26	11.33 / 2.21	11.61 / 2.15	11.88 / 2.10	12.14 / 2.06	12.41 / 2.01
2	6.18 / 4.05	6.64 / 3.77	7.00 / 3.57	7.31 / 3.42	7.58 / 3.30	7.84 / 3.19	8.08 / 3.09	8.30 / 3.01	8.52 / 2.93	8.73 / 2.86	8.93 / 2.80	9.12 / 2.74	9.31 / 2.68	9.50 / 2.63	9.68 / 2.58	9.86 / 2.54	10.03 / 2.49	10.20 / 2.45
3	6.01 / 4.16	6.39 / 3.91	6.69 / 3.74	6.95 / 3.60	7.18 / 3.48	7.39 / 3.38	7.58 / 3.30	7.77 / 3.22	7.94 / 3.15	8.11 / 3.08	8.27 / 3.02	8.43 / 2.97	8.58 / 2.91	8.73 / 2.87	8.87 / 2.82	9.01 / 2.77	9.15 / 2.73	9.28 / 2.69
4	5.90 / 4.23	6.25 / 4.00	6.51 / 3.84	6.73 / 3.71	6.93 / 3.61	7.11 / 3.51	7.28 / 3.43	7.44 / 3.36	7.60 / 3.29	7.74 / 3.23	7.88 / 3.17	8.02 / 3.12	8.15 / 3.07	8.27 / 3.02	8.40 / 2.98	8.52 / 2.94	8.63 / 2.90	8.75 / 2.86
5	5.83 / 4.29	6.14 / 4.07	6.38 / 3.92	6.58 / 3.80	6.76 / 3.70	6.93 / 3.61	7.08 / 3.53	7.23 / 3.46	7.36 / 3.40	7.49 / 3.34	7.62 / 3.28	7.74 / 3.23	7.85 / 3.18	7.97 / 3.14	8.08 / 3.10	8.18 / 3.06	8.29 / 3.02	8.39 / 2.98
6	5.78 / 4.33	6.06 / 4.12	6.29 / 3.98	6.47 / 3.86	6.64 / 3.77	6.79 / 3.68	6.93 / 3.61	7.06 / 3.54	7.19 / 3.48	7.31 / 3.42	7.42 / 3.37	7.53 / 3.32	7.64 / 3.27	7.74 / 3.23	7.84 / 3.19	7.94 / 3.15	8.03 / 3.11	8.13 / 3.08
7	5.73 / 4.36	6.00 / 4.16	6.21 / 4.03	6.39 / 3.92	6.54 / 3.82	6.68 / 3.74	6.81 / 3.67	6.94 / 3.60	7.05 / 3.55	7.16 / 3.49	7.27 / 3.44	7.37 / 3.39	7.47 / 3.35	7.56 / 3.31	7.66 / 3.27	7.75 / 3.23	7.83 / 3.19	7.92 / 3.16
8	5.70 / 4.39	5.95 / 4.20	6.15 / 4.07	6.31 / 3.96	6.46 / 3.87	6.59 / 3.79	6.72 / 3.72	6.83 / 3.66	6.94 / 3.60	7.05 / 3.55	7.15 / 3.50	7.24 / 3.45	7.33 / 3.41	7.42 / 3.37	7.51 / 3.33	7.59 / 3.29	7.68 / 3.26	7.76 / 3.22
9	5.67 / 4.41	5.91 / 4.23	6.10 / 4.10	6.26 / 4.00	6.39 / 3.91	6.52 / 3.83	6.64 / 3.77	6.75 / 3.71	6.85 / 3.65	6.95 / 3.60	7.04 / 3.55	7.13 / 3.50	7.22 / 3.46	7.30 / 3.42	7.39 / 3.38	7.47 / 3.35	7.54 / 3.31	7.62 / 3.28
10	5.64 / 4.43	5.88 / 4.25	6.05 / 4.13	6.20 / 4.03	6.34 / 3.94	6.46 / 3.87	6.57 / 3.81	6.67 / 3.75	6.77 / 3.69	6.87 / 3.64	6.96 / 3.59	7.04 / 3.55	7.13 / 3.51	7.21 / 3.47	7.28 / 3.43	7.36 / 3.40	7.43 / 3.36	7.50 / 3.33
11	5.62 / 4.45	5.84 / 4.28	6.02 / 4.16	6.16 / 4.06	6.29 / 3.98	6.40 / 3.90	6.51 / 3.84	6.61 / 3.78	6.71 / 3.73	6.80 / 3.68	6.88 / 3.63	6.96 / 3.59	7.04 / 3.55	7.12 / 3.51	7.19 / 3.48	7.27 / 3.44	7.34 / 3.41	7.41 / 3.38
12	5.60 / 4.47	5.82 / 4.30	5.98 / 4.18	6.12 / 4.08	6.25 / 4.00	6.36 / 3.93	6.46 / 3.87	6.56 / 3.81	6.65 / 3.76	6.73 / 3.71	6.82 / 3.67	6.89 / 3.63	6.97 / 3.59	7.04 / 3.55	7.12 / 3.51	7.19 / 3.48	7.25 / 3.45	7.32 / 3.42

Years

	1	2	3	4	5	6	7	8	9	10	11	12	13	14	15	16	17	18
13	5.58 4.48	5.79 4.32	5.95 4.20	6.09 4.11	6.21 4.03	6.32 3.96	6.41 3.90	6.51 3.84	6.59 3.79	6.68 3.74	6.76 3.70	6.83 3.66	6.91 3.62	6.98 3.58	7.05 3.55	7.11 3.51	7.18 3.48	7.24 3.45
14	5.57 4.49	5.77 4.33	5.93 4.22	6.06 4.13	6.17 4.05	6.28 3.98	6.37 3.92	6.46 3.87	6.55 3.82	6.63 3.77	6.71 3.73	6.78 3.69	6.85 3.65	6.92 3.61	6.99 3.58	7.05 3.55	7.11 3.52	7.17 3.49
15	5.55 4.50	5.75 4.35	5.90 4.24	6.03 4.15	6.14 4.07	6.24 4.00	6.34 3.95	6.42 3.89	6.51 3.84	6.58 3.80	6.66 3.75	6.73 3.71	6.80 3.68	6.87 3.64	6.93 3.61	6.99 3.58	7.05 3.54	7.11 3.52
16	5.54 4.51	5.73 4.36	5.88 4.25	6.00 4.16	6.11 4.09	6.21 4.02	6.30 3.97	6.39 3.91	6.47 3.87	6.54 3.82	6.62 3.78	6.69 3.74	6.75 3.70	6.82 3.67	6.88 3.63	6.94 3.60	7.00 3.57	7.06 3.54
17	5.53 4.52	5.72 4.37	5.86 4.27	5.98 4.18	6.09 4.11	6.18 4.04	6.27 3.99	6.36 3.93	6.43 3.89	6.51 3.84	6.58 3.80	6.64 3.76	6.71 3.73	6.77 3.69	6.83 3.66	6.89 3.63	6.95 3.60	7.01 3.57
18	5.52 4.53	5.70 4.38	5.84 4.28	5.96 4.19	6.06 4.12	6.16 4.06	6.24 4.00	6.33 3.95	6.40 3.91	6.47 3.86	6.54 3.82	6.61 3.78	6.67 3.75	6.73 3.71	6.79 3.68	6.85 3.65	6.90 3.62	6.96 3.59
19	5.51 4.54	5.69 4.40	5.83 4.29	5.94 4.21	6.04 4.14	6.13 4.08	6.22 4.02	6.30 3.97	6.37 3.92	6.44 3.88	6.51 3.84	6.57 3.80	6.63 3.77	6.69 3.73	6.75 3.70	6.81 3.67	6.86 3.64	6.92 3.61
20	5.50 4.55	5.67 4.41	5.81 4.30	5.92 4.22	6.02 4.15	6.11 4.09	6.19 4.04	6.27 3.99	6.34 3.94	6.41 3.90	6.48 3.86	6.54 3.82	6.60 3.79	6.66 3.75	6.72 3.72	6.77 3.69	6.82 3.66	6.88 3.64
21	5.49 4.56	5.66 4.41	5.80 4.31	5.91 4.23	6.00 4.16	6.09 4.10	6.17 4.05	6.25 4.00	6.32 3.96	6.39 3.91	6.45 3.88	6.51 3.84	6.57 3.80	6.63 3.77	6.68 3.74	6.74 3.71	6.79 3.68	6.84 3.66
22	5.48 4.56	5.65 4.42	5.78 4.32	5.89 4.24	5.99 4.18	6.07 4.12	6.15 4.06	6.23 4.02	6.29 3.97	6.36 3.93	6.42 3.89	6.48 3.86	6.54 3.82	6.60 3.79	6.65 3.76	6.70 3.73	6.75 3.70	6.80 3.67
23	5.47 4.57	5.64 4.43	5.77 4.33	5.88 4.26	5.97 4.19	6.05 4.13	6.13 4.08	6.20 4.03	6.27 3.99	6.34 3.94	6.40 3.91	6.46 3.87	6.51 3.84	6.57 3.81	6.62 3.78	6.67 3.75	6.72 3.72	6.77 3.69
24	5.46 4.58	5.63 4.44	5.76 4.34	5.86 4.27	5.95 4.20	6.04 4.14	6.11 4.09	6.18 4.04	6.25 4.00	6.32 3.96	6.38 3.92	6.43 3.89	6.49 3.85	6.54 3.82	6.59 3.79	6.65 3.76	6.69 3.73	6.74 3.71
25	5.46 4.58	5.62 4.45	5.74 4.35	5.85 4.27	5.94 4.21	6.02 4.15	6.10 4.10	6.17 4.05	6.23 4.01	6.29 3.97	6.35 3.93	6.41 3.90	6.47 3.87	6.52 3.84	6.57 3.81	6.62 3.78	6.67 3.75	6.71 3.72

RANGE OF FUTURE YIELDS FROM INITIAL YIELD OF 6%

BOND MATURITY	Years 1	2	3	4	5	6	7	8	9	10	11	12	13	14	15	16	17	18
1	7.86 / 4.58	8.61 / 4.18	9.21 / 3.91	9.73 / 3.70	10.20 / 3.53	10.64 / 3.38	11.06 / 3.26	11.45 / 3.14	11.84 / 3.04	12.21 / 2.95	12.57 / 2.87	12.92 / 2.79	13.26 / 2.72	13.60 / 2.65	13.93 / 2.59	14.25 / 2.53	14.57 / 2.47	14.89 / 2.42
2	7.42 / 4.85	7.97 / 4.52	8.40 / 4.29	8.77 / 4.11	9.10 / 3.96	9.41 / 3.83	9.69 / 3.71	9.97 / 3.61	10.22 / 3.52	10.47 / 3.44	10.72 / 3.36	10.95 / 3.29	11.18 / 3.22	11.40 / 3.16	11.62 / 3.10	11.83 / 3.04	12.04 / 2.99	12.24 / 2.94
3	7.21 / 4.99	7.67 / 4.69	8.03 / 4.48	8.34 / 4.32	8.61 / 4.18	8.86 / 4.06	9.10 / 3.96	9.32 / 3.86	9.53 / 3.78	9.73 / 3.70	9.92 / 3.63	10.11 / 3.56	10.29 / 3.50	10.47 / 3.44	10.64 / 3.38	10.81 / 3.33	10.98 / 3.28	11.14 / 3.23
4	7.08 / 5.08	7.49 / 4.80	7.81 / 4.61	8.08 / 4.46	8.32 / 4.33	8.54 / 4.22	8.74 / 4.12	8.93 / 4.03	9.12 / 3.95	9.29 / 3.88	9.46 / 3.81	9.62 / 3.74	9.78 / 3.68	9.93 / 3.63	10.08 / 3.57	10.22 / 3.52	10.36 / 3.47	10.50 / 3.43
5	7.00 / 5.15	7.37 / 4.88	7.66 / 4.70	7.90 / 4.56	8.12 / 4.44	8.31 / 4.33	8.50 / 4.24	8.67 / 4.15	8.83 / 4.08	8.99 / 4.00	9.14 / 3.94	9.28 / 3.88	9.42 / 3.82	9.56 / 3.77	9.69 / 3.71	9.82 / 3.67	9.94 / 3.62	10.07 / 3.58
6	6.93 / 5.19	7.28 / 4.95	7.54 / 4.77	7.77 / 4.63	7.97 / 4.52	8.15 / 4.42	8.32 / 4.33	8.48 / 4.25	8.62 / 4.17	8.77 / 4.11	8.90 / 4.04	9.04 / 3.98	9.16 / 3.93	9.29 / 3.88	9.41 / 3.83	9.52 / 3.78	9.64 / 3.73	9.75 / 3.69
7	6.88 / 5.23	7.20 / 5.00	7.45 / 4.83	7.66 / 4.70	7.85 / 4.59	8.02 / 4.49	8.18 / 4.40	8.32 / 4.33	8.46 / 4.25	8.59 / 4.19	8.72 / 4.13	8.84 / 4.07	8.96 / 4.02	9.08 / 3.97	9.19 / 3.92	9.30 / 3.87	9.40 / 3.83	9.50 / 3.79
8	6.84 / 5.27	7.14 / 5.04	7.38 / 4.88	7.58 / 4.75	7.75 / 4.64	7.91 / 4.55	8.06 / 4.47	8.20 / 4.39	8.33 / 4.32	8.45 / 4.26	8.57 / 4.20	8.69 / 4.14	8.80 / 4.09	8.91 / 4.04	9.01 / 4.00	9.11 / 3.95	9.21 / 3.91	9.31 / 3.87
9	6.80 / 5.29	7.09 / 5.08	7.32 / 4.92	7.51 / 4.80	7.67 / 4.69	7.83 / 4.60	7.97 / 4.52	8.10 / 4.45	8.22 / 4.38	8.34 / 4.32	8.45 / 4.26	8.56 / 4.21	8.66 / 4.15	8.77 / 4.11	8.86 / 4.06	8.96 / 4.02	9.05 / 3.98	9.14 / 3.94
10	6.77 / 5.32	7.05 / 5.11	7.27 / 4.96	7.45 / 4.83	7.61 / 4.73	7.75 / 4.64	7.88 / 4.57	8.01 / 4.49	8.13 / 4.43	8.24 / 4.37	8.35 / 4.31	8.45 / 4.26	8.55 / 4.21	8.65 / 4.16	8.74 / 4.12	8.83 / 4.08	8.92 / 4.04	9.01 / 4.00
11	6.74 / 5.34	7.01 / 5.13	7.22 / 4.99	7.39 / 4.87	7.55 / 4.77	7.69 / 4.68	7.81 / 4.61	7.93 / 4.54	8.05 / 4.47	8.15 / 4.41	8.26 / 4.36	8.36 / 4.31	8.45 / 4.26	8.54 / 4.21	8.63 / 4.17	8.72 / 4.13	8.80 / 4.09	8.89 / 4.05
12	6.72 / 5.36	6.98 / 5.16	7.18 / 5.01	7.35 / 4.90	7.49 / 4.80	7.63 / 4.72	7.75 / 4.64	7.87 / 4.58	7.98 / 4.51	8.08 / 4.46	8.18 / 4.40	8.27 / 4.35	8.36 / 4.30	8.45 / 4.26	8.54 / 4.22	8.62 / 4.18	8.70 / 4.14	8.78 / 4.10

Years

	1	2	3	4	5	6	7	8	9	10	11	12	13	14	15	16	17	18
13	6.70 / 5.37	6.95 / 5.18	7.14 / 5.04	7.31 / 4.93	7.45 / 4.83	7.58 / 4.75	7.70 / 4.68	7.81 / 4.61	7.91 / 4.55	8.01 / 4.49	8.11 / 4.44	8.20 / 4.39	8.29 / 4.34	8.37 / 4.30	8.46 / 4.26	8.54 / 4.22	8.61 / 4.18	8.69 / 4.14
14	6.68 / 5.39	6.93 / 5.20	7.11 / 5.06	7.27 / 4.95	7.41 / 4.86	7.53 / 4.78	7.65 / 4.71	7.76 / 4.64	7.86 / 4.58	7.95 / 4.53	8.05 / 4.47	8.14 / 4.43	8.22 / 4.38	8.30 / 4.34	8.38 / 4.29	8.46 / 4.26	8.53 / 4.22	8.61 / 4.18
15	6.66 / 5.40	6.90 / 5.22	7.08 / 5.08	7.24 / 4.98	7.37 / 4.88	7.49 / 4.80	7.60 / 4.73	7.71 / 4.67	7.81 / 4.61	7.90 / 4.56	7.99 / 4.51	8.08 / 4.46	8.16 / 4.41	8.24 / 4.37	8.32 / 4.33	8.39 / 4.29	8.46 / 4.25	8.53 / 4.22
16	6.65 / 5.42	6.88 / 5.23	7.06 / 5.10	7.21 / 5.00	7.34 / 4.91	7.46 / 4.83	7.56 / 4.76	7.67 / 4.70	7.76 / 4.64	7.85 / 4.58	7.94 / 4.53	8.02 / 4.49	8.10 / 4.44	8.18 / 4.40	8.26 / 4.36	8.33 / 4.32	8.40 / 4.29	8.47 / 4.25
17	6.63 / 5.43	6.86 / 5.25	7.03 / 5.12	7.18 / 5.02	7.31 / 4.93	7.42 / 4.85	7.53 / 4.78	7.63 / 4.72	7.72 / 4.66	7.81 / 4.61	7.89 / 4.56	7.97 / 4.51	8.05 / 4.47	8.13 / 4.43	8.20 / 4.39	8.27 / 4.35	8.34 / 4.32	8.41 / 4.28
18	6.62 / 5.44	6.84 / 5.26	7.01 / 5.13	7.15 / 5.03	7.28 / 4.95	7.39 / 4.87	7.49 / 4.80	7.59 / 4.74	7.68 / 4.69	7.77 / 4.63	7.85 / 4.59	7.93 / 4.54	8.01 / 4.50	8.08 / 4.46	8.15 / 4.42	8.22 / 4.38	8.29 / 4.35	8.35 / 4.31
19	6.61 / 5.45	6.83 / 5.27	6.99 / 5.15	7.13 / 5.05	7.25 / 4.96	7.36 / 4.89	7.46 / 4.82	7.56 / 4.76	7.65 / 4.71	7.73 / 4.66	7.81 / 4.61	7.89 / 4.56	7.96 / 4.52	8.03 / 4.48	8.10 / 4.44	8.17 / 4.41	8.24 / 4.37	8.30 / 4.34
20	6.60 / 5.46	6.81 / 5.29	6.97 / 5.16	7.11 / 5.07	7.23 / 4.98	7.33 / 4.91	7.43 / 4.84	7.53 / 4.78	7.61 / 4.73	7.70 / 4.68	7.77 / 4.63	7.85 / 4.59	7.92 / 4.54	7.99 / 4.50	8.06 / 4.47	8.13 / 4.43	8.19 / 4.40	8.25 / 4.36
21	6.58 / 5.47	6.80 / 5.30	6.95 / 5.18	7.09 / 5.08	7.20 / 5.00	7.31 / 4.93	7.41 / 4.86	7.50 / 4.80	7.58 / 4.75	7.66 / 4.70	7.74 / 4.65	7.81 / 4.61	7.88 / 4.57	7.95 / 4.53	8.02 / 4.49	8.08 / 4.45	8.15 / 4.42	8.21 / 4.39
22	6.58 / 5.48	6.78 / 5.31	6.94 / 5.19	7.07 / 5.09	7.18 / 5.01	7.29 / 4.94	7.38 / 4.88	7.47 / 4.82	7.55 / 4.77	7.63 / 4.72	7.71 / 4.67	7.78 / 4.63	7.85 / 4.59	7.92 / 4.55	7.98 / 4.51	8.04 / 4.47	8.11 / 4.44	8.17 / 4.41
23	6.57 / 5.48	6.77 / 5.32	6.92 / 5.20	7.05 / 5.11	7.16 / 5.03	7.26 / 4.96	7.36 / 4.89	7.45 / 4.84	7.53 / 4.78	7.60 / 4.73	7.68 / 4.69	7.75 / 4.65	7.82 / 4.61	7.88 / 4.57	7.95 / 4.53	8.01 / 4.50	8.07 / 4.46	8.13 / 4.43
24	6.56 / 5.49	6.76 / 5.33	6.91 / 5.21	7.03 / 5.12	7.14 / 5.04	7.24 / 4.97	7.34 / 4.91	7.42 / 4.85	7.50 / 4.80	7.58 / 4.75	7.65 / 4.71	7.72 / 4.66	7.79 / 4.62	7.85 / 4.59	7.91 / 4.55	7.97 / 4.51	8.03 / 4.48	8.09 / 4.45
25	6.55 / 5.50	6.75 / 5.34	6.89 / 5.22	7.02 / 5.13	7.13 / 5.05	7.22 / 4.98	7.31 / 4.92	7.40 / 4.87	7.48 / 4.81	7.55 / 4.77	7.62 / 4.72	7.69 / 4.68	7.76 / 4.64	7.82 / 4.60	7.88 / 4.57	7.94 / 4.53	8.00 / 4.50	8.06 / 4.47

RANGE OF FUTURE YIELDS FROM INITIAL YIELD OF 7%

BOND MATURITY	Years																	
	1	2	3	4	5	6	7	8	9	10	11	12	13	14	15	16	17	18
1	9.17 / 5.34	10.05 / 4.88	10.74 / 4.56	11.35 / 4.32	11.90 / 4.12	12.42 / 3.95	12.90 / 3.80	13.36 / 3.67	13.81 / 3.55	14.24 / 3.44	14.66 / 3.34	15.07 / 3.25	15.47 / 3.17	15.86 / 3.09	16.25 / 3.02	16.63 / 2.95	17.00 / 2.88	17.37 / 2.82
2	8.65 / 5.66	9.29 / 5.27	9.80 / 5.00	10.23 / 4.79	10.62 / 4.62	10.97 / 4.47	11.31 / 4.33	11.63 / 4.21	11.93 / 4.11	12.22 / 4.01	12.50 / 3.92	12.77 / 3.84	13.04 / 3.76	13.30 / 3.68	13.55 / 3.62	13.80 / 3.55	14.04 / 3.49	14.28 / 3.43
3	8.41 / 5.82	8.95 / 5.47	9.37 / 5.23	9.73 / 5.04	10.05 / 4.88	10.34 / 4.74	10.61 / 4.62	10.87 / 4.51	11.12 / 4.41	11.35 / 4.32	11.58 / 4.23	11.80 / 4.15	12.01 / 4.08	12.22 / 4.01	12.42 / 3.95	12.62 / 3.88	12.81 / 3.83	13.00 / 3.77
4	8.27 / 5.93	8.74 / 5.60	9.11 / 5.38	9.43 / 5.20	9.71 / 5.05	9.96 / 4.92	10.20 / 4.80	10.42 / 4.70	10.63 / 4.61	10.84 / 4.52	11.03 / 4.44	11.22 / 4.37	11.40 / 4.30	11.58 / 4.23	11.75 / 4.17	11.92 / 4.11	12.09 / 4.05	12.25 / 4.00
5	8.16 / 6.00	8.60 / 5.70	8.93 / 5.49	9.22 / 5.32	9.47 / 5.17	9.70 / 5.05	9.91 / 4.94	10.12 / 4.84	10.31 / 4.75	10.49 / 4.67	10.66 / 4.60	10.83 / 4.52	10.99 / 4.46	11.15 / 4.39	11.31 / 4.33	11.46 / 4.28	11.60 / 4.22	11.75 / 4.17
6	8.09 / 6.06	8.49 / 5.77	8.80 / 5.57	9.06 / 5.41	9.29 / 5.27	9.51 / 5.15	9.70 / 5.05	9.89 / 4.96	10.06 / 4.87	10.23 / 4.79	10.39 / 4.72	10.54 / 4.65	10.69 / 4.58	10.84 / 4.52	10.98 / 4.46	11.11 / 4.41	11.25 / 4.36	11.38 / 4.31
7	8.02 / 6.11	8.40 / 5.83	8.69 / 5.64	8.94 / 5.48	9.16 / 5.35	9.36 / 5.24	9.54 / 5.14	9.71 / 5.05	9.87 / 4.96	10.03 / 4.89	10.18 / 4.82	10.32 / 4.75	10.46 / 4.69	10.59 / 4.63	10.72 / 4.57	10.85 / 4.52	10.97 / 4.47	11.09 / 4.42
8	7.97 / 6.14	8.33 / 5.88	8.61 / 5.69	8.84 / 5.54	9.05 / 5.42	9.23 / 5.31	9.40 / 5.21	9.57 / 5.12	9.72 / 5.04	9.86 / 4.97	10.00 / 4.90	10.14 / 4.83	10.27 / 4.77	10.39 / 4.72	10.51 / 4.66	10.63 / 4.61	10.75 / 4.56	10.86 / 4.51
9	7.93 / 6.18	8.28 / 5.92	8.54 / 5.74	8.76 / 5.60	8.95 / 5.47	9.13 / 5.37	9.29 / 5.27	9.45 / 5.19	9.59 / 5.11	9.73 / 5.04	9.86 / 4.97	9.99 / 4.91	10.11 / 4.85	10.23 / 4.79	10.34 / 4.74	10.45 / 4.69	10.56 / 4.64	10.67 / 4.59
10	7.90 / 6.20	8.23 / 5.96	8.48 / 5.78	8.69 / 5.64	8.87 / 5.52	9.04 / 5.42	9.20 / 5.33	9.34 / 5.24	9.48 / 5.17	9.61 / 5.10	9.74 / 5.03	9.86 / 4.97	9.98 / 4.91	10.09 / 4.86	10.20 / 4.81	10.30 / 4.76	10.41 / 4.71	10.51 / 4.66
11	7.87 / 6.23	8.18 / 5.99	8.42 / 5.82	8.63 / 5.68	8.80 / 5.57	8.97 / 5.46	9.12 / 5.38	9.26 / 5.29	9.39 / 5.22	9.51 / 5.15	9.63 / 5.09	9.75 / 5.03	9.86 / 4.97	9.97 / 4.92	10.07 / 4.87	10.17 / 4.82	10.27 / 4.77	10.37 / 4.73
12	7.84 / 6.25	8.14 / 6.02	8.38 / 5.85	8.57 / 5.72	8.74 / 5.60	8.90 / 5.51	9.04 / 5.42	9.18 / 5.34	9.31 / 5.27	9.43 / 5.20	9.54 / 5.14	9.65 / 5.08	9.76 / 5.02	9.86 / 4.97	9.96 / 4.92	10.06 / 4.87	10.15 / 4.83	10.25 / 4.78

Years

	1	2	3	4	5	6	7	8	9	10	11	12	13	14	15	16	17	18
13	7.81 6.27	8.11 6.04	8.33 5.88	8.52 5.75	8.69 5.64	8.84 5.54	8.98 5.46	9.11 5.38	9.23 5.31	9.35 5.24	9.46 5.18	9.57 5.12	9.67 5.07	9.77 5.02	9.87 4.97	9.96 4.92	10.05 4.88	10.14 4.83
14	7.79 6.29	8.08 6.06	8.30 5.91	8.48 5.78	8.64 5.67	8.79 5.58	8.92 5.49	9.05 5.41	9.17 5.34	9.28 5.28	9.39 5.22	9.49 5.16	9.59 5.11	9.69 5.06	9.78 5.01	9.87 4.96	9.96 4.92	10.04 4.88
15	7.77 6.30	8.05 6.09	8.26 5.93	8.44 5.80	8.60 5.70	8.74 5.61	8.87 5.52	8.99 5.45	9.11 5.38	9.22 5.32	9.32 5.26	9.42 5.20	9.52 5.15	9.61 5.10	9.70 5.05	9.79 5.01	9.87 4.96	9.96 4.92
16	7.75 6.32	8.03 6.10	8.23 5.95	8.41 5.83	8.56 5.72	8.70 5.63	8.82 5.55	8.94 5.48	9.06 5.41	9.16 5.35	9.26 5.29	9.36 5.24	9.45 5.18	9.54 5.13	9.63 5.09	9.72 5.04	9.80 5.00	9.88 4.96
17	7.74 6.33	8.00 6.12	8.21 5.97	8.37 5.85	8.52 5.75	8.66 5.66	8.78 5.58	8.90 5.51	9.01 5.44	9.11 5.38	9.21 5.32	9.30 5.27	9.39 5.22	9.48 5.17	9.57 5.12	9.65 5.08	9.73 5.04	9.81 5.00
18	7.72 6.35	7.98 6.14	8.18 5.99	8.34 5.87	8.49 5.77	8.62 5.68	8.74 5.60	8.86 5.53	8.96 5.47	9.06 5.41	9.16 5.35	9.25 5.30	9.34 5.25	9.42 5.20	9.51 5.15	9.59 5.11	9.67 5.07	9.74 5.03
19	7.71 6.36	7.96 6.15	8.16 6.01	8.32 5.89	8.46 5.79	8.59 5.71	8.71 5.63	8.82 5.56	8.92 5.49	9.02 5.43	9.11 5.38	9.20 5.32	9.29 5.28	9.37 5.23	9.45 5.18	9.53 5.14	9.61 5.10	9.68 5.06
20	7.69 6.37	7.94 6.17	8.13 6.02	8.29 5.91	8.43 5.81	8.56 5.73	8.67 5.65	8.78 5.58	8.88 5.52	8.98 5.46	9.07 5.40	9.16 5.35	9.24 5.30	9.32 5.26	9.40 5.21	9.48 5.17	9.55 5.13	9.63 5.09
21	7.68 6.38	7.93 6.18	8.11 6.04	8.27 5.93	8.40 5.83	8.53 5.75	8.64 5.67	8.75 5.60	8.85 5.54	8.94 5.48	9.03 5.43	9.12 5.38	9.20 5.33	9.28 5.28	9.36 5.24	9.43 5.20	9.50 5.16	9.57 5.12
22	7.67 6.39	7.91 6.19	8.09 6.05	8.25 5.94	8.38 5.85	8.50 5.76	8.61 5.69	8.72 5.62	8.81 5.56	8.91 5.50	8.99 5.45	9.08 5.40	9.16 5.35	9.24 5.30	9.31 5.26	9.39 5.22	9.46 5.18	9.53 5.14
23	7.66 6.40	7.90 6.20	8.08 6.07	8.23 5.96	8.36 5.86	8.48 5.78	8.58 5.71	8.69 5.64	8.78 5.58	8.87 5.52	8.96 5.47	9.04 5.42	9.12 5.37	9.20 5.33	9.27 5.29	9.34 5.24	9.41 5.21	9.48 5.17
24	7.65 6.41	7.88 6.22	8.06 6.08	8.21 5.97	8.33 5.88	8.45 5.80	8.56 5.73	8.66 5.66	8.75 5.60	8.84 5.54	8.93 5.49	9.01 5.44	9.08 5.39	9.16 5.35	9.23 5.31	9.30 5.27	9.37 5.23	9.44 5.19
25	7.64 6.41	7.87 6.23	8.04 6.09	8.19 5.98	8.31 5.89	8.43 5.81	8.53 5.74	8.63 5.68	8.72 5.62	8.81 5.56	8.90 5.51	8.97 5.46	9.05 5.41	9.13 5.37	9.20 5.33	9.27 5.29	9.33 5.25	9.40 5.21

RANGE OF FUTURE YIELDS FROM INITIAL YIELD OF 8%

BOND MATURITY	Years																	
	1	2	3	4	5	6	7	8	9	10	11	12	13	14	15	16	17	18
1	10.48 / 6.11	11.48 / 5.57	12.28 / 5.21	12.97 / 4.93	13.60 / 4.71	14.19 / 4.51	14.74 / 4.34	15.27 / 4.19	15.78 / 4.06	16.27 / 3.93	16.75 / 3.82	17.22 / 3.72	17.68 / 3.62	18.13 / 3.53	18.57 / 3.45	19.00 / 3.37	19.43 / 3.29	19.86 / 3.22
2	9.89 / 6.47	10.62 / 6.03	11.20 / 5.72	11.69 / 5.48	12.13 / 5.28	12.54 / 5.10	12.92 / 4.95	13.29 / 4.82	13.63 / 4.69	13.97 / 4.58	14.29 / 4.48	14.60 / 4.38	14.90 / 4.29	15.20 / 4.21	15.49 / 4.13	15.77 / 4.06	16.05 / 3.99	16.32 / 3.92
3	9.61 / 6.66	10.23 / 6.26	10.71 / 5.98	11.12 / 5.76	11.48 / 5.57	11.82 / 5.42	12.13 / 5.28	12.42 / 5.15	12.70 / 5.04	12.97 / 4.93	13.23 / 4.84	13.48 / 4.75	13.73 / 4.66	13.96 / 4.58	14.19 / 4.51	14.42 / 4.44	14.64 / 4.37	14.85 / 4.31
4	9.45 / 6.77	9.99 / 6.40	10.41 / 6.15	10.77 / 5.94	11.09 / 5.77	11.38 / 5.62	11.66 / 5.49	11.91 / 5.37	12.15 / 5.27	12.39 / 5.17	12.61 / 5.08	12.82 / 4.99	13.03 / 4.91	13.24 / 4.84	13.43 / 4.76	13.63 / 4.70	13.81 / 4.63	14.00 / 4.57
5	9.33 / 6.86	9.83 / 6.51	10.21 / 6.27	10.53 / 6.08	10.82 / 5.91	11.09 / 5.77	11.33 / 5.65	11.56 / 5.54	11.78 / 5.43	11.99 / 5.34	12.19 / 5.25	12.38 / 5.17	12.56 / 5.09	12.74 / 5.02	12.92 / 4.95	13.09 / 4.89	13.26 / 4.83	13.42 / 4.77
6	9.24 / 6.93	9.70 / 6.60	10.06 / 6.36	10.36 / 6.18	10.62 / 6.03	10.86 / 5.89	11.09 / 5.77	11.30 / 5.66	11.50 / 5.57	11.69 / 5.47	11.87 / 5.39	12.05 / 5.31	12.22 / 5.24	12.38 / 5.17	12.54 / 5.10	12.70 / 5.04	12.85 / 4.98	13.00 / 4.92
7	9.17 / 6.98	9.60 / 6.66	9.94 / 6.44	10.22 / 6.26	10.47 / 6.12	10.69 / 5.99	10.90 / 5.87	11.10 / 5.77	11.28 / 5.67	11.46 / 5.58	11.63 / 5.50	11.79 / 5.43	11.95 / 5.36	12.10 / 5.29	12.25 / 5.22	12.39 / 5.16	12.54 / 5.11	12.67 / 5.05
8	9.11 / 7.02	9.52 / 6.72	9.84 / 6.51	10.10 / 6.33	10.34 / 6.19	10.55 / 6.07	10.75 / 5.95	10.93 / 5.85	11.11 / 5.76	11.27 / 5.68	11.43 / 5.60	11.59 / 5.52	11.73 / 5.45	11.88 / 5.39	12.01 / 5.33	12.15 / 5.27	12.28 / 5.21	12.41 / 5.16
9	9.07 / 7.06	9.46 / 6.77	9.76 / 6.56	10.01 / 6.39	10.23 / 6.26	10.43 / 6.13	10.62 / 6.03	10.80 / 5.93	10.96 / 5.84	11.12 / 5.76	11.27 / 5.68	11.41 / 5.61	11.55 / 5.54	11.69 / 5.48	11.82 / 5.42	11.95 / 5.36	12.07 / 5.30	12.19 / 5.25
10	9.03 / 7.09	9.40 / 6.81	9.69 / 6.61	9.93 / 6.45	10.14 / 6.31	10.33 / 6.19	10.51 / 6.09	10.68 / 5.99	10.84 / 5.91	10.99 / 5.83	11.13 / 5.75	11.27 / 5.68	11.40 / 5.61	11.53 / 5.55	11.65 / 5.49	11.77 / 5.44	11.89 / 5.38	12.01 / 5.33
11	8.99 / 7.12	9.35 / 6.84	9.63 / 6.65	9.86 / 6.49	10.06 / 6.36	10.25 / 6.25	10.42 / 6.14	10.58 / 6.05	10.73 / 5.96	10.87 / 5.89	11.01 / 5.81	11.14 / 5.74	11.27 / 5.68	11.39 / 5.62	11.51 / 5.56	11.63 / 5.51	11.74 / 5.45	11.85 / 5.40
12	8.96 / 7.14	9.31 / 6.88	9.57 / 6.69	9.80 / 6.53	9.99 / 6.40	10.17 / 6.29	10.34 / 6.19	10.49 / 6.10	10.64 / 6.02	10.77 / 5.94	10.90 / 5.87	11.03 / 5.80	11.15 / 5.74	11.27 / 5.68	11.39 / 5.62	11.50 / 5.57	11.60 / 5.52	11.71 / 5.47

Years

	18	17	16	15	14	13	12	11	10	9	8	7	6	5	4	3	2	1
13	11.59 5.52	11.49 5.57	11.38 5.62	11.27 5.68	11.16 5.73	11.05 5.79	10.93 5.85	10.81 5.92	10.68 5.99	10.55 6.07	10.41 6.15	10.26 6.24	10.10 6.33	9.93 6.44	9.74 6.57	9.53 6.72	9.27 6.90	8.93 7.17
14	11.48 5.58	11.38 5.62	11.28 5.67	11.18 5.73	11.07 5.78	10.96 5.84	10.85 5.90	10.73 5.97	10.61 6.03	10.48 6.11	10.34 6.19	10.20 6.28	10.04 6.37	9.88 6.48	9.69 6.60	9.48 6.75	9.23 6.93	8.91 7.19
15	11.38 5.62	11.28 5.67	11.19 5.72	11.09 5.77	10.98 5.83	10.88 5.88	10.77 5.94	10.65 6.01	10.53 6.08	10.41 6.15	10.28 6.23	10.14 6.31	9.99 6.41	9.83 6.51	9.65 6.63	9.44 6.78	9.20 6.95	8.88 7.21
16	11.29 5.67	11.20 5.72	11.10 5.76	11.01 5.81	10.91 5.87	10.80 5.92	10.70 5.98	10.59 6.05	10.47 6.11	10.35 6.18	10.22 6.26	10.09 6.35	9.94 6.44	9.78 6.54	9.61 6.66	9.41 6.80	9.17 6.98	8.86 7.22
17	11.21 5.71	11.12 5.76	11.03 5.80	10.93 5.85	10.84 5.91	10.74 5.96	10.63 6.02	10.52 6.08	10.41 6.15	10.29 6.22	10.17 6.29	10.04 6.38	9.89 6.47	9.74 6.57	9.57 6.69	9.38 6.82	9.15 7.00	8.84 7.24
18	11.13 5.75	11.05 5.79	10.96 5.84	10.87 5.89	10.77 5.94	10.67 6.00	10.57 6.05	10.47 6.11	10.36 6.18	10.24 6.25	10.12 6.32	9.99 6.41	9.85 6.50	9.70 6.60	9.54 6.71	9.35 6.85	9.12 7.02	8.83 7.25
19	11.07 5.78	10.98 5.83	10.89 5.88	10.80 5.92	10.71 5.97	10.62 6.03	10.52 6.09	10.41 6.15	10.31 6.21	10.19 6.28	10.08 6.35	9.95 6.43	9.81 6.52	9.67 6.62	9.51 6.73	9.32 6.87	9.10 7.03	8.81 7.27
20	11.00 5.82	10.92 5.86	10.83 5.91	10.75 5.96	10.66 6.01	10.56 6.06	10.47 6.12	10.37 6.17	10.26 6.24	10.15 6.30	10.03 6.38	9.91 6.46	9.78 6.54	9.64 6.64	9.48 6.75	9.30 6.88	9.08 7.05	8.79 7.28
21	10.94 5.85	10.86 5.89	10.78 5.94	10.69 5.99	10.60 6.04	10.51 6.09	10.42 6.14	10.32 6.20	10.22 6.26	10.11 6.33	10.00 6.40	9.88 6.48	9.75 6.57	9.61 6.66	9.45 6.77	9.27 6.90	9.06 7.06	8.78 7.29
22	10.89 5.88	10.81 5.92	10.73 5.97	10.64 6.01	10.56 6.06	10.47 6.11	10.37 6.17	10.28 6.23	10.18 6.29	10.07 6.35	9.96 6.43	9.84 6.50	9.72 6.59	9.58 6.68	9.42 6.79	9.25 6.92	9.04 7.08	8.77 7.30
23	10.84 5.91	10.76 5.95	10.68 5.99	10.60 6.04	10.51 6.09	10.42 6.14	10.33 6.19	10.24 6.25	10.14 6.31	10.04 6.38	9.93 6.45	9.81 6.52	9.69 6.61	9.55 6.70	9.40 6.81	9.23 6.93	9.02 7.09	8.75 7.31
24	10.79 5.93	10.71 5.98	10.63 6.02	10.55 6.07	10.47 6.11	10.38 6.16	10.29 6.22	10.20 6.27	10.10 6.33	10.00 6.40	9.90 6.47	9.78 6.54	9.66 6.63	9.53 6.72	9.38 6.82	9.21 6.95	9.01 7.10	8.74 7.32
25	10.74 5.96	10.67 6.00	10.59 6.04	10.51 6.09	10.43 6.14	10.34 6.19	10.26 6.24	10.17 6.30	10.07 6.36	9.97 6.42	9.87 6.49	9.75 6.56	9.63 6.64	9.50 6.74	9.36 6.84	9.19 6.96	8.99 7.12	8.73 7.33

RANGE OF FUTURE YIELDS FROM INITIAL YIELD OF 9%

BOND MATURITY	1	2	3	4	5	6	7	8	9	10	11	12	13	14	15	16	17	18
									Years									
1	11.79 / 6.87	12.92 / 6.27	13.81 / 5.86	14.59 / 5.55	15.30 / 5.29	15.96 / 5.07	16.59 / 4.88	17.18 / 4.71	17.75 / 4.56	18.31 / 4.42	18.85 / 4.30	19.37 / 4.18	19.89 / 4.07	20.39 / 3.97	20.89 / 3.88	21.38 / 3.79	21.86 / 3.71	22.34 / 3.63
2	11.12 / 7.28	11.95 / 6.78	12.59 / 6.43	13.15 / 6.16	13.65 / 5.93	14.11 / 5.74	14.54 / 5.57	14.95 / 5.42	15.34 / 5.28	15.71 / 5.16	16.07 / 5.04	16.42 / 4.93	16.77 / 4.83	17.10 / 4.74	17.42 / 4.65	17.74 / 4.57	18.06 / 4.49	18.36 / 4.41
3	10.82 / 7.49	11.51 / 7.04	12.05 / 6.72	12.51 / 6.48	12.92 / 6.27	13.29 / 6.09	13.65 / 5.94	13.98 / 5.80	14.29 / 5.67	14.60 / 5.55	14.89 / 5.44	15.17 / 5.34	15.44 / 5.25	15.71 / 5.16	15.97 / 5.07	16.22 / 4.99	16.47 / 4.92	16.71 / 4.85
4	10.63 / 7.62	11.24 / 7.21	11.72 / 6.91	12.12 / 6.68	12.48 / 6.49	12.81 / 6.32	13.11 / 6.18	13.40 / 6.04	13.67 / 5.92	13.93 / 5.81	14.19 / 5.71	14.43 / 5.61	14.66 / 5.52	14.89 / 5.44	15.11 / 5.36	15.33 / 5.28	15.54 / 5.21	15.75 / 5.14
5	10.50 / 7.72	11.06 / 7.33	11.49 / 7.05	11.85 / 6.84	12.18 / 6.65	12.47 / 6.49	12.75 / 6.35	13.01 / 6.23	13.25 / 6.11	13.48 / 6.01	13.71 / 5.91	13.93 / 5.82	14.13 / 5.73	14.34 / 5.65	14.54 / 5.57	14.73 / 5.50	14.92 / 5.43	15.10 / 5.36
6	10.40 / 7.79	10.92 / 7.42	11.31 / 7.16	11.65 / 6.95	11.95 / 6.78	12.22 / 6.63	12.48 / 6.49	12.71 / 6.37	12.94 / 6.26	13.15 / 6.16	13.36 / 6.06	13.55 / 5.98	13.75 / 5.89	13.93 / 5.81	14.11 / 5.74	14.29 / 5.67	14.46 / 5.60	14.63 / 5.54
7	10.32 / 7.85	10.81 / 7.50	11.18 / 7.25	11.49 / 7.05	11.77 / 6.88	12.03 / 6.73	12.26 / 6.60	12.48 / 6.49	12.69 / 6.38	12.89 / 6.28	13.08 / 6.19	13.27 / 6.11	13.44 / 6.03	13.62 / 5.95	13.78 / 5.88	13.94 / 5.81	14.10 / 5.74	14.26 / 5.68
8	10.25 / 7.90	10.72 / 7.56	11.07 / 7.32	11.37 / 7.13	11.63 / 6.96	11.87 / 6.82	12.09 / 6.70	12.30 / 6.59	12.50 / 6.48	12.68 / 6.39	12.86 / 6.30	13.03 / 6.21	13.20 / 6.14	13.36 / 6.06	13.52 / 5.99	13.67 / 5.93	13.82 / 5.86	13.96 / 5.80
9	10.20 / 7.94	10.64 / 7.61	10.98 / 7.38	11.26 / 7.19	11.51 / 7.04	11.74 / 6.90	11.95 / 6.78	12.15 / 6.67	12.33 / 6.57	12.51 / 6.48	12.68 / 6.39	12.84 / 6.31	13.00 / 6.23	13.15 / 6.16	13.30 / 6.09	13.44 / 6.03	13.58 / 5.97	13.72 / 5.91
10	10.15 / 7.98	10.58 / 7.66	10.90 / 7.43	11.17 / 7.25	11.41 / 7.10	11.63 / 6.97	11.83 / 6.85	12.01 / 6.74	12.19 / 6.64	12.36 / 6.55	12.52 / 6.47	12.68 / 6.39	12.83 / 6.32	12.97 / 6.25	13.11 / 6.18	13.25 / 6.12	13.38 / 6.05	13.51 / 6.00
11	10.11 / 8.01	10.52 / 7.70	10.83 / 7.48	11.09 / 7.30	11.32 / 7.16	11.53 / 7.03	11.72 / 6.91	11.90 / 6.81	12.07 / 6.71	12.23 / 6.62	12.39 / 6.54	12.53 / 6.46	12.68 / 6.39	12.81 / 6.32	12.95 / 6.26	13.08 / 6.19	13.21 / 6.13	13.33 / 6.08
12	10.08 / 8.04	10.47 / 7.74	10.77 / 7.52	11.02 / 7.35	11.24 / 7.21	11.44 / 7.08	11.63 / 6.97	11.80 / 6.86	11.96 / 6.77	12.12 / 6.68	12.27 / 6.60	12.41 / 6.53	12.55 / 6.46	12.68 / 6.39	12.81 / 6.32	12.93 / 6.26	13.05 / 6.20	13.17 / 6.15

Years

	1	2	3	4	5	6	7	8	9	10	11	12	13	14	15	16	17	18
13	10.05 / 8.06	10.43 / 7.77	10.72 / 7.56	10.96 / 7.39	11.17 / 7.25	11.37 / 7.13	11.55 / 7.02	11.71 / 6.92	11.87 / 6.82	12.02 / 6.74	12.16 / 6.66	12.30 / 6.59	12.43 / 6.52	12.56 / 6.45	12.68 / 6.39	12.80 / 6.33	12.92 / 6.27	13.04 / 6.21
14	10.02 / 8.09	10.39 / 7.80	10.67 / 7.59	10.90 / 7.43	11.11 / 7.29	11.30 / 7.17	11.47 / 7.06	11.63 / 6.96	11.79 / 6.87	11.93 / 6.79	12.07 / 6.71	12.20 / 6.64	12.33 / 6.57	12.45 / 6.50	12.57 / 6.44	12.69 / 6.38	12.80 / 6.33	12.91 / 6.27
15	9.99 / 8.11	10.35 / 7.82	10.63 / 7.62	10.85 / 7.46	11.06 / 7.33	11.24 / 7.21	11.41 / 7.10	11.56 / 7.00	11.71 / 6.92	11.85 / 6.83	11.99 / 6.76	12.11 / 6.69	12.24 / 6.62	12.36 / 6.55	12.47 / 6.49	12.59 / 6.44	12.69 / 6.38	12.80 / 6.33
16	9.97 / 8.12	10.32 / 7.85	10.59 / 7.65	10.81 / 7.49	11.01 / 7.36	11.18 / 7.24	11.35 / 7.14	11.50 / 7.04	11.64 / 6.96	11.78 / 6.88	11.91 / 6.80	12.03 / 6.73	12.15 / 6.66	12.27 / 6.60	12.38 / 6.54	12.49 / 6.48	12.60 / 6.43	12.70 / 6.38
17	9.95 / 8.14	10.29 / 7.87	10.55 / 7.68	10.77 / 7.52	10.96 / 7.39	11.13 / 7.28	11.29 / 7.17	11.44 / 7.08	11.58 / 6.99	11.71 / 6.92	11.84 / 6.84	11.96 / 6.77	12.08 / 6.71	12.19 / 6.64	12.30 / 6.59	12.41 / 6.53	12.51 / 6.48	12.61 / 6.42
18	9.93 / 8.16	10.26 / 7.89	10.52 / 7.70	10.73 / 7.55	10.92 / 7.42	11.09 / 7.31	11.24 / 7.21	11.39 / 7.11	11.52 / 7.03	11.65 / 6.95	11.78 / 6.88	11.89 / 6.81	12.01 / 6.75	12.12 / 6.68	12.22 / 6.63	12.33 / 6.57	12.43 / 6.52	12.53 / 6.47
19	9.91 / 8.17	10.24 / 7.91	10.49 / 7.72	10.69 / 7.57	10.88 / 7.45	11.04 / 7.34	11.19 / 7.24	11.34 / 7.15	11.47 / 7.06	11.60 / 6.99	11.72 / 6.91	11.83 / 6.85	11.94 / 6.78	12.05 / 6.72	12.15 / 6.66	12.25 / 6.61	12.35 / 6.56	12.45 / 6.51
20	9.89 / 8.19	10.21 / 7.93	10.46 / 7.75	10.66 / 7.60	10.84 / 7.47	11.00 / 7.36	11.15 / 7.26	11.29 / 7.18	11.42 / 7.09	11.54 / 7.02	11.66 / 6.95	11.77 / 6.88	11.88 / 6.82	11.99 / 6.76	12.09 / 6.70	12.19 / 6.65	12.28 / 6.59	12.38 / 6.54
21	9.88 / 8.20	10.19 / 7.95	10.43 / 7.77	10.63 / 7.62	10.81 / 7.50	10.96 / 7.39	11.11 / 7.29	11.25 / 7.20	11.37 / 7.12	11.49 / 7.05	11.61 / 6.98	11.72 / 6.91	11.83 / 6.85	11.93 / 6.79	12.03 / 6.73	12.13 / 6.68	12.22 / 6.63	12.31 / 6.58
22	9.86 / 8.21	10.17 / 7.96	10.41 / 7.78	10.60 / 7.64	10.77 / 7.52	10.93 / 7.41	11.07 / 7.32	11.21 / 7.23	11.33 / 7.15	11.45 / 7.07	11.56 / 7.01	11.67 / 6.94	11.78 / 6.88	11.88 / 6.82	11.97 / 6.77	12.07 / 6.71	12.16 / 6.66	12.25 / 6.61
23	9.85 / 8.22	10.15 / 7.98	10.38 / 7.80	10.58 / 7.66	10.74 / 7.54	10.90 / 7.43	11.04 / 7.34	11.17 / 7.25	11.29 / 7.17	11.41 / 7.10	11.52 / 7.03	11.62 / 6.97	11.73 / 6.91	11.82 / 6.85	11.92 / 6.80	12.01 / 6.74	12.10 / 6.69	12.19 / 6.64
24	9.84 / 8.24	10.14 / 7.99	10.36 / 7.82	10.55 / 7.68	10.72 / 7.56	10.87 / 7.45	11.00 / 7.36	11.13 / 7.28	11.25 / 7.20	11.37 / 7.13	11.48 / 7.06	11.58 / 6.99	11.68 / 6.93	11.78 / 6.88	11.87 / 6.82	11.96 / 6.77	12.05 / 6.72	12.14 / 6.67
25	9.82 / 8.25	10.12 / 8.01	10.34 / 7.83	10.53 / 7.69	10.69 / 7.58	10.84 / 7.47	10.97 / 7.38	11.10 / 7.30	11.22 / 7.22	11.33 / 7.15	11.44 / 7.08	11.54 / 7.02	11.64 / 6.96	11.73 / 6.90	11.82 / 6.85	11.91 / 6.80	12.00 / 6.75	12.08 / 6.70

RANGE OF FUTURE YIELDS FROM INITIAL YIELD OF 10%

BOND MATURITY	Years																	
	1	2	3	4	5	6	7	8	9	10	11	12	13	14	15	16	17	18
1	13.10 / 7.63	14.35 / 6.97	15.35 / 6.52	16.21 / 6.17	17.00 / 5.88	17.74 / 5.64	18.43 / 5.43	19.09 / 5.24	19.73 / 5.07	20.34 / 4.92	20.94 / 4.78	21.53 / 4.65	22.10 / 4.53	22.66 / 4.41	23.21 / 4.31	23.75 / 4.21	24.29 / 4.12	24.82 / 4.03
2	12.36 / 8.09	13.28 / 7.53	13.99 / 7.15	14.61 / 6.84	15.17 / 6.59	15.68 / 6.38	16.16 / 6.19	16.61 / 6.02	17.04 / 5.87	17.46 / 5.73	17.86 / 5.60	18.25 / 5.48	18.63 / 5.37	19.00 / 5.26	19.36 / 5.17	19.71 / 5.07	20.06 / 4.98	20.41 / 4.90
3	12.02 / 8.32	12.79 / 7.82	13.39 / 7.47	13.90 / 7.20	14.35 / 6.97	14.77 / 6.77	15.16 / 6.60	15.53 / 6.44	15.88 / 6.30	16.22 / 6.17	16.54 / 6.05	16.85 / 5.93	17.16 / 5.83	17.45 / 5.73	17.74 / 5.64	18.02 / 5.55	18.30 / 5.47	18.57 / 5.39
4	11.81 / 8.47	12.49 / 8.01	13.02 / 7.68	13.47 / 7.43	13.86 / 7.21	14.23 / 7.03	14.57 / 6.86	14.89 / 6.72	15.19 / 6.58	15.48 / 6.46	15.76 / 6.34	16.03 / 6.24	16.29 / 6.14	16.55 / 6.04	16.79 / 5.96	17.03 / 5.87	17.27 / 5.79	17.50 / 5.71
5	11.66 / 8.58	12.28 / 8.14	12.76 / 7.84	13.17 / 7.59	13.53 / 7.39	13.86 / 7.22	14.16 / 7.06	14.45 / 6.92	14.72 / 6.79	14.98 / 6.67	15.23 / 6.57	15.47 / 6.46	15.71 / 6.37	15.93 / 6.28	16.15 / 6.19	16.36 / 6.11	16.57 / 6.03	16.78 / 5.96
6	11.55 / 8.66	12.13 / 8.25	12.57 / 7.96	12.95 / 7.72	13.28 / 7.53	13.58 / 7.36	13.86 / 7.21	14.13 / 7.08	14.37 / 6.96	14.61 / 6.84	14.84 / 6.74	15.06 / 6.64	15.27 / 6.55	15.48 / 6.46	15.68 / 6.38	15.87 / 6.30	16.06 / 6.22	16.25 / 6.15
7	11.46 / 8.72	12.01 / 8.33	12.42 / 8.05	12.77 / 7.83	13.08 / 7.64	13.36 / 7.48	13.63 / 7.34	13.87 / 7.21	14.10 / 7.09	14.32 / 6.98	14.54 / 6.88	14.74 / 6.78	14.94 / 6.69	15.13 / 6.61	15.31 / 6.53	15.49 / 6.45	15.67 / 6.38	15.84 / 6.31
8	11.39 / 8.78	11.91 / 8.40	12.30 / 8.13	12.63 / 7.92	12.92 / 7.74	13.19 / 7.58	13.43 / 7.44	13.67 / 7.32	13.88 / 7.20	14.09 / 7.10	14.29 / 7.00	14.48 / 6.91	14.67 / 6.82	14.84 / 6.74	15.02 / 6.66	15.19 / 6.58	15.35 / 6.51	15.51 / 6.45
9	11.33 / 8.82	11.82 / 8.46	12.20 / 8.20	12.51 / 7.99	12.79 / 7.82	13.04 / 7.67	13.28 / 7.53	13.49 / 7.41	13.70 / 7.30	13.90 / 7.20	14.09 / 7.10	14.27 / 7.01	14.44 / 6.92	14.61 / 6.84	14.77 / 6.77	14.93 / 6.70	15.09 / 6.63	15.24 / 6.56
10	11.28 / 8.86	11.75 / 8.51	12.11 / 8.26	12.41 / 8.06	12.68 / 7.89	12.92 / 7.74	13.14 / 7.61	13.35 / 7.49	13.55 / 7.38	13.73 / 7.28	13.91 / 7.19	14.08 / 7.10	14.25 / 7.02	14.41 / 6.94	14.57 / 6.87	14.72 / 6.79	14.86 / 6.73	15.01 / 6.66
11	11.24 / 8.90	11.69 / 8.56	12.03 / 8.31	12.32 / 8.12	12.58 / 7.95	12.81 / 7.81	13.02 / 7.68	13.22 / 7.56	13.41 / 7.46	13.59 / 7.36	13.76 / 7.27	13.93 / 7.18	14.09 / 7.10	14.24 / 7.02	14.39 / 6.95	14.53 / 6.88	14.67 / 6.82	14.81 / 6.75
12	11.20 / 8.93	11.63 / 8.60	11.97 / 8.36	12.25 / 8.17	12.49 / 8.01	12.71 / 7.87	12.92 / 7.74	13.11 / 7.63	13.29 / 7.52	13.47 / 7.43	13.63 / 7.34	13.79 / 7.25	13.94 / 7.17	14.09 / 7.10	14.23 / 7.03	14.37 / 6.96	14.51 / 6.89	14.64 / 6.83

	1	2	3	4	5	6	7	8	9	10	11	12	13	14	15	16	17	18
13	11.16 8.96	11.59 8.63	11.91 8.40	12.18 8.21	12.41 8.05	12.63 7.92	12.83 7.79	13.01 7.68	13.19 7.58	13.36 7.49	13.51 7.40	13.67 7.32	13.81 7.24	13.96 7.17	14.09 7.10	14.23 7.03	14.36 6.97	14.48 6.90
14	11.13 8.98	11.54 8.66	11.85 8.44	12.12 8.25	12.35 8.10	12.55 7.96	12.75 7.84	12.93 7.74	13.10 7.64	13.26 7.54	13.41 7.46	13.56 7.38	13.70 7.30	13.84 7.23	13.97 7.16	14.10 7.09	14.22 7.03	14.35 6.97
15	11.10 9.01	11.50 8.69	11.81 8.47	12.06 8.29	12.28 8.14	12.49 8.01	12.67 7.89	12.85 7.78	13.01 7.68	13.17 7.59	13.32 7.51	13.46 7.43	13.60 7.35	13.73 7.28	13.86 7.22	13.98 7.15	14.11 7.09	14.22 7.03
16	11.08 9.03	11.47 8.72	11.76 8.50	12.01 8.33	12.23 8.18	12.43 8.05	12.61 7.93	12.78 7.83	12.94 7.73	13.09 7.64	13.23 7.56	13.37 7.48	13.50 7.40	13.63 7.33	13.76 7.27	13.88 7.20	14.00 7.14	14.11 7.09
17	11.05 9.05	11.43 8.75	11.72 8.53	11.96 8.36	12.18 8.21	12.37 8.08	12.55 7.97	12.71 7.87	12.87 7.77	13.01 7.68	13.15 7.60	13.29 7.52	13.42 7.45	13.55 7.38	13.67 7.32	13.78 7.25	13.90 7.19	14.01 7.14
18	11.03 9.06	11.40 8.77	11.69 8.56	11.92 8.39	12.13 8.24	12.32 8.12	12.49 8.01	12.65 7.90	12.80 7.81	12.95 7.72	13.08 7.64	13.22 7.57	13.34 7.50	13.46 7.43	13.58 7.36	13.70 7.30	13.81 7.24	13.92 7.19
19	11.01 9.08	11.38 8.79	11.65 8.58	11.88 8.42	12.09 8.27	12.27 8.15	12.44 8.04	12.60 7.94	12.74 7.85	12.88 7.76	13.02 7.68	13.15 7.61	13.27 7.54	13.39 7.47	13.50 7.40	13.62 7.3	13.73 7.29	13.83 7.23
20	10.99 9.10	11.35 8.81	11.62 8.61	11.85 8.44	12.04 8.30	12.22 8.18	12.39 8.07	12.54 7.97	12.69 7.88	12.83 7.80	12.96 7.72	13.08 7.64	13.20 7.57	13.32 7.51	13.43 7.44	13.54 7.38	13.65 7.33	13.75 7.27
21	10.97 9.11	11.33 8.83	11.59 8.63	11.81 8.47	12.01 8.33	12.18 8.21	12.34 8.10	12.50 8.00	12.64 7.91	12.77 7.83	12.90 7.75	13.02 7.68	13.14 7.61	13.26 7.54	13.37 7.48	13.47 7.42	13.58 7.37	13.68 7.31
22	10.96 9.13	11.30 8.85	11.56 8.65	11.78 8.49	11.97 8.35	12.14 8.23	12.30 8.13	12.45 8.03	12.59 7.94	12.72 7.86	12.85 7.78	12.97 7.71	13.08 7.64	13.20 7.58	13.30 7.52	13.41 7.46	13.51 7.40	13.61 7.35
23	10.94 9.14	11.28 8.86	11.54 8.67	11.75 8.51	11.94 8.38	12.11 8.26	12.26 8.15	12.41 8.06	12.55 7.97	12.67 7.89	12.80 7.81	12.92 7.74	13.03 7.68	13.14 7.61	13.24 7.55	13.35 7.49	13.45 7.44	13.54 7.38
24	10.93 9.15	11.26 8.88	11.51 8.69	11.72 8.53	11.91 8.40	12.07 8.28	12.23 8.18	12.37 8.08	12.50 8.00	12.63 7.92	12.75 7.84	12.87 7.77	12.98 7.71	13.09 7.64	13.19 7.58	13.29 7.52	13.39 7.47	13.48 7.42
25	10.91 9.16	11.24 8.90	11.49 8.70	11.70 8.55	11.88 8.42	12.04 8.30	12.19 8.20	12.33 8.11	12.46 8.02	12.59 7.94	12.71 7.87	12.82 7.80	12.93 7.73	13.04 7.67	13.14 7.61	13.24 7.55	13.33 7.50	13.43 7.45

Years

BOND MATURITY	Years																	
	1	2	3	4	5	6	7	8	9	10	11	12	13	14	15	16	17	18
1	14.41 8.40	15.79 7.66	16.88 7.17	17.84 6.78	18.70 6.47	19.51 6.20	20.27 5.97	21.00 5.76	21.70 5.58	22.38 5.41	23.04 5.25	23.68 5.11	24.31 4.98	24.92 4.85	25.53 4.74	26.13 4.63	26.72 4.53	27.30 4.43
2	13.60 8.90	14.60 8.29	15.39 7.86	16.07 7.53	16.68 7.25	17.24 7.02	17.77 6.81	18.27 6.62	18.75 6.45	19.20 6.30	19.65 6.16	20.07 6.03	20.49 5.90	20.90 5.79	21.30 5.68	21.69 5.58	22.07 5.48	22.45 5.39
3	13.22 9.15	14.07 8.60	14.72 8.22	15.29 7.92	15.79 7.66	16.25 7.45	16.68 7.25	17.08 7.08	17.47 6.93	17.84 6.78	18.19 6.65	18.54 6.53	18.87 6.41	19.20 6.30	19.51 6.20	19.82 6.10	20.13 6.01	20.42 5.92
4	12.99 9.32	13.74 8.81	14.32 8.45	14.81 8.17	15.25 7.93	15.65 7.73	16.03 7.55	16.38 7.39	16.71 7.24	17.03 7.10	17.34 6.98	17.63 6.86	17.92 6.75	18.20 6.65	18.47 6.55	18.74 6.46	19.00 6.37	19.25 6.29
5	12.83 9.43	13.51 8.96	14.04 8.62	14.48 8.35	14.88 8.13	15.24 7.94	15.58 7.77	15.90 7.61	16.20 7.47	16.48 7.34	16.76 7.22	17.02 7.11	17.28 7.00	17.52 6.90	17.77 6.81	18.00 6.72	18.23 6.64	18.46 6.56
6	12.71 9.52	13.34 9.07	13.83 8.75	14.24 8.50	14.61 8.28	14.94 8.10	15.25 7.94	15.54 7.79	15.81 7.65	16.07 7.53	16.33 7.41	16.57 7.30	16.80 7.20	17.03 7.11	17.25 7.02	17.46 6.93	17.67 6.85	17.88 6.77
7	12.61 9.60	13.21 9.16	13.66 8.86	14.05 8.61	14.39 8.41	14.70 8.23	14.99 8.07	15.26 7.93	15.51 7.80	15.76 7.68	15.99 7.57	16.21 7.46	16.43 7.36	16.64 7.27	16.84 7.18	17.04 7.10	17.24 7.02	17.43 6.94
8	12.53 9.66	13.10 9.24	13.53 8.94	13.89 8.71	14.21 8.51	14.51 8.34	14.78 8.19	15.03 8.05	15.27 7.92	15.50 7.81	15.72 7.70	15.93 7.60	16.13 7.50	16.33 7.41	16.52 7.32	16.71 7.24	16.89 7.17	17.06 7.09
9	12.47 9.71	13.00 9.30	13.42 9.02	13.76 8.79	14.07 8.60	14.35 8.43	14.60 8.29	14.84 8.15	15.07 8.03	15.29 7.91	15.49 7.81	15.69 7.71	15.89 7.62	16.07 7.53	16.25 7.45	16.43 7.37	16.60 7.29	16.76 7.22
10	12.41 9.75	12.93 9.36	13.32 9.08	13.65 8.86	13.94 8.68	14.21 8.52	14.45 8.37	14.68 8.24	14.90 8.12	15.11 8.01	15.30 7.91	15.49 7.81	15.68 7.72	15.85 7.63	16.02 7.55	16.19 7.47	16.35 7.40	16.51 7.33
11	12.36 9.79	12.86 9.41	13.24 9.14	13.55 8.93	13.84 8.75	14.09 8.59	14.33 8.45	14.55 8.32	14.75 8.20	14.95 8.09	15.14 7.99	15.32 7.90	15.49 7.81	15.66 7.73	15.83 7.65	15.99 7.57	16.14 7.50	16.29 7.43
12	12.32 9.82	12.80 9.45	13.16 9.19	13.47 8.98	13.74 8.81	13.99 8.65	14.21 8.51	14.42 8.39	14.62 8.27	14.81 8.17	14.99 8.07	15.17 7.98	15.34 7.89	15.50 7.81	15.65 7.73	15.81 7.65	15.96 7.58	16.10 7.52

Years

	1	2	3	4	5	6	7	8	9	10	11	12	13	14	15	16	17	18
13	12.28 9.85	12.74 9.49	13.10 9.24	13.39 9.03	13.66 8.86	13.89 8.71	14.11 8.57	14.32 8.45	14.51 8.34	14.69 8.24	14.87 8.14	15.03 8.05	15.20 7.96	15.35 7.88	15.50 7.81	15.65 7.73	15.79 7.66	15.93 7.59
14	12.24 9.88	12.70 9.53	13.04 9.28	13.33 9.08	13.58 8.91	13.81 8.76	14.02 8.63	14.22 8.51	14.41 8.40	14.58 8.30	14.75 8.20	14.91 8.11	15.07 8.03	15.22 7.95	15.37 7.87	15.51 7.80	15.65 7.73	15.78 7.67
15	12.21 9.91	12.65 9.56	12.99 9.32	13.27 9.12	13.51 8.95	13.74 8.81	13.94 8.68	14.13 8.56	14.31 8.45	14.49 8.35	14.65 8.26	14.81 8.17	14.96 8.09	15.10 8.01	15.24 7.94	15.38 7.87	15.52 7.80	15.65 7.73
16	12.19 9.93	12.61 9.59	12.94 9.35	13.21 9.16	13.45 9.00	13.67 8.85	13.87 8.73	14.05 8.61	14.23 8.50	14.40 8.40	14.56 8.31	14.71 8.23	14.86 8.15	15.00 8.07	15.13 8.00	15.27 7.93	15.40 7.86	15.52 7.79
17	12.16 9.95	12.58 9.62	12.89 9.38	13.16 9.19	13.39 9.03	13.61 8.89	13.80 8.77	13.98 8.65	14.15 8.55	14.32 8.45	14.47 8.36	14.62 8.28	14.76 8.20	14.90 8.12	15.03 8.05	15.16 7.98	15.29 7.91	15.41 7.85
18	12.13 9.97	12.54 9.65	12.85 9.41	13.11 9.23	13.34 9.07	13.55 8.93	13.74 8.81	13.92 8.70	14.08 8.59	14.24 8.50	14.39 8.41	14.54 8.32	14.68 8.24	14.81 8.17	14.94 8.10	15.07 8.03	15.19 7.97	15.31 7.90
19	12.11 9.99	12.51 9.67	12.82 9.44	13.07 9.26	13.29 9.10	13.50 8.97	13.68 8.84	13.85 8.73	14.02 8.63	14.17 8.54	14.32 8.45	14.46 8.37	14.60 8.29	14.73 8.22	14.85 8.15	14.98 8.08	15.10 8.01	15.21 7.95
20	12.09 10.01	12.48 9.69	12.78 9.47	13.03 9.29	13.25 9.13	13.45 9.00	13.63 8.88	13.80 8.77	13.96 8.67	14.11 8.58	14.25 8.49	14.39 8.41	14.52 8.33	14.65 8.26	14.78 8.19	14.90 8.12	15.01 8.06	15.13 8.00
21	12.07 10.02	12.46 9.71	12.75 9.49	12.99 9.31	13.21 9.16	13.40 9.03	13.58 8.91	13.75 8.80	13.90 8.70	14.05 8.61	14.19 8.53	14.33 8.45	14.46 8.37	14.58 8.30	14.70 8.23	14.82 8.16	14.93 8.10	15.05 8.04
22	12.05 10.04	12.43 9.73	12.72 9.51	12.96 9.34	13.17 9.19	13.36 9.06	13.53 8.94	13.70 8.83	13.85 8.74	13.99 8.65	14.13 8.56	14.26 8.48	14.39 8.41	14.51 8.34	14.63 8.27	14.75 8.20	14.86 8.14	14.97 8.08
23	12.04 10.05	12.41 9.75	12.69 9.53	12.93 9.36	13.13 9.21	13.32 9.09	13.49 8.97	13.65 8.86	13.80 8.77	13.94 8.68	14.08 8.60	14.21 8.52	14.33 8.44	14.45 8.37	14.57 8.31	14.68 8.24	14.79 8.18	14.90 8.12
24	12.02 10.07	12.39 9.77	12.66 9.56	12.89 9.38	13.10 9.24	13.28 9.11	13.45 9.00	13.61 8.89	13.75 8.80	13.89 8.71	14.03 8.63	14.15 8.55	14.28 8.48	14.39 8.41	14.51 8.34	14.62 8.28	14.73 8.22	14.83 8.16
25	12.01 10.08	12.37 9.78	12.64 9.57	12.87 9.40	13.07 9.26	13.25 9.14	13.41 9.02	13.56 8.92	13.71 8.83	13.85 8.74	13.98 8.66	14.10 8.58	14.22 8.51	14.34 8.44	14.45 8.37	14.56 8.31	14.67 8.25	14.77 8.19

RANGE OF FUTURE YIELDS FROM INITIAL YIELD OF 12%

BOND MATURITY	Years																	
	1	2	3	4	5	6	7	8	9	10	11	12	13	14	15	16	17	18
1	15.72 9.16	17.22 8.36	18.42 7.82	19.46 7.40	20.40 7.06	21.28 6.77	22.12 6.51	22.91 6.29	23.67 6.08	24.41 5.90	25.13 5.73	25.83 5.57	26.52 5.43	27.19 5.30	27.85 5.17	28.50 5.05	29.15 4.94	29.78 4.83
2	14.83 9.71	15.93 9.04	16.79 8.58	17.53 8.21	18.20 7.91	18.81 7.65	19.39 7.43	19.93 7.23	20.45 7.04	20.95 6.87	21.43 6.72	21.90 6.58	22.35 6.44	22.80 6.32	23.23 6.20	23.66 6.09	24.08 5.98	24.49 5.88
3	14.42 9.99	15.35 9.38	16.06 8.96	16.68 8.64	17.22 8.36	17.73 8.12	18.19 7.91	18.64 7.73	19.06 7.56	19.46 7.40	19.85 7.25	20.22 7.12	20.59 6.99	20.94 6.88	21.29 6.76	21.63 6.66	21.96 6.56	22.28 6.46
4	14.17 10.16	14.99 9.61	15.62 9.22	16.16 8.91	16.64 8.66	17.08 8.43	17.48 8.24	17.87 8.06	18.23 7.90	18.58 7.75	18.91 7.61	19.24 7.49	19.55 7.37	19.85 7.25	20.15 7.15	20.44 7.05	20.72 6.95	21.00 6.86
5	13.99 10.29	14.74 9.77	15.31 9.40	15.80 9.11	16.23 8.87	16.63 8.66	17.00 8.47	17.34 8.30	17.67 8.15	17.98 8.01	18.28 7.88	18.57 7.76	18.85 7.64	19.12 7.53	19.38 7.43	19.64 7.33	19.89 7.24	20.13 7.15
6	13.86 10.39	14.55 9.89	15.08 9.55	15.53 9.27	15.93 9.04	16.30 8.84	16.63 8.66	16.95 8.50	17.25 8.35	17.54 8.21	17.81 8.09	18.07 7.97	18.33 7.86	18.57 7.75	18.82 7.65	19.05 7.56	19.28 7.47	19.50 7.38
7	13.76 10.47	14.41 10.00	14.90 9.66	15.33 9.40	15.70 9.17	16.04 8.98	16.35 8.81	16.65 8.65	16.92 8.51	17.19 8.38	17.44 8.26	17.69 8.14	17.92 8.03	18.15 7.93	18.38 7.84	18.59 7.75	18.80 7.66	19.01 7.58
8	13.67 10.53	14.29 10.08	14.76 9.76	15.16 9.50	15.51 9.29	15.83 9.10	16.12 8.93	16.40 8.78	16.66 8.64	16.91 8.52	17.15 8.40	17.38 8.29	17.60 8.18	17.81 8.08	18.02 7.99	18.22 7.90	18.42 7.82	18.61 7.74
9	13.60 10.59	14.19 10.15	14.63 9.84	15.01 9.59	15.35 9.38	15.65 9.20	15.93 9.04	16.19 8.89	16.44 8.76	16.68 8.63	16.90 8.52	17.12 8.41	17.33 8.31	17.53 8.21	17.73 8.12	17.92 8.04	18.11 7.95	18.29 7.87
10	13.54 10.64	14.10 10.21	14.53 9.91	14.89 9.67	15.21 9.47	15.50 9.29	15.77 9.13	16.02 8.99	16.25 8.86	16.48 8.74	16.69 8.63	16.90 8.52	17.10 8.42	17.29 8.33	17.48 8.24	17.66 8.15	17.84 8.07	18.01 8.00
11	13.48 10.68	14.03 10.27	14.44 9.97	14.79 9.74	15.09 9.54	15.37 9.37	15.63 9.21	15.87 9.08	16.09 8.95	16.31 8.83	16.51 8.72	16.71 8.62	16.90 8.52	17.09 8.43	17.27 8.34	17.44 8.26	17.61 8.18	17.77 8.10
12	13.44 10.72	13.96 10.31	14.36 10.03	14.69 9.80	14.99 9.61	15.26 9.44	15.50 9.29	15.74 9.15	15.95 9.03	16.16 8.91	16.36 8.80	16.55 8.70	16.73 8.61	16.91 8.52	17.08 8.43	17.24 8.35	17.41 8.27	17.56 8.20

	18	17	16	15	14	13	12	11	10	9	8	7	6	5	4	3	2	1
13	17.38 8.29	17.23 8.36	17.07 8.43	16.91 8.51	16.75 8.60	16.58 8.69	16.40 8.78	16.22 8.88	16.03 8.98	15.83 9.10	15.62 9.22	15.39 9.35	15.16 9.50	14.90 9.67	14.61 9.85	14.29 10.08	13.90 10.36	13.40 10.75
14	17.22 8.36	17.07 8.44	16.92 8.51	16.76 8.59	16.60 8.67	16.44 8.76	16.27 8.85	16.09 8.95	15.91 9.05	15.72 9.16	15.51 9.28	15.30 9.41	15.07 9.56	14.82 9.72	14.54 9.90	14.22 10.12	13.85 10.40	13.36 10.78
15	17.07 8.44	16.93 8.51	16.78 8.58	16.63 8.66	16.48 8.74	16.32 8.83	16.15 8.92	15.98 9.01	15.80 9.11	15.62 9.22	15.42 9.34	15.21 9.47	14.98 9.61	14.74 9.77	14.47 9.95	14.17 10.16	13.80 10.43	13.32 10.81
16	16.93 8.50	16.80 8.57	16.66 8.65	16.51 8.72	16.36 8.80	16.21 8.89	16.05 8.97	15.88 9.07	15.71 9.17	15.52 9.28	15.33 9.39	15.13 9.52	14.91 9.66	14.67 9.81	14.41 9.99	14.11 10.20	13.76 10.46	13.29 10.83
17	16.81 8.56	16.68 8.63	16.54 8.71	16.40 8.78	16.25 8.86	16.10 8.94	15.95 9.03	15.79 9.12	15.62 9.22	15.44 9.33	15.25 9.44	15.05 9.56	14.84 9.70	14.61 9.86	14.36 10.03	14.07 10.24	13.72 10.49	13.26 10.86
18	16.70 8.62	16.57 8.69	16.44 8.76	16.30 8.84	16.16 8.91	16.01 8.99	15.86 9.08	15.70 9.17	15.54 9.27	15.36 9.37	15.18 9.49	14.99 9.61	14.78 9.74	14.55 9.89	14.31 10.07	14.02 10.27	13.68 10.52	13.24 10.88
19	16.60 8.68	16.47 8.74	16.34 8.81	16.21 8.89	16.07 8.96	15.92 9.04	15.78 9.13	15.62 9.22	15.46 9.31	15.29 9.42	15.11 9.53	14.93 9.65	14.72 9.78	14.50 9.93	14.26 10.10	13.98 10.30	13.65 10.55	13.21 10.90
20	16.50 8.73	16.38 8.79	16.25 8.86	16.12 8.93	15.98 9.01	15.84 9.09	15.70 9.17	15.55 9.26	15.39 9.36	15.23 9.46	15.05 9.57	14.87 9.69	14.67 9.82	14.45 9.96	14.21 10.13	13.94 10.33	13.62 10.57	13.19 10.92
21	16.41 8.77	16.29 8.84	16.17 8.91	16.04 8.98	15.91 9.05	15.77 9.13	15.63 9.21	15.48 9.30	15.33 9.40	15.16 9.50	14.99 9.60	14.81 9.72	14.62 9.85	14.41 9.99	14.17 10.16	13.91 10.35	13.59 10.60	13.17 10.93
22	16.33 8.82	16.21 8.88	16.09 8.95	15.96 9.02	15.83 9.09	15.70 9.17	15.56 9.25	15.42 9.34	15.27 9.43	15.11 9.53	14.94 9.64	14.76 9.75	14.57 9.88	14.37 10.02	14.14 10.19	13.87 10.38	13.56 10.62	13.15 10.95
23	16.25 8.86	16.14 8.92	16.02 8.99	15.89 9.06	15.77 9.13	15.64 9.21	15.50 9.29	15.36 9.38	15.21 9.47	15.05 9.57	14.89 9.67	14.72 9.79	14.53 9.91	14.33 10.05	14.10 10.21	13.84 10.40	13.54 10.64	13.13 10.97
24	16.18 8.90	16.07 8.96	15.95 9.03	15.83 9.10	15.70 9.17	15.57 9.25	15.44 9.33	15.30 9.41	15.16 9.50	15.00 9.60	14.84 9.70	14.67 9.81	14.49 9.94	14.29 10.08	14.07 10.24	13.81 10.42	13.51 10.66	13.11 10.98
25	16.11 8.94	16.00 9.00	15.88 9.07	15.77 9.13	15.64 9.21	15.52 9.28	15.39 9.36	15.25 9.44	15.11 9.53	14.96 9.63	14.80 9.73	14.63 9.84	14.45 9.97	14.25 10.10	14.04 10.26	13.79 10.44	13.49 10.67	13.10 10.99

RANGE OF FUTURE YIELDS FROM INITIAL YIELD OF 13%

BOND MATURITY	1	2	3	4	5	6	7	8	9	10	11	12	13	14	15	16	17	18
1	17.03 / 9.92	18.66 / 9.06	19.95 / 8.47	21.08 / 8.02	22.10 / 7.65	23.06 / 7.33	23.96 / 7.05	24.82 / 6.81	25.65 / 6.59	26.45 / 6.39	27.22 / 6.21	27.98 / 6.04	28.73 / 5.88	29.46 / 5.74	30.17 / 5.60	30.88 / 5.47	31.58 / 5.35	32.26 / 5.24
2	16.07 / 10.52	17.26 / 9.79	18.19 / 9.29	18.99 / 8.90	19.72 / 8.57	20.38 / 8.29	21.00 / 8.05	21.59 / 7.83	22.15 / 7.63	22.69 / 7.45	23.22 / 7.28	23.72 / 7.12	24.22 / 6.98	24.70 / 6.84	25.17 / 6.71	25.63 / 6.59	26.08 / 6.48	26.53 / 6.37
3	15.62 / 10.82	16.62 / 10.17	17.40 / 9.71	18.07 / 9.36	18.66 / 9.06	19.20 / 8.80	19.71 / 8.57	20.19 / 8.37	20.65 / 8.19	21.08 / 8.02	21.50 / 7.86	21.91 / 7.71	22.30 / 7.58	22.69 / 7.45	23.06 / 7.33	23.43 / 7.21	23.79 / 7.10	24.14 / 7.00
4	15.35 / 11.01	16.24 / 10.41	16.92 / 9.99	17.50 / 9.65	18.02 / 9.38	18.50 / 9.14	18.94 / 8.92	19.36 / 8.73	19.75 / 8.56	20.13 / 8.40	20.49 / 8.25	20.84 / 8.11	21.18 / 7.98	21.51 / 7.86	21.83 / 7.74	22.14 / 7.63	22.45 / 7.53	22.75 / 7.43
5	15.16 / 11.15	15.97 / 10.58	16.59 / 10.19	17.12 / 9.87	17.59 / 9.61	18.01 / 9.38	18.41 / 9.18	18.79 / 9.00	19.14 / 8.83	19.48 / 8.68	19.80 / 8.53	20.11 / 8.40	20.42 / 8.28	20.71 / 8.16	21.00 / 8.05	21.27 / 7.94	21.55 / 7.84	21.81 / 7.75
6	15.02 / 11.25	15.77 / 10.72	16.34 / 10.34	16.83 / 10.04	17.26 / 9.79	17.66 / 9.57	18.02 / 9.38	18.36 / 9.20	18.69 / 9.04	19.00 / 8.90	19.29 / 8.76	19.58 / 8.63	19.86 / 8.51	20.12 / 8.40	20.38 / 8.29	20.64 / 8.19	20.88 / 8.09	21.13 / 8.00
7	14.90 / 11.34	15.61 / 10.83	16.15 / 10.47	16.60 / 10.18	17.01 / 9.94	17.37 / 9.73	17.71 / 9.54	18.03 / 9.37	18.33 / 9.22	18.62 / 9.08	18.90 / 8.94	19.16 / 8.82	19.42 / 8.70	19.67 / 8.59	19.91 / 8.49	20.14 / 8.39	20.37 / 8.30	20.59 / 8.21
8	14.81 / 11.41	15.48 / 10.92	15.99 / 10.57	16.42 / 10.29	16.80 / 10.06	17.15 / 9.86	17.47 / 9.68	17.77 / 9.51	18.05 / 9.36	18.32 / 9.23	18.58 / 9.10	18.83 / 8.98	19.07 / 8.86	19.30 / 8.76	19.52 / 8.66	19.74 / 8.56	19.96 / 8.47	20.17 / 8.38
9	14.73 / 11.47	15.37 / 11.00	15.85 / 10.66	16.26 / 10.39	16.63 / 10.16	16.95 / 9.97	17.26 / 9.79	17.54 / 9.63	17.81 / 9.49	18.07 / 9.35	18.31 / 9.23	18.55 / 9.11	18.77 / 9.00	18.99 / 8.90	19.21 / 8.80	19.41 / 8.71	19.61 / 8.62	19.81 / 8.53
10	14.67 / 11.52	15.28 / 11.06	15.74 / 10.74	16.13 / 10.48	16.48 / 10.26	16.79 / 10.06	17.08 / 9.89	17.35 / 9.74	17.61 / 9.60	17.85 / 9.47	18.09 / 9.34	18.31 / 9.23	18.53 / 9.12	18.73 / 9.02	18.94 / 8.92	19.13 / 8.83	19.32 / 8.75	19.51 / 8.66
11	14.61 / 11.57	15.20 / 11.12	15.64 / 10.80	16.02 / 10.55	16.35 / 10.34	16.65 / 10.15	16.93 / 9.98	17.19 / 9.83	17.44 / 9.69	17.67 / 9.57	17.89 / 9.45	18.10 / 9.33	18.31 / 9.23	18.51 / 9.13	18.70 / 9.04	18.89 / 8.95	19.07 / 8.86	19.25 / 8.78
12	14.56 / 11.61	15.12 / 11.17	15.56 / 10.86	15.92 / 10.62	16.24 / 10.41	16.53 / 10.22	16.80 / 10.06	17.05 / 9.91	17.28 / 9.78	17.51 / 9.65	17.72 / 9.54	17.93 / 9.43	18.12 / 9.32	18.32 / 9.23	18.50 / 9.13	18.68 / 9.05	18.86 / 8.96	19.03 / 8.88

Years

	1	2	3	4	5	6	7	8	9	10	11	12	13	14	15	16	17	18
13	14.51 / 11.65	15.06 / 11.22	15.48 / 10.92	15.83 / 10.68	16.14 / 10.47	16.42 / 10.29	16.68 / 10.13	16.92 / 9.99	17.15 / 9.86	17.36 / 9.73	17.57 / 9.62	17.77 / 9.51	17.96 / 9.41	18.14 / 9.32	18.32 / 9.22	18.49 / 9.14	18.66 / 9.05	18.83 / 8.98
14	14.47 / 11.68	15.00 / 11.26	15.41 / 10.97	15.75 / 10.73	16.05 / 10.53	16.32 / 10.35	16.57 / 10.20	16.81 / 10.06	17.03 / 9.93	17.23 / 9.81	17.43 / 9.69	17.63 / 9.59	17.81 / 9.49	17.99 / 9.39	18.16 / 9.31	18.33 / 9.22	18.49 / 9.14	18.65 / 9.06
15	14.43 / 11.71	14.95 / 11.30	15.35 / 11.01	15.68 / 10.78	15.97 / 10.58	16.23 / 10.41	16.48 / 10.26	16.70 / 10.12	16.92 / 9.99	17.12 / 9.87	17.31 / 9.76	17.50 / 9.66	17.68 / 9.56	17.85 / 9.47	18.02 / 9.38	18.18 / 9.30	18.34 / 9.22	18.49 / 9.14
16	14.40 / 11.74	14.91 / 11.34	15.29 / 11.05	15.61 / 10.82	15.90 / 10.63	16.15 / 10.46	16.39 / 10.31	16.61 / 10.17	16.82 / 10.05	17.01 / 9.93	17.20 / 9.82	17.38 / 9.72	17.56 / 9.63	17.72 / 9.54	17.89 / 9.45	18.04 / 9.37	18.20 / 9.29	18.35 / 9.21
17	14.37 / 11.76	14.86 / 11.37	15.24 / 11.09	15.55 / 10.87	15.83 / 10.68	16.08 / 10.51	16.31 / 10.36	16.52 / 10.23	16.73 / 10.10	16.92 / 9.99	17.10 / 9.88	17.28 / 9.78	17.45 / 9.69	17.61 / 9.60	17.77 / 9.51	17.92 / 9.43	18.07 / 9.35	18.21 / 9.28
18	14.34 / 11.78	14.82 / 11.40	15.19 / 11.13	15.50 / 10.90	15.77 / 10.72	16.01 / 10.55	16.24 / 10.41	16.45 / 10.28	16.64 / 10.15	16.83 / 10.04	17.01 / 9.94	17.18 / 9.84	17.34 / 9.74	17.50 / 9.66	17.66 / 9.57	17.81 / 9.49	17.95 / 9.41	18.09 / 9.34
19	14.31 / 11.81	14.79 / 11.43	15.15 / 11.16	15.45 / 10.94	15.71 / 10.76	15.95 / 10.60	16.17 / 10.45	16.37 / 10.32	16.57 / 10.20	16.75 / 10.09	16.92 / 9.99	17.09 / 9.89	17.25 / 9.80	17.41 / 9.71	17.56 / 9.63	17.70 / 9.55	17.84 / 9.47	17.98 / 9.40
20	14.29 / 11.83	14.75 / 11.45	15.11 / 11.19	15.40 / 10.97	15.66 / 10.79	15.89 / 10.63	16.11 / 10.49	16.31 / 10.36	16.50 / 10.25	16.67 / 10.14	16.84 / 10.03	17.01 / 9.94	17.16 / 9.85	17.32 / 9.76	17.46 / 9.68	17.60 / 9.60	17.74 / 9.53	17.88 / 9.45
21	14.27 / 11.85	14.72 / 11.48	15.07 / 11.22	15.36 / 11.01	15.61 / 10.83	15.84 / 10.67	16.05 / 10.53	16.24 / 10.40	16.43 / 10.29	16.60 / 10.18	16.77 / 10.08	16.93 / 9.98	17.08 / 9.89	17.23 / 9.81	17.38 / 9.73	17.51 / 9.65	17.65 / 9.58	17.78 / 9.50
22	14.25 / 11.86	14.69 / 11.50	15.03 / 11.24	15.31 / 11.04	15.56 / 10.86	15.79 / 10.70	15.99 / 10.57	16.19 / 10.44	16.37 / 10.33	16.54 / 10.22	16.70 / 10.12	16.86 / 10.02	17.01 / 9.94	17.15 / 9.85	17.29 / 9.77	17.43 / 9.70	17.56 / 9.62	17.69 / 9.55
23	14.23 / 11.88	14.67 / 11.52	15.00 / 11.27	15.28 / 11.06	15.52 / 10.89	15.74 / 10.74	15.94 / 10.60	16.13 / 10.48	16.31 / 10.36	16.48 / 10.26	16.64 / 10.16	16.79 / 10.07	16.94 / 9.98	17.08 / 9.89	17.22 / 9.82	17.35 / 9.74	17.48 / 9.67	17.61 / 9.60
24	14.21 / 11.90	14.64 / 11.54	14.97 / 11.29	15.24 / 11.09	15.48 / 10.92	15.70 / 10.77	15.89 / 10.63	16.08 / 10.51	16.25 / 10.40	16.42 / 10.29	16.58 / 10.20	16.73 / 10.10	16.87 / 10.02	17.01 / 9.93	17.15 / 9.86	17.28 / 9.78	17.40 / 9.71	17.53 / 9.64
25	14.19 / 11.91	14.61 / 11.56	14.94 / 11.31	15.20 / 11.11	15.44 / 10.95	15.65 / 10.80	15.85 / 10.66	16.03 / 10.54	16.20 / 10.43	16.36 / 10.33	16.52 / 10.23	16.67 / 10.14	16.81 / 10.05	16.95 / 9.97	17.08 / 9.89	17.21 / 9.82	17.33 / 9.75	17.45 / 9.68

BOND MATURITY	1	2	3	4	5	6	7	8	9 (Years)	10	11	12	13	14	15	16	17	18
1	18.34 / 10.69	20.09 / 9.76	21.49 / 9.12	22.70 / 8.63	23.80 / 8.23	24.83 / 7.89	25.80 / 7.60	26.73 / 7.33	27.62 / 7.10	28.48 / 6.88	29.32 / 6.69	30.14 / 6.50	30.94 / 6.34	31.72 / 6.18	32.49 / 6.03	33.26 / 5.89	34.01 / 5.76	34.75 / 5.64
2	17.30 / 11.33	18.59 / 10.54	19.59 / 10.00	20.46 / 9.58	21.23 / 9.23	21.95 / 8.93	22.62 / 8.67	23.25 / 8.43	23.86 / 8.22	24.44 / 8.02	25.00 / 7.84	25.55 / 7.67	26.08 / 7.52	26.60 / 7.37	27.10 / 7.23	27.60 / 7.10	28.09 / 6.98	28.57 / 6.86
3	16.83 / 11.65	17.90 / 10.95	18.74 / 10.46	19.45 / 10.07	20.09 / 9.75	20.68 / 9.48	21.23 / 9.23	21.74 / 9.01	22.23 / 8.82	22.70 / 8.63	23.16 / 8.46	23.59 / 8.31	24.02 / 8.16	24.43 / 8.02	24.84 / 7.89	25.23 / 7.77	25.62 / 7.65	26.00 / 7.54
4	16.53 / 11.86	17.49 / 11.21	18.22 / 10.76	18.85 / 10.40	19.41 / 10.10	19.92 / 9.84	20.40 / 9.61	20.84 / 9.40	21.27 / 9.21	21.68 / 9.04	22.07 / 8.88	22.44 / 8.73	22.81 / 8.59	23.16 / 8.46	23.51 / 8.34	23.85 / 8.22	24.18 / 8.11	24.50 / 8.00
5	16.33 / 12.01	17.20 / 11.40	17.87 / 10.97	18.43 / 10.63	18.94 / 10.35	19.40 / 10.10	19.83 / 9.88	20.23 / 9.69	20.61 / 9.51	20.98 / 9.34	21.33 / 9.19	21.66 / 9.05	21.99 / 8.91	22.30 / 8.79	22.61 / 8.67	22.91 / 8.55	23.20 / 8.45	23.49 / 8.34
6	16.17 / 12.12	16.98 / 11.54	17.60 / 11.14	18.12 / 10.81	18.59 / 10.54	19.01 / 10.31	19.41 / 10.10	19.78 / 9.91	20.12 / 9.74	20.46 / 9.58	20.78 / 9.43	21.09 / 9.30	21.38 / 9.17	21.67 / 9.04	21.95 / 8.93	22.22 / 8.82	22.49 / 8.71	22.75 / 8.62
7	16.05 / 12.21	16.81 / 11.66	17.39 / 11.27	17.88 / 10.96	18.31 / 10.70	18.71 / 10.48	19.08 / 10.27	19.42 / 10.09	19.75 / 9.93	20.05 / 9.77	20.35 / 9.63	20.64 / 9.50	20.91 / 9.37	21.18 / 9.25	21.44 / 9.14	21.69 / 9.04	21.94 / 8.93	22.18 / 8.84
8	15.95 / 12.29	16.67 / 11.76	17.22 / 11.38	17.68 / 11.09	18.09 / 10.83	18.46 / 10.62	18.81 / 10.42	19.13 / 10.24	19.44 / 10.08	19.73 / 9.94	20.01 / 9.80	20.27 / 9.67	20.53 / 9.55	20.78 / 9.43	21.03 / 9.32	21.26 / 9.22	21.49 / 9.12	21.72 / 9.03
9	15.87 / 12.35	16.55 / 11.84	17.07 / 11.48	17.51 / 11.19	17.90 / 10.95	18.26 / 10.73	18.59 / 10.55	18.89 / 10.37	19.18 / 10.22	19.46 / 10.07	19.72 / 9.94	19.97 / 9.81	20.22 / 9.69	20.45 / 9.58	20.68 / 9.48	20.91 / 9.38	21.12 / 9.28	21.34 / 9.19
10	15.79 / 12.41	16.45 / 11.91	16.95 / 11.56	17.37 / 11.28	17.75 / 11.04	18.08 / 10.84	18.40 / 10.65	18.69 / 10.49	18.96 / 10.34	19.23 / 10.19	19.48 / 10.06	19.72 / 9.94	19.95 / 9.82	20.17 / 9.72	20.39 / 9.61	20.60 / 9.51	20.81 / 9.42	21.01 / 9.33
11	15.73 / 12.46	16.36 / 11.98	16.85 / 11.63	17.25 / 11.36	17.61 / 11.13	17.93 / 10.93	18.23 / 10.75	18.51 / 10.59	18.78 / 10.44	19.03 / 10.30	19.27 / 10.17	19.50 / 10.05	19.72 / 9.94	19.93 / 9.83	20.14 / 9.73	20.34 / 9.63	20.54 / 9.54	20.73 / 9.45
12	15.68 / 12.50	16.29 / 12.03	16.75 / 11.70	17.14 / 11.43	17.49 / 11.21	17.80 / 11.01	18.09 / 10.84	18.36 / 10.68	18.61 / 10.53	18.85 / 10.40	19.08 / 10.27	19.30 / 10.15	19.52 / 10.04	19.72 / 9.94	19.92 / 9.84	20.12 / 9.74	20.31 / 9.65	20.49 / 9.56

	Years 1	2	3	4	5	6	7	8	9	10	11	12	13	14	15	16	17	18
13	15.63 12.54	16.22 12.08	16.67 11.76	17.05 11.50	17.38 11.28	17.68 11.08	17.96 10.91	18.22 10.76	18.47 10.61	18.70 10.48	18.92 10.36	19.13 10.24	19.34 10.13	19.54 10.03	19.73 9.93	19.92 9.84	20.10 9.75	20.28 9.67
14	15.58 12.58	16.16 12.13	16.60 11.81	16.96 11.56	17.28 11.34	17.58 11.15	17.85 10.98	18.10 10.83	18.34 10.69	18.56 10.56	18.78 10.44	18.98 10.33	19.18 10.22	19.37 10.12	19.56 10.02	19.74 9.93	19.91 9.84	20.09 9.76
15	15.54 12.61	16.10 12.17	16.53 11.86	16.88 11.61	17.20 11.40	17.48 11.21	17.74 11.05	17.99 10.90	18.22 10.76	18.44 10.63	18.64 10.51	18.84 10.40	19.04 10.30	19.22 10.20	19.40 10.10	19.58 10.01	19.75 9.93	19.91 9.84
16	15.51 12.64	16.05 12.21	16.47 11.90	16.81 11.66	17.12 11.45	17.40 11.27	17.65 11.10	17.89 10.96	18.11 10.82	18.32 10.70	18.53 10.58	18.72 10.47	18.91 10.37	19.09 10.27	19.26 10.18	19.43 10.09	19.60 10.00	19.76 9.92
17	15.47 12.67	16.01 12.24	16.41 11.94	16.75 11.70	17.05 11.50	17.32 11.32	17.56 11.16	17.80 11.01	18.01 10.88	18.22 10.76	18.42 10.64	18.61 10.53	18.79 10.43	18.96 10.34	19.13 10.24	19.30 10.16	19.46 10.07	19.61 9.99
18	15.44 12.69	15.97 12.28	16.36 11.98	16.69 11.74	16.98 11.54	17.24 11.37	17.49 11.21	17.71 11.07	17.92 10.94	18.13 10.81	18.32 10.70	18.50 10.59	18.68 10.49	18.85 10.40	19.02 10.31	19.18 10.22	19.33 10.14	19.48 10.06
19	15.42 12.71	15.93 12.31	16.31 12.02	16.63 11.78	16.92 11.58	17.18 11.41	17.41 11.26	17.63 11.12	17.84 10.99	18.04 10.87	18.23 10.75	18.40 10.65	18.58 10.55	18.74 10.46	18.91 10.37	19.06 10.28	19.22 10.20	19.36 10.12
20	15.39 12.74	15.89 12.34	16.27 12.05	16.58 11.82	16.86 11.62	17.11 11.45	17.35 11.30	17.56 11.16	17.76 11.03	17.96 10.92	18.14 10.80	18.32 10.70	18.48 10.60	18.65 10.51	18.81 10.42	18.96 10.34	19.11 10.26	19.25 10.18
21	15.36 12.76	15.86 12.36	16.23 12.08	16.54 11.85	16.81 11.66	17.06 11.49	17.28 11.34	17.49 11.20	17.69 11.08	17.88 10.96	18.06 10.85	18.23 10.75	18.40 10.65	18.56 10.56	18.71 10.47	18.86 10.39	19.01 10.31	19.15 10.24
22	15.34 12.78	15.82 12.39	16.19 12.11	16.49 11.88	16.76 11.69	17.00 11.53	17.22 11.38	17.43 11.24	17.63 11.12	17.81 11.00	17.99 10.90	18.15 10.80	18.32 10.70	18.47 10.61	18.62 10.52	18.77 10.44	18.91 10.36	19.05 10.29
23	15.32 12.79	15.79 12.41	16.15 12.14	16.45 11.91	16.71 11.73	16.95 11.56	17.17 11.42	17.37 11.28	17.56 11.16	17.74 11.05	17.92 10.94	18.08 10.84	18.24 10.75	18.39 10.66	18.54 10.57	18.69 10.49	18.83 10.41	18.96 10.34
24	15.30 12.81	15.77 12.43	16.12 12.16	16.41 11.94	16.67 11.76	16.90 11.60	17.12 11.45	17.32 11.32	17.50 11.20	17.68 11.08	17.85 10.98	18.01 10.88	18.17 10.79	18.32 10.70	18.47 10.61	18.61 10.53	18.74 10.46	18.88 10.38
25	15.28 12.83	15.74 12.45	16.08 12.19	16.37 11.97	16.63 11.79	16.86 11.63	17.07 11.48	17.26 11.35	17.45 11.23	17.62 11.12	17.79 11.02	17.95 10.92	18.10 10.83	18.25 10.74	18.39 10.66	18.53 10.58	18.67 10.50	18.80 10.43

RANGE OF FUTURE YIELDS FROM INITIAL YIELD OF 15%

Years

BOND MATURITY	1	2	3	4	5	6	7	8	9	10	11	12	13	14	15	16	17	18
1	19.65 11.45	21.53 10.45	23.02 9.77	24.32 9.25	25.50 8.82	26.60 8.46	27.64 8.14	28.64 7.86	29.59 7.60	30.52 7.37	31.41 7.16	32.29 6.97	33.15 6.79	33.99 6.62	34.82 6.46	35.63 6.31	36.43 6.18	37.23 6.04
2	18.54 12.14	19.92 11.30	20.99 10.72	21.92 10.27	22.75 9.89	23.52 9.57	24.23 9.28	24.91 9.03	25.56 8.80	26.19 8.59	26.79 8.40	27.37 8.22	27.94 8.05	28.50 7.90	29.04 7.75	29.57 7.61	30.09 7.48	30.61 7.35
3	18.03 12.48	19.18 11.73	20.08 11.21	20.84 10.79	21.53 10.45	22.16 10.15	22.74 9.89	23.30 9.66	23.82 9.45	24.33 9.25	24.81 9.07	25.28 8.90	25.73 8.74	26.18 8.60	26.61 8.46	27.03 8.32	27.45 8.20	27.85 8.08
4	17.71 12.70	18.74 12.01	19.53 11.52	20.20 11.14	20.80 10.82	21.34 10.54	21.85 10.30	22.33 10.07	22.79 9.87	23.22 9.69	23.64 9.52	24.05 9.36	24.44 9.21	24.82 9.07	25.19 8.93	25.55 8.81	25.90 8.69	26.25 8.57
5	17.49 12.86	18.43 12.21	19.14 11.75	19.75 11.39	20.29 11.09	20.79 10.82	21.24 10.59	21.68 10.38	22.08 10.19	22.47 10.01	22.85 9.85	23.21 9.69	23.56 9.55	23.90 9.42	24.23 9.29	24.55 9.17	24.86 9.05	25.17 8.94
6	17.33 12.99	18.19 12.37	18.86 11.93	19.42 11.59	19.92 11.30	20.37 11.04	20.79 10.82	21.19 10.62	21.56 10.43	21.92 10.26	22.26 10.11	22.59 9.96	22.91 9.82	23.22 9.69	23.52 9.57	23.81 9.45	24.10 9.34	24.38 9.23
7	17.20 13.08	18.01 12.49	18.63 12.08	19.16 11.75	19.62 11.47	20.05 11.22	20.44 11.01	20.81 10.81	21.16 10.64	21.49 10.47	21.80 10.32	22.11 10.18	22.41 10.04	22.69 9.92	22.97 9.80	23.24 9.68	23.50 9.57	23.76 9.47
8	17.09 13.17	17.86 12.60	18.45 12.20	18.94 11.88	19.38 11.61	19.78 11.37	20.15 11.16	20.50 10.98	20.83 10.80	21.14 10.64	21.44 10.50	21.72 10.36	22.00 10.23	22.27 10.10	22.53 9.99	22.78 9.88	23.03 9.77	23.27 9.67
9	17.00 13.24	17.73 12.69	18.29 12.30	18.77 11.99	19.18 11.73	19.56 11.50	19.91 11.30	20.24 11.12	20.55 10.95	20.85 10.79	21.13 10.65	21.40 10.51	21.66 10.39	21.91 10.27	22.16 10.15	22.40 10.05	22.63 9.94	22.86 9.84
10	16.92 13.30	17.63 12.76	18.16 12.39	18.61 12.09	19.01 11.83	19.38 11.61	19.71 11.42	20.02 11.24	20.32 11.07	20.60 10.92	20.87 10.78	21.13 10.65	21.38 10.53	21.62 10.41	21.85 10.30	22.08 10.19	22.30 10.09	22.51 9.99
11	16.86 13.35	17.53 12.83	18.05 12.47	18.48 12.17	18.87 11.93	19.21 11.71	19.53 11.52	19.83 11.34	20.12 11.18	20.39 11.04	20.64 10.90	20.89 10.77	21.13 10.65	21.36 10.53	21.58 10.43	21.80 10.32	22.01 10.22	22.22 10.13
12	16.80 13.40	17.45 12.89	17.95 12.54	18.37 12.25	18.74 12.01	19.07 11.80	19.38 11.61	19.67 11.44	19.94 11.28	20.20 11.14	20.45 11.00	20.68 10.88	20.91 10.76	21.13 10.65	21.35 10.54	21.56 10.44	21.76 10.34	21.96 10.25

Years

	1	2	3	4	5	6	7	8	9	10	11	12	13	14	15	16	17	18
13	16.74 13.44	17.38 12.95	17.86 12.60	18.27 12.32	18.62 12.08	18.95 11.88	19.24 11.69	19.52 11.53	19.78 11.37	20.03 11.23	20.27 11.10	20.50 10.98	20.72 10.86	20.93 10.75	21.14 10.64	21.34 10.54	21.54 10.45	21.73 10.36
14	16.70 13.48	17.31 13.00	17.78 12.65	18.17 12.38	18.52 12.15	18.83 11.95	19.12 11.77	19.39 11.60	19.65 11.45	19.89 11.31	20.12 11.18	20.34 11.06	20.55 10.95	20.76 10.84	20.96 10.74	21.15 10.64	21.34 10.55	21.52 10.46
15	16.65 13.51	17.25 13.04	17.71 12.71	18.09 12.44	18.43 12.21	18.73 12.01	19.01 11.84	19.27 11.67	19.52 11.53	19.75 11.39	19.98 11.26	20.19 11.14	20.40 11.03	20.60 10.92	20.79 10.82	20.98 10.73	21.16 10.63	21.34 10.55
16	16.62 13.54	17.20 13.08	17.64 12.75	18.01 12.49	18.34 12.27	18.64 12.07	18.91 11.90	19.16 11.74	19.40 11.60	19.63 11.46	19.85 11.34	20.06 11.22	20.26 11.11	20.45 11.00	20.64 10.90	20.82 10.81	21.00 10.72	21.17 10.63
17	16.58 13.57	17.15 13.12	17.58 12.80	17.95 12.54	18.26 12.32	18.55 12.13	18.82 11.96	19.07 11.80	19.30 11.66	19.52 11.53	19.73 11.40	19.93 11.29	20.13 11.18	20.32 11.07	20.50 10.98	20.68 10.88	20.85 10.79	21.02 10.71
18	16.55 13.60	17.11 13.15	17.53 12.84	17.88 12.58	18.19 12.37	18.48 12.18	18.73 12.01	18.98 11.86	19.20 11.72	19.42 11.59	19.63 11.46	19.82 11.35	20.01 11.24	20.20 11.14	20.37 11.04	20.55 10.95	20.71 10.86	20.88 10.78
19	16.52 13.62	17.06 13.19	17.48 12.87	17.82 12.62	18.13 12.41	18.40 12.23	18.66 12.06	18.89 11.91	19.12 11.77	19.33 11.64	19.53 11.52	19.72 11.41	19.90 11.30	20.08 11.20	20.26 11.11	20.42 11.02	20.59 10.93	20.75 10.84
20	16.49 13.65	17.02 13.22	17.43 12.91	17.77 12.66	18.07 12.45	18.34 12.27	18.58 12.11	18.82 11.96	19.03 11.82	19.24 11.70	19.44 11.58	19.62 11.47	19.80 11.36	19.98 11.26	20.15 11.17	20.31 11.08	20.47 10.99	20.63 10.91
21	16.46 13.67	16.99 13.24	17.39 12.94	17.72 12.70	18.01 12.49	18.27 12.31	18.52 12.15	18.74 12.00	18.96 11.87	19.16 11.74	19.35 11.63	19.53 11.52	19.71 11.41	19.88 11.32	20.05 11.22	20.21 11.13	20.36 11.05	20.52 10.97
22	16.44 13.69	16.95 13.27	17.34 12.97	17.67 12.73	17.96 12.53	18.22 12.35	18.45 12.19	18.68 12.05	18.88 11.91	19.08 11.79	19.27 11.68	19.45 11.57	19.63 11.46	19.79 11.37	19.95 11.28	20.11 11.19	20.26 11.10	20.41 11.02
23	16.41 13.71	16.92 13.30	17.30 13.00	17.63 12.77	17.91 12.56	18.16 12.39	18.40 12.23	18.61 12.09	18.82 11.96	19.01 11.83	19.20 11.72	19.37 11.61	19.54 11.51	19.71 11.42	19.87 11.33	20.02 11.24	20.17 11.15	20.32 11.07
24	16.39 13.73	16.89 13.32	17.27 13.03	17.58 12.80	17.86 12.60	18.11 12.42	18.34 12.27	18.55 12.13	18.75 12.00	18.95 11.88	19.13 11.76	19.30 11.66	19.47 11.56	19.63 11.46	19.78 11.37	19.94 11.29	20.08 11.20	20.23 11.12
25	16.37 13.74	16.86 13.34	17.23 13.06	17.54 12.82	17.82 12.63	18.06 12.46	18.29 12.30	18.50 12.16	18.70 12.04	18.88 11.92	19.06 11.80	19.23 11.70	19.40 11.60	19.55 11.51	19.71 11.42	19.86 11.33	20.00 11.25	20.14 11.17

RANGE OF FUTURE YIELDS FROM INITIAL YIELD OF 16%

BOND MATURITY	1	2	3	4	5	6	7	8	9	10	11	12	13	14	15	16	17	18
									Years									
1	20.96 / 12.21	22.96 / 11.15	24.55 / 10.43	25.94 / 9.87	27.20 / 9.41	28.38 / 9.02	29.49 / 8.68	30.55 / 8.38	31.56 / 8.11	32.55 / 7.86	33.51 / 7.64	34.44 / 7.43	35.36 / 7.24	36.25 / 7.06	37.14 / 6.89	38.01 / 6.74	38.86 / 6.59	39.71 / 6.45
2	19.78 / 12.95	21.24 / 12.05	22.39 / 11.43	23.38 / 10.95	24.27 / 10.55	25.08 / 10.21	25.85 / 9.90	26.57 / 9.63	27.27 / 9.39	27.93 / 9.17	28.58 / 8.96	29.20 / 8.77	29.81 / 8.59	30.40 / 8.42	30.98 / 8.26	31.54 / 8.12	32.10 / 7.97	32.65 / 7.84
3	19.23 / 13.31	20.46 / 12.51	21.42 / 11.95	22.23 / 11.51	22.96 / 11.15	23.63 / 10.83	24.26 / 10.55	24.85 / 10.30	25.41 / 10.07	25.95 / 9.87	26.46 / 9.67	26.96 / 9.49	27.45 / 9.33	27.92 / 9.17	28.38 / 9.02	28.83 / 8.88	29.28 / 8.74	29.71 / 8.62
4	18.89 / 13.55	19.98 / 12.81	20.83 / 12.29	21.54 / 11.88	22.18 / 11.54	22.77 / 11.24	23.31 / 10.98	23.82 / 10.75	24.31 / 10.53	24.77 / 10.33	25.22 / 10.15	25.65 / 9.98	26.07 / 9.82	26.47 / 9.67	26.87 / 9.53	27.25 / 9.39	27.63 / 9.27	28.00 / 9.14
5	18.66 / 13.72	19.65 / 13.03	20.42 / 12.54	21.07 / 12.15	21.65 / 11.83	22.17 / 11.55	22.66 / 11.30	23.12 / 11.07	23.56 / 10.87	23.97 / 10.68	24.37 / 10.50	24.76 / 10.34	25.13 / 10.19	25.49 / 10.04	25.84 / 9.91	26.18 / 9.78	26.52 / 9.65	26.85 / 9.54
6	18.48 / 13.85	19.41 / 13.19	20.11 / 12.73	20.71 / 12.36	21.24 / 12.05	21.73 / 11.78	22.18 / 11.54	22.60 / 11.33	23.00 / 11.13	23.38 / 10.95	23.75 / 10.78	24.10 / 10.62	24.44 / 10.48	24.77 / 10.34	25.09 / 10.20	25.40 / 10.08	25.70 / 9.96	26.00 / 9.85
7	18.34 / 13.96	19.21 / 13.33	19.87 / 12.88	20.43 / 12.53	20.93 / 12.23	21.38 / 11.97	21.80 / 11.74	22.19 / 11.53	22.57 / 11.34	22.92 / 11.17	23.26 / 11.01	23.58 / 10.85	23.90 / 10.71	24.20 / 10.58	24.50 / 10.45	24.79 / 10.33	25.07 / 10.21	25.35 / 10.10
8	18.23 / 14.04	19.05 / 13.44	19.68 / 13.01	20.21 / 12.67	20.68 / 12.38	21.10 / 12.13	21.50 / 11.91	21.87 / 11.71	22.21 / 11.52	22.55 / 11.35	22.86 / 11.20	23.17 / 11.05	23.47 / 10.91	23.75 / 10.78	24.03 / 10.65	24.30 / 10.54	24.56 / 10.42	24.82 / 10.31
9	18.13 / 14.12	18.92 / 13.53	19.51 / 13.12	20.02 / 12.79	20.46 / 12.51	20.87 / 12.27	21.24 / 12.05	21.59 / 11.86	21.92 / 11.68	22.24 / 11.51	22.54 / 11.36	22.83 / 11.22	23.11 / 11.08	23.38 / 10.95	23.64 / 10.83	23.89 / 10.71	24.14 / 10.60	24.38 / 10.50
10	18.05 / 14.18	18.80 / 13.62	19.37 / 13.21	19.86 / 12.89	20.28 / 12.62	20.67 / 12.39	21.02 / 12.18	21.36 / 11.99	21.67 / 11.81	21.97 / 11.65	22.26 / 11.50	22.53 / 11.36	22.80 / 11.23	23.06 / 11.10	23.31 / 10.98	23.55 / 10.87	23.78 / 10.76	24.01 / 10.66
11	17.98 / 14.24	18.70 / 13.69	19.25 / 13.30	19.72 / 12.98	20.12 / 12.72	20.49 / 12.49	20.84 / 12.29	21.16 / 12.10	21.46 / 11.93	21.75 / 11.77	22.02 / 11.63	22.28 / 11.49	22.54 / 11.36	22.78 / 11.24	23.02 / 11.12	23.25 / 11.01	23.48 / 10.90	23.70 / 10.80
12	17.92 / 14.29	18.62 / 13.75	19.15 / 13.37	19.59 / 13.07	19.99 / 12.81	20.34 / 12.58	20.67 / 12.38	20.98 / 12.20	21.27 / 12.04	21.55 / 11.88	21.81 / 11.74	22.06 / 11.60	22.31 / 11.48	22.54 / 11.36	22.77 / 11.24	22.99 / 11.13	23.21 / 11.03	23.42 / 10.93

Years

	1	2	3	4	5	6	7	8	9	10	11	12	13	14	15	16	17	18
13	17.86 / 14.33	18.54 / 13.81	19.05 / 13.44	19.48 / 13.14	19.86 / 12.89	20.21 / 12.67	20.53 / 12.47	20.82 / 12.29	21.10 / 12.13	21.37 / 11.98	21.62 / 11.84	21.87 / 11.71	22.10 / 11.58	22.33 / 11.46	22.55 / 11.35	22.76 / 11.25	22.97 / 11.14	23.17 / 11.05
14	17.81 / 14.37	18.47 / 13.86	18.97 / 13.50	19.38 / 13.21	19.75 / 12.96	20.09 / 12.74	20.40 / 12.55	20.68 / 12.38	20.95 / 12.22	21.21 / 12.07	21.46 / 11.93	21.69 / 11.80	21.92 / 11.68	22.14 / 11.56	22.35 / 11.45	22.56 / 11.35	22.76 / 11.25	22.95 / 11.15
15	17.77 / 14.41	18.40 / 13.91	18.89 / 13.55	19.30 / 13.27	19.65 / 13.02	19.98 / 12.81	20.28 / 12.62	20.56 / 12.45	20.82 / 12.30	21.07 / 12.15	21.31 / 12.01	21.54 / 11.89	21.76 / 11.77	21.97 / 11.65	22.17 / 11.54	22.37 / 11.44	22.57 / 11.34	22.76 / 11.25
16	17.72 / 14.44	18.35 / 13.95	18.82 / 13.60	19.22 / 13.32	19.56 / 13.08	19.88 / 12.88	20.17 / 12.69	20.44 / 12.52	20.70 / 12.37	20.94 / 12.23	21.17 / 12.09	21.39 / 11.97	21.61 / 11.85	21.81 / 11.74	22.01 / 11.63	22.21 / 11.53	22.40 / 11.43	22.58 / 11.34
17	17.69 / 14.48	18.29 / 13.99	18.76 / 13.65	19.14 / 13.37	19.48 / 13.14	19.79 / 12.94	20.07 / 12.75	20.34 / 12.59	20.59 / 12.44	20.82 / 12.29	21.05 / 12.16	21.26 / 12.04	21.47 / 11.92	21.67 / 11.81	21.87 / 11.71	22.05 / 11.61	22.24 / 11.51	22.42 / 11.42
18	17.65 / 14.50	18.25 / 14.03	18.70 / 13.69	19.07 / 13.42	19.41 / 13.19	19.71 / 12.99	19.98 / 12.81	20.24 / 12.65	20.48 / 12.50	20.71 / 12.36	20.93 / 12.23	21.14 / 12.11	21.35 / 11.99	21.54 / 11.88	21.73 / 11.78	21.92 / 11.68	22.09 / 11.59	22.27 / 11.50
19	17.62 / 14.53	18.20 / 14.07	18.64 / 13.73	19.01 / 13.47	19.34 / 13.24	19.63 / 13.04	19.90 / 12.86	20.15 / 12.70	20.39 / 12.56	20.61 / 12.42	20.83 / 12.29	21.03 / 12.17	21.23 / 12.06	21.42 / 11.95	21.61 / 11.85	21.79 / 11.75	21.96 / 11.66	22.13 / 11.57
20	17.59 / 14.56	18.16 / 14.10	18.59 / 13.77	18.95 / 13.51	19.27 / 13.28	19.56 / 13.09	19.82 / 12.91	20.07 / 12.76	20.30 / 12.61	20.52 / 12.47	20.73 / 12.35	20.93 / 12.23	21.13 / 12.12	21.31 / 12.01	21.49 / 11.91	21.67 / 11.82	21.84 / 11.72	22.00 / 11.63
21	17.56 / 14.58	18.12 / 14.13	18.54 / 13.80	18.90 / 13.55	19.21 / 13.33	19.49 / 13.13	19.75 / 12.96	19.99 / 12.80	20.22 / 12.66	20.44 / 12.53	20.64 / 12.40	20.84 / 12.29	21.03 / 12.18	21.21 / 12.07	21.38 / 11.97	21.56 / 11.88	21.72 / 11.79	21.88 / 11.70
22	17.53 / 14.60	18.08 / 14.16	18.50 / 13.84	18.85 / 13.58	19.15 / 13.37	19.43 / 13.18	19.68 / 13.01	19.92 / 12.85	20.14 / 12.71	20.35 / 12.58	20.56 / 12.45	20.75 / 12.34	20.93 / 12.23	21.11 / 12.13	21.28 / 12.03	21.45 / 11.93	21.62 / 11.84	21.77 / 11.76
23	17.51 / 14.62	18.05 / 14.18	18.46 / 13.87	18.80 / 13.62	19.10 / 13.40	19.37 / 13.21	19.62 / 13.05	19.85 / 12.89	20.07 / 12.75	20.28 / 12.62	20.48 / 12.50	20.67 / 12.39	20.85 / 12.28	21.02 / 12.18	21.19 / 12.08	21.36 / 11.99	21.52 / 11.90	21.67 / 11.81
24	17.49 / 14.64	18.02 / 14.21	18.42 / 13.90	18.76 / 13.65	19.05 / 13.44	19.32 / 13.25	19.56 / 13.09	19.79 / 12.94	20.01 / 12.80	20.21 / 12.67	20.40 / 12.55	20.59 / 12.43	20.77 / 12.33	20.94 / 12.23	21.10 / 12.13	21.26 / 12.04	21.42 / 11.95	21.57 / 11.87
25	17.46 / 14.66	17.99 / 14.23	18.38 / 13.93	18.71 / 13.68	19.00 / 13.47	19.27 / 13.29	19.51 / 13.12	19.73 / 12.97	19.94 / 12.84	20.14 / 12.71	20.33 / 12.59	20.51 / 12.48	20.69 / 12.37	20.86 / 12.27	21.02 / 12.18	21.18 / 12.09	21.33 / 12.00	21.48 / 11.92

APPENDIX C
Range of Future Prices

The tables in this Appendix show the range of future prices for 5, 10, 15, and 20 year maturities and various future years for present yields from 1 to 14 percent. Each table shows the range of future prices for a single maturity and various future years up to maturity.

WHAT TABLE C–1 SHOWS

1. The maturity of the bond: 5 years.
2. The number of years from now: 1 year.
3. The present yield on the bond: 4 percent.
4. The *low* probable price five years from now: $97.40.
5. The *high* probable price 10 years from now: $102.30.
6. The price at maturity: $100.

The range of prices shown in these tables have a two-thirds probability. Thus, for the five year maturity, the probability is two-thirds that prices a year from now will lie between $97.40 and $102.30. There is a 1-in-6 chance that prices will drop below $97.40 and a 1-in-6 chance that prices will rise above $102.30.

The range of prices is based on the range of yields given in Appendix B. The range of yields was derived from Salomon U.S. yield index data, 1950–1979.

TABLE C–1

Range of Future Prices

RANGE OF FUTURE PRICES OF 5 YEAR BOND

Initial Yield	0	1	2	3	4	5
1.0	100.0	99.3	99.2	99.2	99.4	100.0
1.0	100.0	100.6	100.6	100.6	100.4	100.0
2.0	100.0	98.6	98.4	98.5	98.8	100.0
2.0	100.0	101.2	101.3	101.1	100.8	100.0
3.0	100.0	98.0	97.7	97.7	98.2	100.0
3.0	100.0	101.7	101.9	101.7	101.1	100.0
4.0	100.0	97.4	97.0	97.1	97.7	100.0
4.0	100.0	102.3	102.5	102.2	101.5	100.0
5.0	100.0	96.9	96.3	96.4	97.1	100.0
5.0	100.0	102.8	103.0	102.7	101.9	100.0
6.0	100.0	96.3	95.7	95.7	96.6	100.0
6.0	100.0	103.3	103.6	103.2	102.2	100.0
7.0	100.0	95.8	95.1	95.1	96.1	100.0
7.0	100.0	103.7	104.1	103.7	102.6	100.0
8.0	100.0	95.4	94.5	94.5	95.6	100.0
8.0	100.0	104.2	104.6	104.2	102.9	100.0
9.0	100.0	94.9	93.9	94.0	95.1	100.0
9.0	100.0	104.6	105.1	104.7	103.3	100.0
10.0	100.0	94.5	93.4	93.4	94.7	100.0
10.0	100.0	105.0	105.6	105.1	103.6	100.0
11.0	100.0	94.1	92.9	92.9	94.2	100.0
11.0	100.0	105.4	106.1	105.6	103.9	100.0
12.0	100.0	93.7	92.4	92.4	93.8	100.0
12.0	100.0	105.8	106.6	106.1	104.3	100.0
13.0	100.0	93.3	91.9	91.9	93.3	100.0
13.0	100.0	106.2	107.0	106.5	104.6	100.0
14.0	100.0	93.0	91.5	91.4	92.9	100.0
14.0	100.0	106.5	107.5	106.9	104.9	100.0

RANGE OF FUTURE PRICES OF 5 YEAR BOND

Initial Yield	0	1	2	3	4	5
1.0	100.0	99.3	99.2	99.2	99.4	100.0
1.0	100.0	100.6	100.6	100.6	100.4	100.0
2.0	100.0	98.6	98.4	98.5	98.8	100.0
2.0	100.0	101.2	101.3	101.1	100.8	100.0
3.0	100.0	98.0	97.7	97.7	98.2	100.0
3.0	100.0	101.7	101.9	101.7	101.1	100.0
4.0	100.0	97.4	97.0	97.1	97.7	100.0
4.0	100.0	102.3	102.5	102.2	101.5	100.0
5.0	100.0	96.9	96.3	96.4	97.1	100.0
5.0	100.0	102.8	103.0	102.7	101.9	100.0
6.0	100.0	96.3	95.7	95.7	96.6	100.0
6.0	100.0	103.3	103.6	103.2	102.2	100.0
7.0	100.0	95.8	95.1	95.1	96.1	100.0
7.0	100.0	103.7	104.1	103.7	102.6	100.0
8.0	100.0	95.4	94.5	94.5	95.6	100.0
8.0	100.0	104.2	104.6	104.2	102.9	100.0
9.0	100.0	94.9	93.9	94.0	95.1	100.0
9.0	100.0	104.6	105.1	104.7	103.3	100.0
10.0	100.0	94.5	93.4	93.4	94.7	100.0
10.0	100.0	105.0	105.6	105.1	103.6	100.0
11.0	100.0	94.1	92.9	92.9	94.2	100.0
11.0	100.0	105.4	106.1	105.6	103.9	100.0
12.0	100.0	93.7	92.4	92.4	93.8	100.0
12.0	100.0	105.8	106.6	106.1	104.3	100.0
13.0	100.0	93.3	91.9	91.9	93.3	100.0
13.0	100.0	106.2	107.0	106.5	104.6	100.0
14.0	100.0	93.0	91.5	91.4	92.9	100.0
14.0	100.0	106.5	107.5	106.9	104.9	100.0

RANGE OF FUTURE PRICES OF 10 YEAR BOND

Initial Yield	0	1	2	3	4	5	6	7	8	9	10
1.0	100.0	98.9	98.6	98.4	98.3	98.3	98.4	98.5	98.7	99.0	100.0
1.0	100.0	101.0	101.2	101.3	101.3	101.3	101.2	101.0	100.8	100.5	100.0
2.0	100.0	97.9	97.3	96.9	96.8	96.7	96.8	97.1	97.5	98.1	100.0
2.0	100.0	101.9	102.4	102.6	102.6	102.5	102.3	102.0	101.6	101.0	100.0
3.0	100.0	96.9	96.1	95.6	95.4	95.3	95.4	95.7	96.3	97.2	100.0
3.0	100.0	102.8	103.4	103.7	103.8	103.7	103.4	102.9	102.3	101.5	100.0
4.0	100.0	96.1	95.0	94.4	94.1	94.0	94.1	94.5	95.2	96.4	100.0
4.0	100.0	103.6	104.4	104.8	104.9	104.8	104.4	103.9	103.1	101.9	100.0
5.0	100.0	95.4	94.1	93.3	92.9	92.7	92.9	93.3	94.1	95.6	100.0
5.0	100.0	104.3	105.3	105.8	106.0	105.9	105.5	104.8	103.8	102.4	100.0
6.0	100.0	94.7	93.2	92.3	91.8	91.6	91.7	92.2	93.1	94.8	100.0
6.0	100.0	105.0	106.2	106.8	107.0	106.9	106.4	105.7	104.5	102.9	100.0
7.0	100.0	94.2	92.4	91.4	90.8	90.5	90.6	91.1	92.1	94.0	100.0
7.0	100.0	105.6	107.0	107.7	108.0	107.9	107.4	106.5	105.2	103.3	100.0
8.0	100.0	93.6	91.7	90.6	89.8	89.5	89.6	90.1	91.2	93.3	100.0
8.0	100.0	106.1	107.7	108.6	108.9	108.8	108.3	107.4	105.9	103.8	100.0
9.0	100.0	93.1	91.1	89.8	89.0	88.6	88.6	89.1	90.3	92.6	100.0
9.0	100.0	106.6	108.4	109.4	109.8	109.7	109.2	108.2	106.6	104.2	100.0
10.0	100.0	92.7	90.5	89.1	88.2	87.7	87.7	88.2	89.5	91.9	100.0
10.0	100.0	107.1	109.1	110.1	110.6	110.6	110.1	109.0	107.3	104.7	100.0
11.0	100.0	92.3	90.0	88.5	87.5	87.0	86.9	87.4	88.7	91.2	100.0
11.0	100.0	107.5	109.7	110.8	111.4	111.4	110.9	109.8	108.0	105.1	100.0
12.0	100.0	92.0	89.5	87.9	86.8	86.2	86.1	86.6	87.9	90.6	100.0
12.0	100.0	107.9	110.2	111.5	112.1	112.2	111.7	110.5	108.6	105.6	100.0
13.0	100.0	91.7	89.1	87.3	86.2	85.5	85.4	85.8	87.1	89.9	100.0
13.0	100.0	108.3	110.7	112.1	112.9	113.0	112.5	111.3	109.2	106.0	100.0
14.0	100.0	91.4	88.7	86.9	85.6	84.9	84.6	85.1	86.4	89.3	100.0
14.0	100.0	108.7	111.2	112.7	113.5	113.7	113.2	112.0	109.9	106.4	100.0

RANGE OF FUTURE PRICES OF 15 YEAR BOND

Initial Yield	0	1	2	3	4	5	6	7
1.0	100.0	98.5	98.1	97.8	97.6	97.5	97.4	97.4
1.0	100.0	101.3	101.7	101.9	102.0	102.0	102.0	102.0
2.0	100.0	97.3	96.5	95.9	95.6	95.3	95.2	95.1
2.0	100.0	102.5	103.2	103.5	103.8	103.9	103.9	103.8
3.0	100.0	96.3	95.1	94.3	93.8	93.4	93.2	93.1
3.0	100.0	103.5	104.5	105.1	105.4	105.6	105.6	105.6
4.0	100.0	95.4	93.9	92.9	92.3	91.8	91.4	91.3
4.0	100.0	104.4	105.7	106.4	106.9	107.1	107.2	107.2
5.0	100.0	94.6	92.9	91.8	90.9	90.3	89.9	89.6
5.0	100.0	105.2	106.7	107.6	108.2	108.6	108.7	108.7
6.0	100.0	93.9	92.0	90.7	89.8	89.0	88.5	88.2
6.0	100.0	105.9	107.6	108.7	109.5	109.9	110.1	110.1
7.0	100.0	93.4	91.3	89.8	88.7	87.9	87.3	86.9
7.0	100.0	106.5	108.5	109.7	110.6	111.1	111.4	111.5
8.0	100.0	92.9	90.6	89.1	87.9	86.9	86.2	85.7
8.0	100.0	107.0	109.2	110.6	111.6	112.2	112.6	112.7
9.0	100.0	92.5	90.1	88.4	87.1	86.1	85.3	84.7
9.0	100.0	107.5	109.9	111.4	112.5	113.3	113.7	113.9
10.0	100.0	92.2	89.6	87.8	86.4	85.3	84.4	83.8
10.0	100.0	107.9	110.5	112.2	113.4	114.2	114.8	115.0
11.0	100.0	91.9	89.2	87.3	85.8	84.6	83.7	82.9
11.0	100.0	108.3	111.0	112.8	114.2	115.1	115.7	116.0
12.0	100.0	91.6	88.8	86.9	85.3	84.0	83.0	82.2
12.0	100.0	108.6	111.5	113.4	114.9	115.9	116.6	117.0
13.0	100.0	91.4	88.5	86.5	84.8	83.5	82.4	81.5
13.0	100.0	108.9	111.9	114.0	115.5	116.7	117.5	117.9
14.0	100.0	91.2	88.3	86.1	84.4	83.0	81.8	80.9
14.0	100.0	109.2	112.3	114.4	116.1	117.4	118.3	118.8

8	9	10	11	12	13	14	15
97.4	97.5	97.6	97.8	98.0	98.3	98.8	100.0
101.9	101.8	101.6	101.4	101.2	100.9	100.6	100.0
95.1	95.2	95.4	95.7	96.2	96.7	97.6	100.0
103.7	103.5	103.2	102.8	102.4	101.8	101.1	100.0
93.1	93.2	93.4	93.8	94.4	95.2	96.4	100.0
105.4	105.1	104.7	104.2	103.5	102.7	101.7	100.0
91.2	91.3	91.6	92.1	92.8	93.8	95.4	100.0
107.0	106.6	106.2	105.5	104.7	103.6	102.2	100.0
89.5	89.6	89.9	90.4	91.2	92.4	94.3	100.0
108.5	108.1	107.5	106.8	105.8	104.5	102.7	100.0
88.0	88.1	88.4	88.9	89.8	91.2	93.3	100.0
109.9	109.5	108.9	108.0	106.8	105.3	103.3	100.0
86.7	86.7	86.9	87.5	88.4	89.9	92.4	100.0
111.3	110.9	110.2	109.2	107.9	106.1	103.8	100.0
85.5	85.4	85.6	86.2	87.2	88.8	91.4	100.0
112.6	112.1	111.4	110.4	108.9	107.0	104.3	100.0
84.3	84.2	84.4	84.9	86.0	87.7	90.5	100.0
113.8	113.4	112.6	111.5	109.9	107.8	104.8	100.0
83.3	83.2	83.3	83.8	84.8	86.6	89.7	100.0
114.9	114.5	113.8	112.6	110.9	108.6	105.4	100.0
82.4	82.2	82.3	82.7	83.7	85.6	88.9	100.0
116.0	115.6	114.9	113.6	111.8	109.4	105.9	100.0
81.6	81.3	81.3	81.7	82.7	84.6	88.1	100.0
117.1	116.7	115.9	114.7	112.8	110.1	106.4	100.0
80.8	80.5	80.4	80.8	81.8	83.7	87.3	100.0
118.0	117.7	117.0	115.7	113.7	110.9	106.9	100.0
80.1	79.7	79.6	79.9	80.9	82.8	86.5	100.0
119.0	118.7	117.9	116.6	114.6	111.6	107.4	100.0

RANGE OF FUTURE PRICES OF 20 YEAR BOND

Initial Yield	0	1	2	3	4	5	6	7	8	9
1.0	100.0	98.3	97.7	97.4	97.1	96.9	96.7	96.6	96.6	96.5
1.0	100.0	101.6	102.0	102.3	102.5	102.6	102.7	102.7	102.7	102.7
2.0	100.0	96.9	95.9	95.2	94.7	94.3	94.0	93.8	93.7	93.6
2.0	100.0	102.9	103.8	104.3	104.7	104.9	105.1	105.2	105.2	105.1
3.0	100.0	95.8	94.4	93.5	92.8	92.2	91.8	91.4	91.2	91.0
3.0	100.0	104.0	105.2	106.0	106.6	106.9	107.2	107.3	107.4	107.4
4.0	100.0	94.9	93.2	92.1	91.2	90.5	89.9	89.5	89.1	88.9
4.0	100.0	105.0	106.5	107.5	108.2	108.7	109.1	109.3	109.4	109.4
5.0	100.0	94.1	92.2	90.9	89.8	89.0	88.3	87.8	87.3	87.0
5.0	100.0	105.8	107.6	108.8	109.6	110.3	110.8	111.1	111.3	111.3
6.0	100.0	93.5	91.4	89.9	88.8	87.8	87.0	86.4	85.8	85.4
6.0	100.0	106.4	108.5	109.9	110.9	111.7	112.3	112.7	112.9	113.0
7.0	100.0	93.1	90.8	89.2	87.9	86.8	85.9	85.2	84.5	84.0
7.0	100.0	107.0	109.2	110.8	112.0	112.9	113.6	114.1	114.5	114.6
8.0	100.0	92.7	90.2	88.5	87.1	86.0	85.0	84.1	83.4	82.9
8.0	100.0	107.4	109.9	111.6	112.9	114.0	114.8	115.4	115.8	116.1
9.0	100.0	92.3	89.8	88.0	86.5	85.3	84.2	83.3	82.5	81.8
9.0	100.0	107.8	110.5	112.3	113.8	114.9	115.9	116.6	117.1	117.4
10.0	100.0	92.1	89.5	87.5	86.0	84.7	83.5	82.5	81.7	80.9
10.0	100.0	108.2	110.9	112.9	114.5	115.8	116.8	117.6	118.2	118.6
11.0	100.0	91.9	89.2	87.2	85.6	84.2	83.0	81.9	81.0	80.2
11.0	100.0	108.5	111.4	113.5	115.2	116.5	117.7	118.6	119.3	119.8
12.0	100.0	91.7	88.9	86.9	85.2	83.8	82.5	81.4	80.4	79.5
12.0	100.0	108.7	111.7	113.9	115.7	117.2	118.4	119.4	120.2	120.8
13.0	100.0	91.5	88.7	86.6	84.9	83.4	82.1	80.9	79.9	78.9
13.0	100.0	108.9	112.0	114.3	116.2	117.8	119.1	120.2	121.1	121.8
14.0	100.0	91.4	88.5	86.4	84.7	83.1	81.8	80.5	79.4	78.4
14.0	100.0	109.1	112.3	114.7	116.7	118.3	119.7	120.9	121.9	122.7

10	11	12	13	14	15	16	17	18	19	20
96.5	96.6	96.6	96.7	96.9	97.1	97.3	97.6	98.0	98.5	100.0
102.6	102.5	102.4	102.3	102.1	101.9	101.6	101.3	101.0	100.6	100.0
93.5	93.6	93.7	93.8	94.1	94.4	94.8	95.4	96.1	97.1	100.0
105.0	104.9	104.7	104.4	104.1	103.7	103.2	102.7	102.0	101.2	100.0
91.0	91.0	91.1	91.3	91.6	92.0	92.5	93.3	94.3	95.7	100.0
107.3	107.1	106.8	106.4	106.0	105.4	104.7	104.0	103.0	101.8	100.0
88.7	88.7	88.8	89.0	89.3	89.8	90.4	91.3	92.6	94.4	100.0
109.3	109.1	108.8	108.3	107.8	107.1	106.2	105.2	104.0	102.4	100.0
86.8	86.7	86.7	86.9	87.2	87.7	88.5	89.5	91.0	93.2	100.0
111.2	111.0	110.7	110.2	109.5	108.7	107.7	106.4	104.9	103.0	100.0
85.1	85.0	84.9	85.1	85.4	85.9	86.7	87.8	89.5	92.0	100.0
113.0	112.8	112.4	111.9	111.2	110.3	109.1	107.7	105.9	103.5	100.0
83.7	83.4	83.3	83.4	83.7	84.2	85.0	86.2	88.0	90.9	100.0
114.6	114.5	114.1	113.5	112.8	111.8	110.5	108.8	106.8	104.1	100.0
82.4	82.1	81.9	81.9	82.2	82.7	83.5	84.8	86.7	89.8	100.0
116.1	116.0	115.7	115.1	114.3	113.2	111.8	110.0	107.7	104.7	100.0
81.3	80.9	80.7	80.6	80.8	81.2	82.0	83.4	85.4	88.8	100.0
117.5	117.5	117.1	116.6	115.8	114.6	113.1	111.1	108.6	105.3	100.0
80.3	79.9	79.5	79.4	79.5	79.9	80.7	82.0	84.2	87.8	100.0
118.8	118.8	118.5	118.0	117.2	116.0	114.3	112.2	109.5	105.8	100.0
79.5	78.9	78.5	78.3	78.4	78.7	79.5	80.8	83.0	86.8	100.0
120.1	120.1	119.9	119.3	118.5	117.3	115.6	113.3	110.4	106.4	100.0
78.7	78.1	77.6	77.4	77.3	77.6	78.3	79.7	81.9	85.9	100.0
121.2	121.3	121.1	120.6	119.8	118.5	116.8	114.4	111.2	106.9	100.0
78.1	77.4	76.8	76.5	76.4	76.6	77.3	78.6	80.9	85.0	100.0
122.2	122.4	122.3	121.8	121.0	119.7	117.9	115.4	112.1	107.5	100.0
77.5	76.7	76.1	75.7	75.5	75.7	76.3	77.5	79.9	84.1	100.0
123.2	123.4	123.4	123.0	122.2	120.9	119.1	116.5	112.9	108.0	100.0

APPENDIX D
Glossary

Appreciation. Appreciation is the increase in the market value of the bond or bond portfolio.

Basis Point. One hundredth of 1 percent. 100 basis points is 1 percent.

Bill. A bill does not carry a coupon or pay income specifically designated as such, but is priced at a discount on original offering. The income received is represented by the difference between the purchase price and the maturity value.

Bond. A bond is a certificate of long-term debt (usually for $1,000) issued by a corporation or government agency. It normally pays interest semiannually and can be redeemed at maturity for the face value of the bond.

Bond principal. The face value of the bond. The term also refers to the amount you originally invest.

Bond rating. A bond rating is the rating given by one of the bond rating services. The rating is designed to reflect the quality of the bond, which means the certainty with which income and principal will be paid.

Call. The redemption of a bond by the issuer by repayment of principal prior to maturity. Not all bonds are callable.

Coupon. Detachable pieces of paper that can be taken to the bank, or other paying agent, and redeemed for the amount of the coupon. A $1,000 principal bond with a 10 percent yield pays one $50 coupon every six months. Registered bonds do not have coupons.

Current yield. The current yield is computed by dividing the annual coupon by the purchase price, and it gives your current return. If you are interested in current income, then the current yield is an important figure to know. While it is much simpler to calculate, the current yield is less useful than yield to maturity for comparing different bonds.

Difference interval. The time interval over which we compute differences in yields for the purpose of measuring volatility. A month, two months, . . . up to six or seven years.

Discount.   A bond price which is less than the face value of the bond, or at a discount from par.

Duration.   Duration refers to the length of time it takes to get half your money back when you calculate the money received on a discounted basis so that a dollar received at maturity is worth less than a dollar received today. Thus, duration supplies information not given by the yield to maturity.

Floating rate.   An interest rate that is not fixed, but fluctuates.

Income.   When you invest in a bond, you do so, generally, for the return you receive in the form of interest income.

Income return.   Refers to the return generated by interest. It excludes changes in the price of the bond or bond portfolio.

Long-term bonds.   Bonds with many years to maturity.

Maturity.   The date at which the bond matures and also the number of years until the bond matures.

Money market fund.   A short-term bond fund with a floating interest rate, redeemable daily at cost.

Par.   The face value of the bond. A bond priced at par will carry a price of $100, the par or redemption value. Although bonds are issued in units of $1000, they are priced in units of $100.

Perpetuity.   A perpetuity pays only income, not principal, and has no maturity.

Premium.   The amount over face value at which bonds are selling.

Principal.   Your investment to be used to generate income or appreciation. It also refers to the face value of the bond, or to the amount you invest in the bond.

Short-term bonds.   Bonds with only a few years to maturity.

Square root of time.   If designate time by the letter t, the square root of time is $t^{.5}$.

Standard deviation.   A common statistical measure for describing the degree of variation in a set of numbers.

Total return is a measure of the return on your investment. It includes income and price change in the value of the bond. It is generally computed on a compound annual basis, the same way that yield to maturity is calculated, but for actual past performance rather than future return. It is not very useful as an indicator of future return.

Volatility.   As used here, volatility refers to the degree to which interest rates fluctuate. Interest rates with a high degree of fluctuation are said to be volatile, and vice versa. We measure the degree of volatility with the standard deviation (of changes in rates).

Years to maturity.   The number of years (and months) remaining until the bond matures and is redeemed.

Yield.   The annual income in interest which a bond returns expressed as a percentage of the purchase price. See current yield, yield to maturity.

Yield curve.   The yield curve is a chart showing the yield to maturity on the vertical axis and the maturity on the horizontal axis. You place a dot for the yield for each maturity on the chart. If you connect the dots with a line, you obtain a yield curve. An upward sloping yield curve slopes up to the right (higher yields for longer bonds), and a downward sloping yield curve slopes down to the right (higher yields for shorter bonds).

Yield to maturity.   The effective return on a bond if it is held to maturity. The yield to maturity gives an equivalent figure for all kinds of bonds, irrespective of whether coupons are large, small, or nonexistent, or whether the bond is selling at a discount or premium. The method of computing yield to maturity is equivalent to that used in determining the interest on a savings account.

Zero coupon bond.   A noninterest bearing obligation that is sold at a discount and has no coupon.

APPENDIX E
References

1. Bachelier, Louis. *Theory of Speculation,* Paris: Gauthier-Villers, 1900. In *The Random Character of Stock Market Prices.* trans. P. E. Cootner. Cambridge, Mass.: MIT Press, 1964.

2. Durand, David. *Basic Yields of Corporate Bonds, 1900–1942.* Technical Paper 3, National Bureau of Economic Research, New York, 1947.

3. Feller, W. *An Introduction to Probability Theory and Its Applications,* vol. 1, 2nd ed. New York: John Wiley & Sons, 1957, p. 344.

4. Fong, H. Gifford, and Frank J. Fabozzi. *Fixed Income Portfolio Management.* Homewood, Ill.: Dow Jones-Irwin, 1985.

5. Homer, Sidney. *A History of Interest Rates.* New Brunswick, N.J.: Rutgers University Press, 1963.

6. Macaulay, Frederick R. *The Movements of Interest Rates, Bond Yields and Stock Prices in the United States since 1956.* New York: National Bureau of Economic Research, 1938.

7. Malkiel, Burton G. *The Term Structure of Interest Rates.* Princeton, N.J.: Princeton University Press, 1966.

8. Murphy, J. E., and M. F. M. Osborne. "Predicting the Volatility of Interest Rates." *Journal of Portfolio Management,* Winter 1985.

9. Osborne, M. F. M. "Brownian Motion in the Stock Market." *Operations Research* 7, 1959, pp. 145–73.

10. Osborne, M. F. M. *The Stock Market and Finance from a Physicist's Viewpoint,* Temple Hills, Md.: Published by the author, 1977.

11. Osborne, M. F. M. "Random Walks in Earnings and Fixed Income Securities." Paper presented at a seminar, Institute for Quantitative Research in Finance, Columbia University, April 1968.

12. Osborne, M. F. M., and J. E. Murphy. "Brownian Motion in the Bond Market." Paper presented to the Eastern Finance Association, New York, April 27–30, 1983.

13. Osborne, M. F. M., and J. E. Murphy. "Financial Analogs of Physical Brownian Motion, as Illustrated by Earnings." *The Financial Review* 19, no. 2, 1984, pp. 153–72.

14. Salomon Brothers. *An Analytical Record of Yields and Yield Spreads*. New York, 1979.

15. Standard & Poor's Corp. *Security Price Index Record*. New York.

References 8 and 12 describe work on fluctuations in interest rates that are the basis of this book. Reference 1 is the initial work on randomness in very short-term bond prices (rentes), not yields. References 9, 11, and 13 describe the approach used here as applied to other kinds of financial data. References 3 and 10 discuss some of the underlying theory and issues. References 2, 5, 6, 7, 14, and 15 provided yield data for the original study of fluctuations in interest rates.

Index